演讲的艺术

The Art of Public Speaking

第十版（中国版）

TENTH EDITION
Specially adapted for Chinese readers

STEPHEN E. LUCAS（美）
University of Wisconsin–Madison

with

YIN SUYA
Richard Stockton College of New Jersey

外语教学与研究出版社
FOREIGN LANGUAGE TEACHING AND RESEARCH PRESS
北京 BEIJING

京权图字：01-2010-1290

图书在版编目(CIP)数据

演讲的艺术：第10版＝The Art of Public Speaking, Tenth Edition：英文 /（美）卢卡斯（Lucas, S. E.）著. —北京：外语教学与研究出版社，2009. 12（2013.1 重印）
ISBN 978－7－5600－9239－3

Ⅰ. ①演… Ⅱ. ①卢… Ⅲ. ①演讲—语言艺术—高等学校—教材—英文 Ⅳ. ①H019

中国版本图书馆CIP数据核字（2010）第000939号
审图号：GS (2010) 401号

出 版 人：蔡剑峰
项目负责：陈　静
责任编辑：陈　静
封面设计：牛茜茜
版式设计：梁　东
出版发行：外语教学与研究出版社
社　　址：北京市西三环北路19号（100089）
网　　址：http://www.fltrp.com
印　　刷：北京方嘉彩色印刷有限责任公司
开　　本：850×1168　1／16
印　　张：18.5
版　　次：2010年4月第1版　2013年1月第7次印刷
书　　号：ISBN 978－7－5600－9239－3
定　　价：48.90元（含CD–ROM光盘1张）
*　*　*
购书咨询：（010）88819929　电子邮箱：club@fltrp.com
如有印刷、装订质量问题，请与出版社联系
联系电话：（010）61207896　电子邮箱：zhijian@fltrp.com
制售盗版必究 举报查实奖励
版权保护办公室举报电话：（010）88817519
物料号：192390101

About the Author

Professor of Communication Arts and Evjue-Bascom Professor in the Humanities at the University of Wisconsin, Stephen E. Lucas has been recognized for his work as both a scholar and a teacher.

His first book, *Portents of Rebellion: Rhetoric and Revolution in Philadelphia, 1765–1776*, received the Golden Anniversary Award of the National Communication Association in 1977 and was nominated for a Pulitzer Prize. His essay "The Rhetorical Ancestry of the Declaration of Independence" (1998) received the Golden Anniversary Monograph Award of the National Communication Association, and in 2009 he received the same organization's Distinguished Scholar Award. His most recent book is *Words of a Century: The Top 100 American Speeches, 1900–1999* (Oxford University Press, 2009).

Professor Lucas is also author of *The Art of Public Speaking*, which is used at more than 1,000 colleges and universities around the world. One of the most influential textbooks of its time, regardless of academic discipline, it has established the paradigm for current approaches to the teaching of public speaking. In 2004, it received both the William Holmes McGuffey Longevity Award and the Textbook Excellence Award from the Text and Academic Authors Association.

A member of the Wisconsin Teaching Academy, Professor Lucas has received numerous teaching awards, including the University of Wisconsin Chancellor's Award for Excellence in Teaching and the National Communication Association's Donald Ecroyd Award for Outstanding Teaching in Higher Education. His numerous pedagogical innovations have had a profound impact in the United States and beyond.

Professor Lucas first came to China in 2001. In addition to serving as a judge at the 21st Century Cup National English Speaking Competition and the FLTRP Cup National English Debating Competition, he has become known as a commentator for the CCTV Cup English Speaking Contest. He has lectured at many Chinese universities, has presented workshops on public speaking instruction for Chinese professors, and has been a featured guest on CCTV International's *Dialogue* and on China Radio International. He has also worked with numerous visiting scholars from China in his seminars and teacher-training sessions at the University of Wisconsin.

Stephen Lucas and his wife, Patty, live in Madison, Wisconsin, and have two sons, Jeff and Ryan. His interests include travel, sports, art, and photography.

序一

能言善道 说话的艺术

两千多年前，孔夫子周游列国，力劝各地诸侯一切要以民为先，做君王就应该为老百姓着想。他能受到主政者的善待就是因为他有一张很会说话的嘴巴，而且说得头头是道。所谓言之有物，能言人之不能言，能道人之不能道，这当然是有口才之人才能做得到。现在外研社要出一本课本，英文的书名是 *The Art of Public Speaking*，中文该译为“演讲的艺术”。

在此我想回顾一下我个人的经历。我从小就喜欢读书，尤其喜欢在学校参加演讲比赛。中学时还经常代表学校去参加各学校的学生演讲比赛，拿到了多项冠军，也由此养成了我在不同时期、不同环境中与人雄辩（的习惯），而且兴趣甚高，每次旗开得胜，有不少自满。我大学毕业后第一份工作是新闻记者，做的是采访各地大小人物的工作，因此也得到了不少生活的经验，尤其是如何应付各种不同的考验与挑战，而其中最大的挑战之一该是如何能言善辩，不能让对方以言论来把自己打倒。

我在美国多年来以写作和演讲谋生，乐此不倦。因为做得好，总有些成就感，而且增加自信，无论在任何场合都能抬起头，无人敢欺。美国的退休总统大多都以出书和演讲为生财之道。老布什、克林顿、基辛格（他不是总统，只是国务卿），都在退休后投身讲坛，一次演讲比他们全年的薪俸还要高。当然这现象只是在美国，其他地域还未迎头赶上。

三言两语只想一道能言的好处。二十一世纪的社会更是一个无时无地都有竞争的社会，若不能有点说话的才能，定会吃亏。为此我劝年轻的学子要多多训练您的口才，不要被语言打倒。每时每刻善用您的言语技能，为您带来无比的成功。

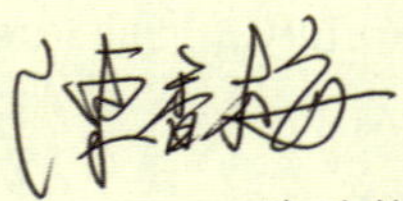

陈香梅

于美国华盛顿

序二

演讲的力量

提到演讲，我们都很熟悉。我们既曾被历史上的许多著名演讲感动过，也在被现代社会中各类风格独特的演讲影响着。无论是闻一多先生为真理、正义而战的“最后一次演讲”，还是马丁·路德·金为争取平等、呼唤自由的“我有一个梦想”，无论是杨澜女士充满东方魅力的申奥演讲，还是奥巴马总统慷慨激昂的竞选演说，都让我们感受到演讲所承载的思想之深与语言之美。这就是演讲的力量。一个成功的演讲者能够激励起千百万人，一次打动人心的演说能使人终身难忘。

可能有人会说：“我不打算竞选，也没有太多机会发表重要正式讲话，甚至没有机会做任何公共发言，为什么要学习演讲？”实际上，除了演讲台上、聚光灯下、公共场合的演讲，演讲在生活中还有更多更深远的意义。我曾走访过欧美国家的不少大学，注意到一些知名大学往往把演讲与写作这两门课程作为全校学生的必修课，有的大学在强调学生必须具有的综合素质时往往把交流与公共演讲的能力列在前位。在日本、新加坡等国家，政府工作人员要进行三个月到半年的演讲训练才能上岗工作，可见对演讲的重视程度。系统的演讲训练不仅有助于增强一个人的表达能力，更有利于其开拓思路、增强自信，提高沟通技巧。在注重交流、合作与效率的当今社会，这是一位高素质人才所应具备的重要能力。特别是当下我们强调培养大学生的创新思维和能力，就我自己的体会，通过对学生交流、演讲和论辩能力的培养可以使他们更具逻辑推理、言辞表达、哲理思辨。在创新人才的培养中和在不同国家与文化之间的沟通中，这一能力显得尤为重要。

对大学生而言，练习英语演讲是提高英语表达能力的有效方法，同时更是了解中西文化、培养思维能力的重要手段。一个成功的演讲者，除了有较强的语言能力与记忆力之外，还需要有敏锐的观察力、敏捷的思维力与准确的判断力。通过演讲的准备，你可以逐步学会去了解他人的背景、兴趣、信仰与态度，去了解其他文化的优秀历史传承，从而更好地与不同类型的人沟通与相处；通过演讲稿的撰写，你可以练习将思想和材料组织得更有条理，表达准确而又清楚；而通过在演讲台上的表达，你可以克服对公众讲话时的恐惧，变得更加自信。英语演讲，能帮助你练习用简明、清晰、有力的语言表达自己的观点，也能使你在国际交流的场合，以更开阔的视野、更自信的姿态、更得体的方式介绍中国的文化，发表独到的见解，维护国家尊严，弘扬民族精神。

在教育部近期公示的《国家中长期教育改革和发展规划纲要（2010-2020年）》（征求意见稿）中明确提出，教育要“适应国家经济社会对外开放的要求，培养大批具有国际视野、通晓国际规则、能够参与国际事务与国际竞争的国际化人才”。我相信英语演讲有助于培养这样的国际化人才。实际上，目前国内许多高校已充分认识到英语演讲的重要性，并已相继开设了此类课程。四川大学从2002年起就开设了英语演讲课，并将“演讲艺术”与“论辩艺术”、“交流艺术”并列，作为全校的公选课，着重培养学生的综合素质。在川大，英语演讲课不是口语课，也不是理论课和知识课，而是“英语+演讲”的特殊课型，“集听、说、读、写、视之大成”，与其他课程相辅相成，学生在其他课上的学习成果都可以在演讲课上得到充分体现。这门课无论对教师还是对学生来说都是一个学习、思考与创新的平台，既有助于语言能力提高，也有助于综合素质培养。

在目前高校探讨新的语言教学方法、关注学生的创新能力培养的环境与背景下，外研社将Stephen E. Lucas教授的经典著作、被誉为“演讲圣经”的《演讲的艺术》引入中国，并结合中国文化和中国大学生的特点，针对中国英语演讲课程的需要策划与出版《演讲的艺术》（中国版），可谓是非常有远见。这种“量身定制”的改编方式既可以保留原书的精髓，又可以融入中国的文化，既利于教师课堂操作，又便于学生吸收提高。对英语演讲教师而言，讲授这本教材本身就是向演讲大师学习演讲教学的方法；对学生而言，阅读这本书就像聆听大师讲解交流艺术与沟通技巧，可获得启迪终生的收益。《演讲的艺术》展现的是演讲的艺术，但又绝不仅仅是演讲，更是与人交流的艺术，是生活的艺术，是人人都应该具备的能力。

演讲给人力量，而这种力量的传达需要一种有效的方式，从作者传递给教师，从教师传递给学生，从一个人传递给周边的其他人。我相信，由Lucas教授精心编写的《演讲的艺术》（中国版），能带给中国的学习者这种震撼人心的力量。

石坚
四川大学副校长
2010年4月9日

Preface

The Art of Public Speaking has long been the leading book on its subject in the West, and I am deeply grateful for the favorable reception it has received in China. In preparing this adaptation of the 10th edition, I have retained the original book's balance between theory and practice. Firmly grounded in classical and contemporary theories of rhetoric, it offers full coverage of all major aspects of speech preparation and presentation.

It also follows David Hume's advice that "He who would teach eloquence must do it chiefly by examples." The book contains a large number of outlines, speech extracts, and sample speeches that illustrate the principles of effective public speaking. In addition, it comes with a CD-ROM that allows readers to see those principles in action. The CD-ROM contains more than 50 speech videos, as well as a variety of other teaching and learning materials.

As with previous editions, this adaptation reflects my belief that the most important part of speaking is thinking. One cannot give a successful speech without having something of substance to say. Nor can one be truly successful without a strong ethical foundation. Regardless of the audience or situation, the goal of public speaking is to communicate worthy thoughts in an effective manner.

While keeping the essence of the original book, I have taken several steps to harmonize it with the needs, interests, and experiences of Chinese readers.

First, I have reduced its length by judicious editing and conceptual refinement. English public speaking is a new course in China, and, unlike public speaking courses in American universities, it is not taught in the students' native tongue. As a result, it has somewhat different educational objectives and pedagogical methods. In adjusting to those differences, I have deleted material that is not germane to the course in China, and I have reworked other material to make it more suitable for the course. The result is a more concise book designed to meet the needs of students and teachers at Chinese universities.

Second, I have incorporated numerous Chinese examples that will relate the principles of English public speaking more directly to the cultural experiences of readers in China. Because English public speaking is a language course as well as a speech course, I use Western examples when they are the best choice to illustrate key skills and concepts. However, because public speaking, like other forms of communication, is culturally based, I use Chinese examples when they will be more effective than Western ones. In this regard, the adaptation can be thought of as a Western book with Chinese characteristics.

Third, unlike Western editions of *The Art of Public Speaking*, this adaptation includes a chapter on speaking in competitions. It has been my privilege to participate in both the 21st Century Cup and the CCTV Cup as a judge, question master, and commentator. I never cease to be impressed by the achievements of the students and the dedication of their tutors. These competitions are exceedingly rigorous, and they have played a major role in promoting the quality and popularity of English public speaking throughout China. Writing the chapter on competitions has been one of the most enjoyable aspects of preparing this adaptation, and I hope it will be of value to contestants and tutors alike.

When I made my first trip to China in 2001, I could not have imagined the growth that would take place in English public speaking during the subsequent decade. It has been my privilege to lecture at many Chinese universities and to meet students and teachers from all parts of the nation. Their enthusiasm for English learning in general and for public speaking in particular are truly inspiring. It is to them that this adaptation of *The Art of Public Speaking* is dedicated.

Acknowledgments

Many people have contributed to this book over the years. Huang Zhenhua, Jiang Bo, and Chen Yinghui, all of whom were then at the Chinese consulate in Chicago, helped facilitate my first visit to China in October 2001, which is the genesis of everything that has followed. Li Ping, director of the School of International Studies at the University of International Business and Economics, in Beijing, invited me to present several lectures and to meet with students, administrators, and faculty.

During that visit, Zhu Yinghuang, editor in chief of *China Daily*, extended an invitation to attend the 2002 21st Century Cup in Chengdu, thereby starting an enduring association with that competition. Over the years, Nie Lisheng, editor in chief of *21st Century*, and Huang Qing, managing editor of *China Daily*, have extended many kindnesses, including permission to include in the book speeches from the 21st Century Cup.

Three months before I arrived in Beijing, China received the bid to host the 2008 Olympic Games. Liu Qi, Mayor of Beijing and chair of the Beijing Organizing Committee for the XXIX Olympiad, graciously met with me and provided insight into the preparation of the speeches presented to the IOC at its July 13, 2001, meeting in Moscow.

In 2004, Foreign Language Teaching and Research Press published the 8th edition of *The Art of Public Speaking*. I owe much to Li Pengyi, then President of FLTRP; to current FLTRP President Yu Chunchi; to Vice President Xu Jianzhong; and to Higher English Education Publishing Managing Director Chang Xiaoling.

Also in 2004, I was invited to serve as a commentator at the CCTV Cup English Speaking Contest. Among the people I have worked with at CCTV-9 over the years, special thanks go to Director Wang Xi, Producer He Yujie, and fellow commentators Peng Wenlan and Chen Xiaowei.

In 2007, the First National Symposium on English Public Speaking was held in Beijing; the Second National Symposium was held in 2009. I was honored to present keynote addresses at both of these pathbreaking conferences, and I am grateful to the participants who shared with me their ideas about *The Art of Public Speaking*.

I have learned much about Chinese pedagogy and culture from the visiting scholars who have worked with me at the University of Wisconsin, including Ren Wen, Su Yurong, Gu Qiubei, Chen Zhihong, Liao Jinjin, Yang Huimin, Liu Aihua, Xu Haiyan, Zhang Chunyue, Liu Jia, Han Ning and Li Zhikun.

My visits to Chinese universities have provided opportunities to establish connections with English-language educators in China and to test ideas related to the book. I am especially grateful to Professor Cheng Musheng of Tsinghua University, Dean Cheng Xiaotang of Beijing Normal University, Dean Fu Li of Harbin Institute of Technology, Dean Gong Wenxiang of Peking University, Professor Jia Guodong of Renmin University, Deputy Dean Li Youwen of Beijing Foreign Studies University, Professor Liu Sen of East China Normal University, Vice President Ma Yulu of East China University of Science and Technology, Professor Mao Sihui of Macao Polytechnic Institute, Dean Mei Deming of Shanghai International Studies University, Vice Dean Shang Xiaoming of Heilongjiang University, Dean Wang Lifei of the University of International Business and Economics, Dean Wang Tongshun of Shanghai Jiaotong University, Professor Yang Huizhong of Shanghai Jiaotong University, and Dean Zhang Chunbai of East China Normal University.

In addition to the people at FLTRP mentioned earlier, I also wish to thank Duan Changcheng, Li Shujing, and especially Liu Xiangdong, who has helped in ways too numerous to recount. Zhao Chunmei was the project editor during early stages of this project. Chen Jing was responsible for subsequent stages and guided the book to completion. I could not have asked for better editors.

Nor should I neglect the people at McGraw-Hill who played a role in the book. International publishing can be a complex enterprise. Ed Stanford, President of McGraw-Hill Higher Education; Michael Hays, Managing Director of Global Publishing; and Jerene Tan, Director of Educational Publishing at McGraw-Hill Asia, were instrumental in expediting the process. Michael Xia, Selina Tang, and Fan Ying helped with a variety of details during my visits to China.

Margaret Procario's careful proofreading has improved the book substantively as well as stylistically. Sarah Jedd helped me select sample speeches from the 21st Century Cup and the CCTV Cup.

Wang Shenggang, of the China Association for Education Exchange, provided generous hospitality, while Xu Cuying and Jiang Jiajie assisted during their postings at the Chinese consulate in Chicago.

Few people in China have had greater experience in English public speaking than Chen Xiangmei. I am deeply honored by her endorsement of the book. I am thankful as well to Shi Jian, Vice President of Sichuan University, for his preface.

Above all, I am indebted to Yin Suya, who as second author collaborated with me on this project from its conception. In addition to her contributions to the book, she has worked tirelessly in behalf of all my activities in China. Her vision, initiative, and perseverance have been invaluable.

Finally, as in my other books, I owe more than I can express to my wife, Patty. Her love and support make everything possible.

Stephen E. Lucas
Madison, Wisconsin

导读

演讲论辩修辞自古希腊时代起就一直是西方教育的重要组成部分。始于先秦时期的中国修辞学尽管没有形成西方修辞学研究中的演说和论辩传统，但中国历史上也并不乏“羽扇纶巾，谈笑间，樯橹灰飞烟灭”的论辩大师。演讲论辩修辞在中国和西方都有着很强的实用性；事实上，古往今来，从东方到西方，演讲论辩的能力始终与个人的前途和国家的命运息息相关。古人云：片语可以兴邦，一言可以辱国。西汉的刘向在《战国策·东周》“秦兴师临周而求九鼎”一文中讲述了东周的重臣颜率如何利用自己的智慧和口才维护了本国的尊严和利益，正可谓：一人之辩，重于九鼎之宝；三寸之舌，强于百万之师。

有些读者可能会认为演讲的艺术主要是指演讲者的口才、风度和语言修养。也有人会认为，演讲的艺术是指当众讲话时运用声音、表情以及身体语言的技巧。而事实上，演讲作为一门艺术所涵盖的内容远不止这些简单的概念。爱好演讲的读者可以借助《演讲的艺术》一书来全面、深入地了解演讲的要素和组成部分，从而达到掌握这门艺术的目的。

如国内很多英语演讲爱好者所知，《演讲的艺术》是一本深受中外大学生读者欢迎的传播学基础教程。本教程以传播学的基本理论和概念为出发点，详尽地讲解了演讲所涉及的每个环节和步骤。这些环节和步骤包括：克服怯场、选题立意、了解听众、论证观点、巧用语言、撰写讲稿以及排练演示等。本教程也专门介绍了各类演讲的不同用途，如：传播知识、雄辩说理、激情励志、引见致辞、颁奖致辞、受奖致辞、祝酒致辞以及竞技口才等。

克服怯场是演讲训练的第一个环节。为了帮助读者排除紧张心理，本书第三章布置了一个简短的作业作为演讲的热身练习。这个作业是一个两分钟左右的有备演讲，演讲的话题可以是介绍自己本人，也可以是介绍他人。介绍的内容要包括自己或他人的背景、性格、信仰和追求。因为时间的限制，演讲者必须合理地设计段落大意和中心思想，以避免讲稿过长。讲稿的字数应在300字左右。为了使演讲有创意和感染力，演讲者可以设计独具匠心的开头和结尾，并使用富有戏剧性或冒险性的素材。当然，所有的情节都必须是真实的，不可虚构。为达到锻炼的目的，建议读者用半脱稿的方式完成演讲。

选题立意是演讲成功的基础。本书的第四章介绍了选择演讲话题的主要方法，如盘点法、分类法等。这一章还讲解了如何确定演讲的总体目的、具体目的和中心思想。演讲的总体目的取决于演讲所属的种类。比如，说明性演讲的总体目的是传播知识，教育听众；说服性演讲的总体目的是雄辩说理，说服听众；而纪念性演讲的总体目的是激情励志，鼓舞听众。当然，说服性演讲必定要包含说明性演讲的成分，而纪念性演讲也必定要包含说明性演讲和说服性演讲的成分。

演讲的具体目的是演讲内容的高度概括。比如，一个以中国旗袍为话题的演讲，其总体目的是传播知识，而其具体目的则可以定为，“让听众了解中国旗袍的起源、款式以及文化影响。”演讲的中心思想是演讲的要点，也是对演讲具体目的的进一部解释。这里还以中国旗袍这一话题为例，基于上面提到的具体目的，其中心思想则应是，“中国旗袍起源于上世纪二十年代，其款式众多，并对中国妇女产生了重要的文化影响。”通过学习第四章的内容，读者可以掌握选题的技巧，学会如何确定演讲的总体目的，以及如何规划起草与演讲的时限相应的具体目的和中心思想。

分析听众是演讲成功的一个不可忽略的环节。要想演讲达到预期的效果，演讲者要对听众进行充分的了解，这包括了解听众的人数、演讲的场景、听众的文化特征，以及听众对演讲话题、演讲者及演讲场合的态度。本书的第五章从理论上阐述了以听众为中心和了解听众心理的重要性，并且系统地讲解了分析听众和收集有关听众信息的具体步骤和方法。

从某种意义上讲，如果说口才是演讲成功的重要条件，那么了解听众则是演讲成功的必要条件。据《吕氏春秋·必己》记载，一次孔子的马跑到地里吃了一个农民的庄稼，农民将马扣留。一向以能言善辩著称的子贡请求去说服那农民，他道理讲透，好话说尽，马也没要回来。可是有个刚刚跟随孔子学习的粗俗的人只说了一句话，马就要回来了。那个农民听了粗人的话说：“说话都像你这么清楚就好了，怎么能像刚刚那个人那样！”子贡的口才在农民面前无用武之地，这是因为他不了解农民，因此也不知道如何与农民交流。可见，如果没有对听众的充分了解，再好的口才也不会有任何的说服力或感染力。

论证观点是演讲成功的前提。因为，没有充分的论据，再有力的论点也是站不住脚的。本书的第六章介绍了三种论据，即例证、数据和证言。演讲者可以集中收集论据，也可以通过平时的积累为演讲储备论据。在这一章中，读者可以接触大量的各类论据的实例，以及论据在演讲中的用法。学习这一章的要点是掌握如何识别和收集每一种不同的论据，以及如何在演讲中恰当地使用论据，并准确、清楚地说明其出处。

撰写讲稿是演讲成功的关键环节。演讲者要具备自己撰写讲稿的能力，这对国内的大多数英语演讲爱好者来说也许是一个不小的挑战。《演讲的艺术》一书用大量的篇幅详细地介绍了英语演讲辞写作的过程、步骤、方法和技巧。本书第九章讲解了讲稿提纲和演讲提纲的区别和这两种提纲的准备方法。讲稿提纲是指用提纲形式准备的演讲辞的全文，而演讲提纲则只包括演讲辞的要点。第七章介绍了组织讲稿提纲的一些具体步骤，如确定段落大意、为段落大意排序、为段落大意填充内容和使用连接词串连讲稿全文等。第八章介绍了演讲辞开头和结尾的写作方法，这其中包括演讲辞开头和结尾的各自的组成成分。演讲辞的开头一般包含四个成分：引起听众的注意和兴趣、搭建交流平台以便与听众彼此心会意通、建立和证明演讲者的可信度、介绍演讲的要点。演讲辞的结束语首先要示意演讲已接近尾声，然后进一步深化演讲的中心思想。当然，要从根本上提高英语演讲辞写作的水平，单凭阅读课本的有关章节是不够的。希望读者在掌握本教程所传授的写作要领的同时，能经常地、有选择地阅读中英文书籍和报刊杂志，用以激发灵感，积累素材，充实语汇，并用以保持与时俱进的精神。

巧用语言是增强演讲辞力度和效果的必要手段。正如本书第十章所说，演讲者首先应该对语言有较好的驾驭能力，语言表达要准确、鲜明和生动。对于国内的大学生读者和其他各行各业的英语演讲爱好者来说，在扩大英语单词量的同时，还要掌握词语的内涵和外延，练习使用实词和听众耳熟能详的词语，以及学会如何识别和删除赘词。在此基础上，演讲者还应恰到好处地使用富有表现力和艺术美感的方法或手段，来提升语言的表现力和演讲的感染力。本书的第十章介绍了两大类修辞格，一类用于加强语言的形象性，如明喻、暗喻、双关等；另一类用于加强语言的韵律性，如重复、排比、头韵、对照等。

美国黑人民权运动领袖马丁·路德·金的著名演讲“我有一个梦想”是巧用修辞手法的范例。其中脍炙人口的名句，“我有一个梦想……”，“让自由之声响彻……”，都是通过重复和排比的手法使演讲辞更加铿锵有力、震撼人心。在这篇演讲辞中，金同时也使用了大量的形象词语来唤起听众的觉醒和共鸣。例如，他把《解放宣言》比作灯塔的光芒、把种族隔离和种族歧视形容成枷锁、把黑人的生存环境描绘成贫困的孤岛等。而“欢乐的黎明，漫长的黑夜”，“种族隔离的荒凉深谷，种族平等的阳关大道”，“种族不平等的流沙，充满手足情的磐石”等一系列的对照修辞手段又使金的演讲辞琅琅上口、丝丝入扣。

语言修养离不开政治和文化背景的依托。通过阅读第十章的最后两节，读者还可以领悟到演讲者的语言不但要精彩独到，还要分寸得体，要适合于演讲的场合、听众、话题和演讲者本身，而且不能包含任何歧视。演讲者说话的艺术往往与自身的政治见识和文化素养紧密相连，比如，在香港回归的谈判桌上与英方代表既唇枪舌剑，又不失风度的原新华社香港分社社长周南就一向被称为诗人外交家。一次周南在香港总商会发表演讲时，有人就中国人民解放军驻港部队能否更名进行提问，周南当场引用了莎剧《罗密欧与朱丽叶》的道白作答：“What's in a name? That which we call a rose by any other name would smell as sweet."（"名字本身有什么意义？我们称之为玫瑰的花朵，换一个别的名字，它的香味还是同样芬芳。"）周南在此种场合表现出的机敏睿智和分寸得体博得在场所有听众的叹服和敬佩。

对于国内的读者来说，语言修养还包括演讲者的母语修养。一个不热爱或不尊重母语文化的人，英语讲得无论多么流利，都不会成为合格的文化传播者。中华民族的文化博大精深、源远流长，使全天下的炎黄子孙都引以为荣，也使整个世界为之瞩目和景仰。中国古典文学中的名文、名诗和名句经常被中外政要在重要场合引用，以促进国际间的政治和文化交流。

2009年7月27日，美国总统奥巴马在华盛顿罗纳德·里根大厦和国际贸易中心为美中战略与经济对话的致辞中引用了《孟子·尽心下》中的语句："山径之蹊间，介然用之而成路；为间不用，则茅塞之矣"（"A trail through the mountains, if used, becomes a path in a short time, but, if unused, becomes blocked by grass in an equally short time."），以敦促中美两国应为后代共同开辟一条通往未来的坦途，并要防止两国间的合作之路被不利因素所阻断。2010年3月14日，温家宝总理在人民大会堂金色大厅就第十一届全国人民代表大会第三次会议闭幕举行的记者会上，曾多次引用古语和诗文。在回答法新社记者关于中美关系的提问时，他引用了宋朝王安石《登飞来峰》中的诗句，"不畏浮云遮望眼，自缘身在最高层"（"I have no fear of the clouds that may block my sight, as I am already at the top of the height."），用以表明中国政府高瞻远瞩、审时度势、从容大度地把握中美两国之间关系的姿态。

传播知识是说解性演讲的主要用途。说解性演讲有着很宽的使用范围。就《演讲的艺术》一书的读者而言，会经常用到说解性演讲的人包括：用英语授课的教学人员，英语为第一外语的大中院校学生，国际活动或赛事的义务工作者，外交人员，外事人员，准备到英语国家留学或工作的人员，外企雇员，国际航班的空服员，英语导游、导购、销售人员，酒店和餐饮业的管理人员，以及其他各行各业的涉外工作人员。本书第十三章第一节介绍了四种不同的说解性演讲。第一种是介绍物件的，比如向听众介绍戈壁滩、电脑、股票市场、四川面具、湘绣和中国熊猫等。第二种是描述过程的，例如为听众讲解台风的形成、指导听众书写个人简历或向听众介绍如何打太极拳。第三种是陈述事件的，这包括向听众陈述失眠、婚姻、世界杯、海啸和网络犯罪等事件。第四种是诠释概念的，比如向听众解释什么是进化论、军事理论、教育哲学以及激励法原理等。这一章节还讲解了如何根据演讲的时限来确定说解性演讲的具体目的、中心思想和段落大意，以及段落大意的排序方法。读者可以通过学习这一章节提供的范例来掌握诸如时间法、空间法和话题法等说解性演讲段落大意的排序方式。第十三章的第二节提醒读者在作说解性演讲时不要高估听众的理解能力，不要拘泥技术细节，要使想法人格化，避免语言抽象化，并要有独创性，第三节为读者提供了说解性演讲的范文及专家点评。

雄辩说理是说服性演讲的主要特色。就本书的读者而言，说服性演讲的使用范围包括：对外籍人士进行健康保健、交通安全、旅行安全等宣传，向外企、外商、外籍人士募捐，签证面试，外企求职面试，外企竞岗演讲，对外招商引资洽谈，各种涉外谈判，对外商品广告、营销、促销等。说服性演讲比说解性演讲更具挑战性，因为它要求演讲者有较高的可信度、充足的证据、较强的推理能力和充沛的情感。本书的第十四章用递进的方法介绍了三种论辩形式的内容和相关性。这三种论辩形式由低到高可排列为事实性论辩、价值性论辩和政策性论辩。事实性论辩旨在论证某一事实的真伪，比如，吸烟是否对身体有害，莎翁的戏剧是否出自他人之手等。此类论辩的目的是说服听众同意某种观点。价值性论辩主要是论证某种想法或行为的对与否、正义与否、道德与否等。价值性论辩的核心是演讲者的价值判断标准，例如，若是演讲者认为“脚踏车是最理想的陆地交通工具”，那么这位演讲者首先要界定“最理想”的判断标准，以便为接下来的论证奠定基础。价值性论辩的最终目的是要听众接受演讲者所倡导的价值观。价值性论辩必然包含事实性论辩的成分，而政策性论辩既涵盖事实性论辩又涵盖价值性论辩。政策性论辩能直接改变或影响听众的行为，所以是更具实用价值的说服性演讲。政策性论辩又细分为针对机构政策的说服性演讲和针对个体政策的说服性演讲。比如，“说服听众同意将演讲设为英语专业的必修课”所针对的是机构政策，而“说服听众定期义务献血”所针对的是个体政策。针对机构政策的说服性演讲只力求听众同意演讲者的建议是必要的、可行的；而针对个体政策的说服性演讲则力求听众采用演讲者的建议，并立即付诸行动。政策性论辩的段落大意有下列几种排序法：问题—出路法、问题—成因—出路法、动机序列法和优势对比法。需要提及的是，动机序列法最适用于针对个体政策的说服性演讲；这也可以解释为什么西方广告商专门采用动机序列法编排商业广告词的内容。第十四章第六节介绍了说理的手段和技巧以及常见的说理谬误，第七节为读者提供了说服性演讲的范文及专家点评。

激情励志是纪念性演讲的总体目的。就本书的读者而言，纪念性演讲适用于：英语演讲比赛的自选题演讲，各种涉外场合的节日庆典致辞、毕业典礼致辞、就职演说、悼辞，以及其他涉外场合的献词等。纪念性演讲通常用来赞颂某一人物（屈原、秋瑾、钱学森等），某一群体（都市清洁工、天安门国旗班、中国航天员等），某一机构（中国红十字会、希望工程、中国历史博物馆等），某一情操（五四运动的精神、虎门销烟的民族气节、重阳节的尊老传统等）。成功的纪念性演讲既要包括说解性和说服性成分，又要通过恰当的修辞手段达到激情励志的效果。本书的第十五章最后一节提供了纪念性演讲的范文和专家点评。本章还介绍了其他几种用于特殊场合的演讲，比如，引见辞、颁奖辞、受奖辞以及祝酒辞等。

竞技口才是演讲的一种特殊用途。由CCTV和外研社联合主办的“CCTV杯全国英语演讲大赛”以及由中国日报和大型跨国公司联合主办的“21世纪杯全国英语演讲比赛”是目前国内最大规模的英语演讲赛事。本书的第一作者斯蒂文·卢卡斯博士曾多次担任上述两个大赛的提问评委和点评专家。在本书的最后一章，卢卡斯博士讲解了有备演讲、即兴演讲、现场问答和分组辩论的有关技巧，并点评了一些获奖作品。

排练演示涵盖演示的方式、演讲者声音的运用以及演讲者肢体语言的运用。本书第十一章第二节介绍了四种不同的演示方式：读稿式演示、背诵式演示、即兴式演示和提纲式演示，其中提纲式演示是本教程的教学重点。提纲式演示是一种半即兴演讲，演讲者通过演讲提纲和即兴发挥相结合的方式来完成演讲。本章的第三节探讨了用声的一些基本要领，比如如何控制或运用音量、音调、语速、停顿以及吐字发音等。在此特别值得读者注意的是，当你在演讲或辩论中提及欧美品牌名称或其他专有名词时，应该使用该词的英语读音，避免用中文读音来替代。比如，不应把“Nike”误读成“耐克”，把“Coca-Cola”误读成“可口可乐”，或把“Versace”误读成“范思哲”。本章的第四节讨论了演讲者如何注意个人形象、台上举止、手势运用，以及如何与听众保持目光接触。

在此，我们至诚感谢美国国会图书馆和中国驻美国大使馆的全力支持和帮助。中国驻美使馆尤少忠公使衔参赞专程安排本书的两位作者与深受国人尊敬的陈香梅女士在华盛顿会面。陈香梅女士曾被八位美国总统委以重任，并被誉为“中美民间大使”。她不仅是享誉太平洋两岸的著名作家，还是出色的演说家。她于上世纪60年代初曾师从乔治亚城大学特别教授学习演讲。在她的私人相册中，我们看到了她在美国各地巡讲的足迹。其中有一幅照片记载了她去美国通用电器公司演讲的情景。从照片的说明中我们得知，陈香梅女士是历史上第一位在美国通用电器公司演讲的女性。为了使中国的大学生读者充分地认识到英语演讲与口才的重要性，陈香梅女士欣然命笔为本书作序。在感到荣幸和激动之余，我们更要以陈香梅女士为楷模，为弘扬中国文化、增进国际交流作出贡献。荀子曰：“无冥冥之志者，无昭昭之明；无惛惛之事者，无赫赫之功。”我们希望以此古训与读者朋友共勉。

殷苏娅于美国新泽西
2010年3月20日

殷苏娅毕业于美国威斯康星大学麦迪逊分校新闻与大众传播学院，并获得新闻与大众传播学硕士学位和大众传播学博士学位。殷苏娅现在任职于美国新泽西州理查德·斯特哥顿学院，为传播学专业副教授，主要研究领域为广告、新闻写作、国际传播和中美关系。

Contents in Brief

Contents

PART 1 INTRODUCTION TO PUBLIC SPEAKING

CHAPTER 1

Speaking in Public 2

CHAPTER 2

Speaking Confidently and Ethically 16

CHAPTER 3

Giving Your First Speech 32

CHAPTER 4

Selecting a Topic and a Purpose 44

PART 2 SPEECH PREPARATION: GETTING STARTED

CHAPTER 5

Analyzing the Audience 58

CHAPTER 6

Supporting Your Ideas 72

CHAPTER 7

Organizing the Body of the Speech 88

CHAPTER 8

Beginning and Ending the Speech 102

CHAPTER 9

Outlining the Speech 118

PART 4 PRESENTING THE SPEECH

CHAPTER 10

Using Language 130

CHAPTER 11

Delivering the Speech 146

CHAPTER 12

Using Visual Aids 160

CHAPTER 13

Speaking to Inform 176

CHAPTER 14

Speaking to Persuade 192

CHAPTER 15

Speaking on Special Occasions 222

CHAPTER 16

Speaking in Competitions 234

APPENDIX

Speeches for Appreciation and Analysis A1

The Art of
Public Speaking

1 Speaking in Public

It was 3:00 p.m. Moscow time on July 13, 2001. Beijing's delegation was set to start its presentation to the 112th Session of the International Olympic Committee. Three hours later, the Committee would announce its selection of the host city for the 2008 Summer Olympic Games. Earlier in the day, Osaka, Paris, Toronto, and Istanbul had presented their cases to the IOC. Now it was Beijing's turn.

After making a brief statement, delegation chair He Zhenliang introduced Vice Premier Li Lanqing, who spoke on behalf of the Chinese government. As Vice Premier Li began speaking, he knew how high the stakes were. China had looked to this moment since losing the bid for the 2000 Games to Sydney by a mere two votes. The hopes of the nation were riding on the IOC's decision.

Speaking entirely in English, Vice Premier Li said: "China embraces the Olympic spirit and has always been a staunch supporter behind the IOC initiatives." He pledged that the government "will honor each and every commitment it has made in Beijing's Candidature File and will do whatever it can to assist Beijing to fulfill its promises."

Not only would an Olympic Games in Beijing serve the interests of the Chinese people, Li explained, it would also "promote the Olympic spirit and contribute to peace and friendship, stability and development in the world." He concluded by expressing China's desire to welcome "all guests with open arms." Quoting Confucius, he exclaimed: "Is it not a delight after all to have friends come from afar!"

When Vice Premier Li finished, he was greeted with applause. His speech was followed by remarks from the other members of Beijing's delegation. They systematically discussed every aspect of the bid. Beijing, they showed, had the experience, the resources, the technology, and the commitment to make the Games a success for participants and spectators alike. "If you honor Beijing with the right to host the 2008 Olympic Games," He Zhenliang told the IOC in his closing speech, "I can assure you" that "Beijing will make you proud of the decision you make here today."

When the IOC voted at 6:00 p.m., it awarded the 2008 Summer Games to Beijing. Even other cities who had bid for the Games praised the speeches of the Chinese representatives. "They had a compelling argument," said John Bitove, chief of the Toronto delegation. "Their presentation today pushed all the right buttons." The dream had become reality.

For nations, as for individuals, public speaking is a vital way of expressing ideas and achieving objectives. Although many factors—historical, economic, geopolitical—contributed to Beijing's selection as host city of the 2008 Olympic Games, that selection also depended on the Chinese delegation's ability to present a persuasive case in English when the IOC gathered to make its decision. This took a great deal of planning, untold hours of work, and a perfect presentation when it was China's turn to speak. No matter how strong China's position was in fact, the Games would not have come to Beijing without the confident and eloquent speeches of the Chinese delegation on that historic afternoon in Moscow.

The Power of Public Speaking

Throughout history people have used public speaking as a vital means of communication. What the Greek leader Pericles said more than 2,500 years ago is still true today: "One who forms a judgment on any point but cannot explain" it clearly "might as well never have thought at all on the subject."[1] Public speaking, as its name implies, is a way of making your ideas public—of sharing them with other people and of influencing other people.

During modern times many women and men around the globe have spread their ideas and influence through public speaking.[2] The list includes Mahatma Gandhi, Eleanor Roosevelt, Winston Churchill, Nelson Mandela, Ronald Reagan, Martin Luther King, Bill Clinton, and Barack Obama. In China, leaders such as Sun Yat-sen, Mao Zedong, and Deng Xiaoping employed the power of the spoken word to change the course of history.[3]

As you read these names, you may think to yourself, "That's fine. Good for them. But what does that have to do with me? I don't plan to be a national leader or a philosopher or a crusader for any cause." Nevertheless, the need for public speaking will almost surely touch you sometime in your life—maybe tomorrow, maybe not for five years. Can you imagine yourself in either of these situations?

One of your classmates is seriously ill and needs treatment. The medical expense, however, is beyond what your classmate and his family can afford. At a regular meeting of the University Students' Union, you stand up and deliver a sincere, moving speech urging a fundraising drive to help your classmate. Many students reach out their hands to help, and your classmate receives the treatment he needs.

You are one of seven management trainees in a multinational corporation with offices in China. One of you will get the lower management job that has just opened. There is to be a large staff meeting at which each of the trainees will discuss—in English—the project he or she has been developing. One by one your colleagues make their presentations. They have no experience in public speaking and are intimidated by the higher-ranking managers present. Their speeches are awkward and stumbling. You, however, call upon all the skills you learned in your public speaking class and deliver a talk that is clear, well-reasoned, and articulate. You get the job.

Fantasies? Not really. Either of these situations could occur. Public speaking is a form of empowerment. It can—and often does—make a difference in things people care about very much. Even if you spend the rest of your life primarily in a Chinese environment, you will have need for English public speaking. To mention just a few situations, you might give a presentation at an international conference, a product demonstration to global buyers, a toast at a dinner in honor of foreign guests, or a tour of a Chinese historic site for overseas friends or associates.

Study after study has shown that even in highly specialized fields, employers consistently rank the ability to communicate at or near the top of the skills they look for when deciding whom to hire and whom to promote. More than 90 percent of employees at multinational companies in Asia, Europe, and Latin America believe the use of English is "critical" or "important" to their positions.[4] In a survey of nearly 500 business administrative personnel and professionals in China, speaking and listening were ranked as the most important English skills required in their jobs.[5] The ability to speak effectively is so prized that college graduates in China are increasingly being asked to give a presentation as part of their job interview.

The need for public speaking arises in many situations. Here Dr. Jim Thomas explains the surgical procedures used in a pioneering operation at Children's Medical Center in Dallas, Texas.

In short, the need for Chinese students to have effective skills of English public speaking will only grow in future years. Not only will these skills be crucial to your personal success as you work and live in a world shaped by globalization, they will be vital to China's success as it competes with other nations of the world in the 21st century.

The Tradition of Public Speaking

Given the importance of public speaking, it's not surprising that it has been taught and studied around the globe for thousands of years. Almost all cultures have an equivalent of the English word "orator" to designate someone with special skills in public speaking.[6]

orator
A person with special skills in public speaking.

The oldest known handbook on effective speech was written on papyrus in Egypt some 4,500 years ago. In classical Greece and Rome, public speaking was studied extensively and played a central role in civic life. Aristotle's *Rhetoric*, composed during the third century B.C., is still considered the most important work on its subject.[7] Over the centuries, many other notable Western thinkers have dealt with issues of rhetoric,[8] speech, and language. In recent years, communication researchers have provided an increasingly scientific basis for understanding the methods and strategies of effective speech.

rhetoric
The art of effective communication between a speaker (or writer) and an audience.

The earliest record of public speaking practices in China can be traced to the *Book of History* (*Shangshu*), which exemplifies two types of speech: taking oath (*shi*) and imperial mandate (*gao*).[9] The *Intrigues of the Warring States* (*Zhanguo Ce*) records hundreds of discourses from the Warring States period. During the Tang Dynasty, several new persuasive genres were introduced by Chinese Buddhists, including sermons and sutra lectures.[10] Although there is no single term in Mandarin that corresponds exactly with "rhetoric," Chinese history is replete with conceptualizations and practices of discourse that include public speaking, artistic expression, persuasion, advising, and argumentation.[11] The current interest in English public speaking is a manifestation of China's long tradition of attention to the discursive arts.

Public Speaking and Intercultural Communicative Competence

Speechmaking becomes more complex as cultural diversity increases. Part of the complexity stems from the differences in language from culture to culture. Nothing separates one culture from another more than language. Not only do words change from language to language, but so do ways of thinking and of seeing the world. Language and culture are so closely bound that "we communicate the way we do because we are raised in a particular culture and learn its language, rules, and norms."[12]

intercultural communicative competence
The ability to respect diversity and to communicate effectively in cross-cultural situations.

If you are going to be an effective public speaker in English, you will need to be a culturally competent communicator. Intercultural communicative competence requires thinking and acting in ways that acknowledge and respect cultural diversity. Among other things, culturally competent communicators are sensitive to different cultural backgrounds and seek to understand the world from various points of view. Intercultural communicative competence builds upon traditional communicative competence but adds the awareness and skills required to make one's way in an interdependent, culturally diverse world. The optimal outcome is not just linguistic fluency, but cultural fluency.[13]

When talking to a cross-cultural audience, you must be especially alert to how cultural factors will affect responses to your message. Try to put yourself in your listeners' place and to hear your speech through their ears. Avoid words or phrases that might cause misunderstanding. When researching the speech, keep an eye out for examples, comparisons, and other supporting materials that are relevant to your listeners. Above all, recognize that your cultural assumptions and practices will not be shared—and perhaps not even understood—by all members of your audience. Show respect for the cultural values and expectations of the people who have come to hear you speak.

This does not mean, however, that you should devalue your own culture. Quite the contrary. Developing intercultural communicative competence requires attention to and respect for one's native language and culture as well as for the audience's language and culture.[14] There is no inherent conflict between being a competent English public speaker and being fully Chinese.

Nor is it necessary to avoid references to Chinese history and cultural heritage when speaking in cross-cultural situations. It would make sense, when addressing an English-speaking audience, to quote Bill Gates or J. K. Rowling, but it would make equal sense to quote Confucius, Sunzi, or Zhou Enlai, all of whom are recognized around the world. Intercultural communicative competence allows you to combine your Chinese heritage and English public speaking skills to maximum advantage.[15]

The critical thinking skills you develop in researching and organizing your speeches can be applied in many forms of communication, including meetings and group projects.

Public Speaking and Critical Thinking

Because public speaking is an act of strategic communication, it involves the use of English as a working language—the kind of language employed every day by people in business, law, government, and education. Having command of a language at this level is not just a matter of mastering vocabulary tests, going through pronunciation drills, or memorizing the rules of grammar. It is, rather, a matter of using the language in a full range of real-life situations that include everything from highly formal speeches in front of large audiences to one-on-one negotiations and interpersonal exchanges. All these situations require critical thinking.

To some extent, critical thinking is a matter of logic—of being able to spot weaknesses in other people's arguments and to avoid them in your own. It also involves related skills such as distinguishing fact from opinion, judging the credibility of statements, and assessing the soundness of evidence. In the broadest sense, critical thinking is focused, organized thinking—the ability to see clearly the relationships among ideas.[16] It has often been said that there are few new ideas in the world, only reorganized ideas. The greatest thinkers, scientists, and inventors have often taken information that was readily available and put it together differently to produce new insights. That, too, is critical thinking.

critical thinking
Focused, organized thinking about such things as the logical relationships among ideas, the soundness of evidence, and the differences between fact and opinion.

The skills you use in public speaking can help you become a more effective thinker in a number of ways. As you plan the structure of your speeches, you will learn how to organize your thoughts logically and cohesively. As you work on expressing your ideas in clear, accurate language, you will enhance your ability to think clearly and accurately. As you study the role of evidence and reasoning in speechmaking, you will see how they can be used in other forms of communication as well. If you take full advantage of your speech class, you will be able to enhance your skills as a critical thinker in many circumstances.[17]

Public Speaking and Conversation

The average adult spends about 30 percent of his or her waking hours in conversation. By the time you read this book, you must have spent many hours perfecting the art of conversation. If you communicate well in daily talk, you can learn to communicate well in public speaking.

SIMILARITIES BETWEEN PUBLIC SPEAKING AND CONVERSATION

You may not realize it, but public speaking requires many of the skills used in ordinary conversation. These skills include:

1. *Organizing your thoughts logically.* Suppose you are giving someone directions to your apartment. You don't convey the directions in random order. Instead, you take your listener systematically, step by step, from his or her apartment to your apartment. You organize your message.

2. *Tailoring your message to the audience.* Imagine that you are a biology major. Two people ask you how pearls are formed. One is your uncle, who majored in science as a university student. The other is your nine-year-old niece. You answer as follows:

> To your uncle: "When any irritant, say a grain of sand, gets inside the oyster's shell, the oyster automatically secretes a substance called nacre, which is mostly calcium carbonate. The nacre accumulates around the irritant core to form the pearl."
>
> To your niece: "Imagine you're an oyster on the ocean floor. A grain of sand gets inside your shell and makes you uncomfortable. So you decide to cover it up. The covering builds up around the grain of sand to make a pearl."

3. *Telling a story for maximum impact.* Suppose you are telling a friend about a funny incident at last week's track meet. You don't begin with the punch line ("Lihua fell out of the stands right onto the track. Here's how it started. . . ."). Instead, you carefully build up your story, adjusting your words and tone of voice to get the best effect.

4. *Adapting to listener feedback.* Whenever you talk with someone, you are aware of that person's verbal, facial, and physical reactions. For example, when you tell your boyfriend or girlfriend that you need to study instead of going to a movie on Saturday night, you notice an unmistakable look of unhappiness on his or her face. So you say, "Okay, let's go to the early show; then I can study later."

Each day, in casual conversation, you do all these things many times without thinking about them. You already possess these communication skills, all of which are among the most important skills you will need for public speaking.

Many skills used in conversation also apply in public speaking. As you learn to speak more effectively, you may also learn to communicate more effectively in other situations.

DIFFERENCES BETWEEN PUBLIC SPEAKING AND CONVERSATION

Despite their similarities, public speaking and everyday conversation are not identical. Imagine that you are telling a story to a friend. Then imagine yourself telling the story to a group of seven or eight friends. Now imagine telling the same story to 20 or 30 people. As the size of your audience grows, you will find yourself adapting to three major differences between conversation and public speaking:

1. *Public speaking is more highly structured.* It usually imposes strict time limitations on the speaker. In most cases, the situation does not allow listeners to interrupt with questions or commentary. The speaker must accomplish her or his purpose in the speech itself. When preparing the speech, the speaker must anticipate questions that might arise in the minds of listeners and answer them. Consequently, public speaking demands much more detailed planning and preparation than ordinary conversation.

2. *Public speaking requires more formal language.* Slang, jargon, and bad grammar have little place in public speeches. Even in the United States and Europe, where dress codes and social mores have become more and more informal, listeners usually react negatively to speakers who do not elevate and polish their language when addressing an audience. A speech should be "special."

3. *Public speaking requires a different method of delivery.* When conversing informally, most people talk quietly, interject stock phrases such as "well" and "you know," adopt a casual posture, and use what are called vocalized pauses ("uh," "er," "um"). Effective public speakers, however, adjust their voices to be heard clearly throughout the audience. They assume a more erect posture. They avoid distracting mannerisms and verbal habits.

With study and practice, you will be able to master these differences and expand your conversational skills into speechmaking.

The Speech Communication Process

As you begin your first speeches, you may find it helpful to understand what occurs when one person talks to another. Regardless of the kind of speech communication involved, there are seven elements—speaker, message, channel, listener, feedback, interference, and situation. Here we shall focus on how these elements interact when a public speaker addresses an audience.

SPEAKER

speaker
The person who is presenting an oral message to a listener.

Speech communication begins with a speaker. Your success as a speaker depends on *you*—your personal credibility, your knowledge of the subject, your preparation of the speech, your manner of speaking, your sensitivity to the audience and the occasion. But successful speaking also requires enthusiasm. You can't expect people to be interested in what you say unless you are interested yourself.

You can learn all the techniques of effective speechmaking, but before they can be of much use, you must first have something to say—something that sparks your own enthusiasm.

MESSAGE

message
Whatever a speaker communicates to someone else.

The message is whatever a speaker communicates to someone else. Your goal in public speaking is to have your *intended* message be the message that is *actually* communicated. Achieving this depends both on what you say (the verbal message) and on how you say it (the nonverbal message).

Getting the verbal message just right requires work. You must narrow your topic down to something you can discuss adequately in the time allowed for the speech. You must do research and choose supporting details to make your ideas clear and convincing. You must organize your ideas so listeners can follow them without getting lost. And you must express your message in words that are accurate, clear, vivid, and appropriate.

In addition to the message you send with words, you send a message with your tone of voice, appearance, gestures, facial expression, and eye contact. One of your jobs as a speaker is to make sure your nonverbal message does not distract from your verbal message.

CHANNEL

channel
The means by which a message is communicated.

The channel is the means by which a message is communicated. Public speakers may use one or more of several channels, each of which will affect the message received by the audience.

Consider a speech to Congress by the President of the United States. The speech is carried to the nation by the channels of radio and television. For the radio audience, the message is conveyed entirely by the President's voice. For the television audience, the message is conveyed by both the President's voice and the televised image. The people in Congress have a more direct channel. They not only hear the President's voice as amplified through a microphone, but also see him and the setting firsthand.

In a public speaking class, your channel is the most direct of all. Your listeners will see you and hear you without any electronic intervention.

LISTENER

The listener is the person who receives the communicated message. Without a listener, there is no communication.

listener
The person who receives the speaker's message.

Everything a speaker says is filtered through a listener's *frame of reference*—the total of his or her knowledge, experience, goals, values, and attitudes. Because a speaker and a listener are different people, they can never have exactly the same frame of reference. And because a listener's frame of reference can never be exactly the same as a speaker's, the meaning of a message will never be exactly the same to a listener as to a speaker.

frame of reference
The sum of a person's knowledge, experience, goals, values, and attitudes.

To be an effective public speaker, you need to take account of your listeners' frames of reference. You must be *audience-centered.* You will quickly lose your listeners' attention if your presentation is either too basic or too sophisticated. You will also lose your audience if you do not relate to their experience, interests, knowledge, and values. When you make a speech that causes listeners to say "That is important to *me*," you will almost always be successful.

FEEDBACK

Feedback refers to the messages—usually nonverbal—that are sent from a listenter to a speaker. Do listeners lean forward in their seats, as if paying close attention? Do they applaud in approval? Do they laugh at your jokes? Do they have quizzical looks on their faces? Do they shuffle their feet and gaze at the clock?

feedback
The messages, usually nonverbal, sent from a listener to a speaker.

The message sent by these reactions could be "I am fascinated," "I am bored," "I agree with you," "I don't agree with you," or any number of others. As a speaker, you need to be alert to these reactions and adjust your message accordingly.

INTERFERENCE

Interference is anything that impedes the communication of a message. In public speaking there are two kinds of interference. One is *external* to the audience—traffic outside the building, people conversing in the hall, a room that is stifling hot or freezing cold. Any of these can distract listeners from what a speaker is saying.

interference
Anything that impedes the communication of a message.

A second kind of interference is *internal* and comes from within the audience. Perhaps one of your listeners has a toothache. She may be so distracted by the pain that she doesn't pay attention to your speech. Another listener could be worrying about the CET. Yet another could be brooding about an argument with his girlfriend.

As a speaker, you must try to hold your listeners' attention despite these kinds of interference. In the chapters that follow, you will find many ways to do this.

• **FIGURE 1.1**

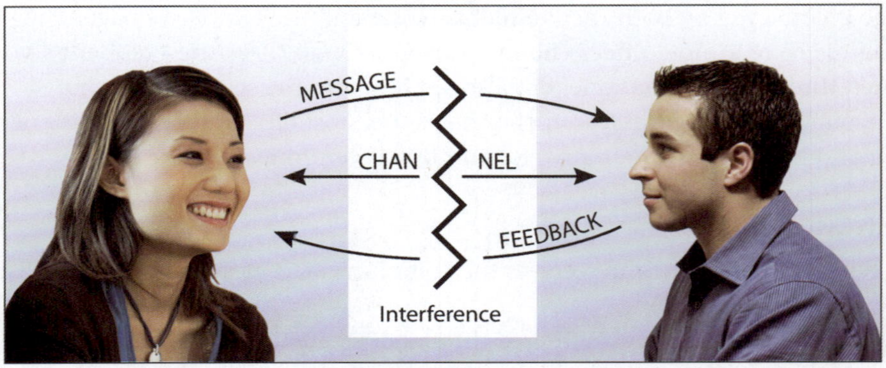

SITUATION

situation
The time and place in which speech communication occurs.

The situation is the time and place in which speech communication occurs. Certain situations—funerals, weddings, graduation ceremonies—require certain kinds of speeches. Physical setting is also important. It makes a great deal of difference whether a speech is presented indoors or out, to a densely packed crowd or to a handful of scattered souls. When you adjust to the situation of a public speech, you are only doing on a larger scale what you do every day in conversation.

A complete model of the speech communication process is shown in Figure 1.1 above.[18]

THE SPEECH COMMUNICATION PROCESS: EXAMPLE WITH COMMENTARY

The following example shows how the various components of the speech communication process interact:

Situation It was 5:15 p.m., and the international sales conference of computer giant Lexstar had been going on in Shenzhen all day. A series of new-product presentations to buyers from the company's largest global customers had taken much longer than expected.

Speaker Cindy Chen was worried. As a marketing manager for the T-Series of laptops, she was the last speaker of the day. When she rose to address the audience, she knew she faced a difficult situation. She had been allotted 45 minutes for her presentation, and the meeting was scheduled to end in 15 minutes. What's more, sales of her product line depended in large part on this presentation.

Channel
Interference Cindy stepped to the microphone and began to speak. She could see members of the audience looking at their watches; she knew they were eager to get to dinner after a long day of speeches.

Adapting to Interference "Good afternoon," Cindy said, "and thanks for your attention. I know everyone is ready for dinner—I certainly am. I was given 45 minutes for my presentation, but with your kind cooperation, I'll do my best to finish in half an hour. I think you'll find the time

Internet Connection

As we shall see throughout this book, there are many Internet resources for public speakers. One of those resources is an extensive collection of speeches from world history, which you can access at the History Place: Great Speeches Collection (www.historyplace.com/speeches/previous.htm).

Founded in 2005, the Professional Speakers Association of China provides networking and training activities for its members. You can learn about the association at www.chinaspeakers.org/new1/index1.php.

worthwhile, because the computers I am going to tell you about are priced right to increase your customer base." Cindy was relieved to see several people smiling as they settled back in their seats.

Message Now that she had the audience's attention, Cindy presented each new computer in the T-Series as briefly as she could. She streamlined her planned presentation to emphasize the features that would be most appealing to buyers from different countries. She ended by promising to contact anyone who needed more information. She quickly added her e-mail address to her PowerPoint slides and was encouraged to see people writing it down.

Feedback As promised, Cindy finished in under half an hour. "And that's it!" she concluded. "Let's eat!" Later, the marketing director complimented her on dealing so well with a tough situation. "You did a great job," the director said. "Next year we'll try to make all the presentations as efficient as yours."

SUMMARY

People throughout history have used public speaking as a vital means of communication and empowerment. Because you will live the rest of your life in a globalized world, the need for English public speaking will almost surely touch you at some time.

To be successful giving speeches in English, you need to be a culturally competent communicator. You must show respect for the cultural values and expectations of the people who come to hear you. This does not mean that you have to devalue your own culture. There is no inherent conflict between being a competent English public speaker and being fully Chinese.

Because public speaking involves the use of English as a working language, it requires critical thinking skills. Critical thinking helps you organize your ideas, spot weaknesses in other people's reasoning, and avoid them in your own.

There are many similarities between public speaking and conversation, but there are also important differences. First, public speaking requires more detailed preparation than ordinary conversation. Second, it requires more formal language. Third, it demands that speakers adjust their voices to the larger audience and work at avoiding distracting physical mannerisms and verbal habits.

The speech communication process includes seven elements: speaker, message, channel, listener, feedback, interference, and situation. The interaction of these elements determines the outcome of any public speech.

KEY TERMS

Key-Term Exercise
Check your knowledge with the Key-Term Exercise for this chapter.

orator *(5)*
rhetoric *(5)*
intercultural communicative competence *(6)*
critical thinking *(7)*
speaker *(10)*
message *(10)*
channel *(10)*
listener *(11)*
frame of reference *(11)*
feedback *(11)*
interference *(11)*
situation *(12)*

EXERCISES FOR THINKING AND SPEAKING

1. Divide a sheet of paper into two columns. Label one column "Characteristics of an Effective Public Speaker." Label the other column "Characteristics of an Ineffective Public Speaker." In the columns, list and briefly explain what you believe to be the five most important characteristics of effective and ineffective speakers. Be prepared to discuss your ideas in class.

2. On the basis of the lists you developed for Exercise 1, candidly evaluate your own strengths and weaknesses as a speaker. Identify the three primary aspects of speechmaking you most want to improve.

3. Identify a famous orator in Chinese history. Learn enough about the orator that you can explain to your classmates something about his or her skills and achievements as a speaker. (For example, in 630 B.C., Zhu Zhiwu successfully persuaded Qin Mugong to withdraw.)

4. Think of a situation in which you sought to understand the message of, or to convey your own message to, someone from a different culture. The situation might have involved either public speaking or everyday conversation. What did the situation—and its outcome—reveal about the process of communicating cross-culturally? If you could approach the same situation again, what changes would you make to communicate more effectively?

5. Analyze the text and video of Yang Lan's "Cultural Programs and the 2008 Olympic Games," which is printed in the appendix of speeches for appreciation and analysis at the end of the book. Evaluate the speech in light of the criteria for public speaking and intercultural communicative competence discussed on page 6 of this chapter.

Public Speaking in Your Career

After graduating from college, you accepted a job at a local consulting firm. Knowing that you took a public speaking class in college, the head of the human relations department has asked you to participate in a company-wide workshop on communication skills. The director wants you to discuss the value of public speaking and the relationship between public speaking and everyday conversation. Prepare a 1–2 minute speech with a focus on these two subjects.

2 Speaking Confidently and Ethically

- Becoming a Confident Speaker
  - Nervousness Is Normal
  - Dealing with Nervousness
- Being an Ethical Speaker
  - Guidelines for Ethical Speaking
  - Plagiarism

If you are like most people, you are nervous about the prospect of giving a speech in public. Stage fright is a global phenomenon that cuts across language, culture, and national borders. What the American comedian Jerry Seinfeld said in jest sometimes seems literally true: "Given a choice, at a funeral most of us would rather be the one in the coffin than the one giving the eulogy."

In addition to dealing with stage fright, public speakers face questions of ethics whenever they address an audience. The goal of public speaking is to gain a desired response from listeners—but not at any cost. Speechmaking is a form of power and therefore carries with it heavy ethical responsibilities.

In this chapter, we will give you skills and information that will help you speak ethically and confidently.

Becoming a Confident Speaker

stage fright Anxiety over the prospect of giving a speech in front of an audience.

If you are worried about stage fright, you may feel better knowing that you are not alone. Even in the United States, where public speaking is highly popular, a 2005 national survey showed that 42 percent of respondents identified giving a speech as their top fear. In comparison, only 28 percent said they were afraid of dying.[1]

In a different study, researchers concentrated on social situations and, again, asked their subjects to list their greatest fears. Here is how they answered:[2]

Greatest Fear	Percent Naming
A party with strangers	74
Giving a speech	70
Asked personal questions in public	65
Meeting a date's parents	59
First day on a new job	59
Victim of a practical joke	56
Talking with someone in authority	53
Job interview	46

Again, speechmaking ranks near the top in provoking anxiety.

NERVOUSNESS IS NORMAL

Stage fright is such a common occurrence that some of the greatest public speakers in history have suffered from it, including Mahatma Gandhi, Abraham Lincoln, and Winston Churchill. The famous Roman orator Cicero said, "I turn pale at the outset of a speech and quake in every limb and in my soul."[3]

More recently, Li Yang had to overcome a serious bout of stage fright before presenting his first Crazy English lecture. Leonardo DiCaprio was once so nervous about giving an acceptance speech that he hoped he would not win the Academy Award for which he had been nominated. Eighty-one percent of business executives say public speaking is the most nerve-wracking experience they face.[4]

Actually, most people tend to be anxious before doing something important in public. Actors are nervous before a play, musicians are nervous before a concert, athletes are nervous before a big game. The ones who succeed have learned to use their nervousness to their advantage. Listen to tennis star Roger Federer speaking before his 2009 Wimbledon title match against Andy Roddick. Asked by a reporter whether he still gets nervous playing in such a big event, Federer responded: "Oh, yes, the tension always comes back for any Grand Slam final. I'll have to play my very best to win." Putting his butterflies to good use, Federer beat Roddick in an epic five-set match to set the all-time record for Grand Slam tennis championships in a career.

Much the same thing happens in speechmaking. Most experienced speakers have stage fright before taking the floor, but their nervousness is a healthy sign that they are getting "psyched up" for a good effort. Novelist and lecturer I. A. R. Wylie explains, "Now after many years of practice I am, I suppose, really a 'practiced speaker.' But I rarely rise to my feet without a throat constricted with terror and a furiously thumping heart. When, for some reason, I *am* cool and self-assured, the speech is always a failure."[5]

In other words, it is perfectly normal—even desirable—to be nervous at the start of a speech. Your body is responding as it would to any stressful situation—by producing extra *adrenaline*. This sudden shot of adrenaline is what makes your heart race, your hands shake, your knees knock, and your skin perspire. Every public speaker experiences all these reactions to some extent. The question is: How can you control your nervousness and make it work for you rather than against you?

adrenaline
A hormone released into the bloodstream in response to physical or mental stress.

DEALING WITH NERVOUSNESS

Rather than trying to eliminate every trace of stage fright, you should aim at transforming it from a negative force into what one expert calls *positive nervousness*—"a zesty, enthusiastic, lively feeling with a slight edge to it. . . . It's still nervousness, but it feels different. You're no longer victimized by it; instead, you're vitalized by it. You're in control of it."[6]

positive nervousness
Controlled nervousness that helps energize a speaker for his or her presentation.

Don't think of yourself as having stage fright. Instead, think of it as "stage excitement" or "stage enthusiasm."[7] It can help you get focused and energized in the same way that it helps athletes, musicians, and others get primed for a game or a concert. Think of it as a normal part of giving a successful speech.

Here are a number of time-tested ways you can turn your nervousness from a negative force into a positive one.

Acquire Speaking Experience

Think back to your first day at kindergarten, your first date, your first day at a new job. You were probably nervous in each situation because you were facing something new and unknown. Once you became accustomed to the situation, it was no longer threatening. So it is with public speaking. For most people, the biggest part of stage fright is fear of the unknown. The more you learn about public speaking and the more speeches you give, the less threatening speechmaking will become.

Learning to give a speech is not much different from learning any other skill—it proceeds by trial and error. As time goes on, your fears about public speaking will gradually recede until they are replaced by only a healthy nervousness before you rise to speak.

Terrified early in his career by the prospect of giving a public speech, today Leonardo DiCaprio is an accomplished speaker who confidently addresses audiences around the globe.

Prepare, Prepare, Prepare

Another key to gaining confidence is to pick speech topics you truly care about—and then to prepare your speeches so thoroughly that you cannot help but be successful. A standard rule is that each minute of speaking time requires one to two hours of preparation time—perhaps more, depending on the amount of research needed for the speech. This may seem like a lot of time, but the rewards are well worth it. One professional speech consultant estimates that proper preparation can reduce stage fright by up to 75 percent.[8]

Imagine that the day for your speech has arrived. You have studied your audience and selected a topic which you know will interest them. You have researched the speech thoroughly and practiced it several times until it feels absolutely comfortable. You have even tried it out before two or three trusted friends. How can you help but be confident of success?

Think Positively

Confidence is mostly the well-known power of positive thinking. If you think you can do it, you usually can. On the other hand, if you predict disaster and doom, that is almost always what you will get. This is especially true when it comes to public speaking. Speakers who think negatively about themselves and the speech experience are much more likely to be overcome by stage fright than are speakers who think positively.

Here are some ways you can transform negative thoughts into positive ones as you work on your speeches:

Negative Thought	Positive Thought
I wish I didn't have to give this speech.	This speech is a chance for me to share my ideas and gain experience as a speaker.
I'm not a great public speaker.	No one's perfect, but I'm getting better with each speech I give.
I'm always nervous when I give a speech.	Everyone's nervous. If other people can handle it, I can too.
No one will be interested in what I have to say.	I have a good topic and I'm fully prepared. Of course they'll be interested.

Many psychologists believe that the ratio of positive to negative thoughts in regard to stressful activities such as speechmaking should be at least five to one. That is, for each negative thought, you should counter with a minimum of five positive ones. Doing so will not make your nerves go away completely, but it will help keep them under control so you can concentrate on communicating your ideas rather than on brooding about your fears and anxieties.

Use the Power of Visualization

visualization
Mental imaging in which a speaker vividly pictures himself or herself giving a successful presentation.

Visualization is closely related to positive thinking. It is used by athletes, musicians, actors, speakers, and others to enhance their performance in stressful situations.

The key to visualization is creating a vivid mental blueprint in which you see yourself succeeding in your speech. Picture yourself rising to speak. See yourself at the lectern, poised and self-assured, making eye contact with your audience and delivering your introduction in a firm, clear voice. Feel your confidence growing as your listeners get more and more caught up in what you are saying. Imagine your sense of achievement as you conclude the speech knowing you have done your very best.

As you create these images in your mind's eye, be realistic but stay focused on the positive aspects of your speech. Don't allow negative images to eclipse the positive ones. Acknowledge your nervousness, but picture yourself overcoming it to give a vibrant, articulate presentation. If one part of the speech always seems to give you trouble, visualize yourself getting through it without any hitches. The more lucid your mental pictures, the more successful you are likely to be.

This visualization should be repeated several times in the days before you speak. It doesn't guarantee that every speech will turn out exactly the way you want—and it certainly is no substitute for thorough preparation. But used in conjunction with the other methods of combating stage fright, it is a proven way to help control your nerves and to craft a successful presentation.

Know That Most Nervousness Is Not Visible

Many novice speakers are worried about appearing nervous to the audience. It's hard to speak with poise and assurance if you think you look tense and insecure. Fortunately, only a fraction of the turmoil you feel inside is visible on the outside. "Your nervous

Speaking with Confidence **Checklist**

	YES	NO
1. Am I enthusiastic about my speech topic?	☐	☐
2. Have I thoroughly developed the content of my speech?	☐	☐
3. Have I worked on the introduction so my speech will get off to a good start?	☐	☐
4. Have I worked on the conclusion so my speech will end on a strong note?	☐	☐
5. Have I rehearsed my speech orally until I am confident about its delivery?	☐	☐
6. Have I worked on turning negative thoughts about my speech into positive ones?	☐	☐
7. Do I realize that nervousness is normal, even among experienced speakers?	☐	☐
8. Do I understand that most nervousness is not visible to the audience?	☐	☐
9. Am I focused on communicating with my audience, rather than on worrying about my nerves?	☐	☐
10. Have I visualized myself speaking confidently and getting a positive response from the audience?	☐	☐

system may be giving you a thousand shocks," says one experienced speaker, "but the viewer can see only a few of them."[9]

Even though your palms are sweating and your heart is pounding, your listeners probably won't realize how tense you are—especially if you do your best to act cool and confident on the outside. As one speaker remarked after watching himself on video, "I was amazed at how calm I looked. I assumed everyone would be able to see how scared I was, but now that I know they can't, I won't be nearly so nervous in the future. It really helps to know that you look in control even though you may not feel that way."

Don't Expect Perfection

It may also help to know that there is no such thing as a perfect speech. At some point in every presentation, every speaker says or does something that does not come across exactly as he or she had planned. Fortunately, such moments are usually not evident to the audience. Why? Because the audience does not know what the speaker *plans* to say. It hears only what the speaker *does* say. If you momentarily lose your place, reverse the order of a couple statements, or forget to pause at a certain spot, no one need be the wiser. When such moments occur, just proceed as if nothing happened.

Even if you do make an obvious mistake during a speech, that is not a catastrophe. You will not lose face or your audience. If you have ever listened to Martin Luther King's "I Have a Dream," you may recall that he stumbles over his words twice during the speech. Most likely, however, you don't remember. Why? Because you were focusing on King's message rather than on the fine points of his delivery.

As you work on your speeches, make sure you prepare thoroughly and do all you can to get your message across to your listeners. But don't panic about being perfect or about what will happen if you make a mistake. Once you free your mind of these burdens, you will find it much easier to approach your speeches with confidence and enthusiasm.

Additional Tips

Besides the six points just discussed, there are several additional tips that can help you deal with nervousness. They include:

- Be at your best physically and mentally. It's not a good idea to stay up until 3:00 a.m. the night before your speech. A good night's sleep will serve you better.
- As you are waiting to speak, quietly tighten and relax your leg muscles, or squeeze your hands together and then release them. Such actions help reduce tension by providing an outlet for your extra adrenaline.
- Take a couple slow, deep breaths before you start to speak. Most people, when they are tense, take short, shallow breaths, which only reinforces their anxiety. Deep breathing breaks this cycle of tension and helps calm your nerves.
- Work especially hard on your introduction. Research has shown that a speaker's anxiety level begins to drop significantly after the first 30 to 60 seconds of a presentation.[10] Once you get through the introduction, you should find smoother sailing the rest of the way.
- Make eye contact with members of your audience. Remember that they are individual people, not a blur of faces. And they want you to succeed.
- Concentrate on communicating with your audience rather than on worrying about your stage fright. If you get caught up in your speech, your audience will too.
- Use visual aids. They create interest, draw attention away from you, and make you feel less self-conscious.

If you are like most people, you will find your speech class to be a very positive experience. As one student at the University of International Business and Economics, in Beijing, wrote on her course evaluation at the end of the term: "I have gained so much through this course. I'm more confident than I was before. Though I still feel nervous when I'm going to give a speech, I know I can handle the situation. I like to give a talk in public now. I don't fear any kind of speech."

Public speaking is a vital mode of communication in most cultures around the world. Here former South African President Nelson Mandela speaks on behalf of the United Nations Children's Fund.

The best part about confidence is that it nurtures itself. After you score your first triumph, you will be that much more confident the next time. And as you become a more confident public speaker, you will likely become more confident in other areas of your life as well.

Being an Ethical Speaker

Ethics is the branch of philosophy that deals with issues of right and wrong in human affairs. Questions of ethics arise whenever we ask whether a course of action is moral or immoral, fair or unfair, just or unjust, honest or dishonest.

ethics
The branch of philosophy that deals with issues of right and wrong in human affairs.

We face such questions daily in almost every part of our lives. The researcher must decide whether to shade her data "just a bit" in order to gain credit for an important scientific breakthrough. The shopper must decide what to do with the extra change mistakenly given by the clerk at the store. The student must decide whether to say anything about a friend he has seen cheating on an exam.

Questions of ethics also come into play whenever a public speaker faces an audience. In an ideal world, as the Greek philosopher Plato noted, all public speakers would be truthful and devoted to the good of society. Yet history tells us that the power of speech is often abused—sometimes with disastrous results. Adolf Hitler was unquestionably a persuasive speaker. His oratory galvanized the German people, but his aims were horrifying and his tactics despicable. He remains to this day the ultimate example of why the power of the spoken word needs to be guided by a strong sense of ethical integrity.

GUIDELINES FOR ETHICAL SPEAKING

Sound ethical decisions involve weighing a potential course of action against a set of ethical standards or guidelines. Just as there are guidelines for ethical behavior in other areas of life, so are there guidelines for ethical conduct in public speaking.

Make Sure Your Goals Are Ethically Sound

Your first responsibility as a speaker is to ask whether your goals are ethically sound. During World War II, Hitler stirred the German people to condone war, invasion, and genocide. More recently, we have seen business leaders who defraud investors of their savings and politicians who betray the public trust for personal gain. There can be no doubt that these are not worthy goals.

But think back for a moment to the examples of speechmaking given in Chapter 1. What do the speakers hope to accomplish? Support Beijing's bid for the 2008 Summer Olympic Games. Report on a business project. Help a classmate who is ill. Few people would question that these goals are ethically sound.

As with other ethical issues, there can be gray areas when it comes to assessing a speaker's goals—areas in which reasonable people with well-defined standards of right and wrong can legitimately disagree. But this is not a reason to avoid asking ethical questions. If you are to be a responsible public speaker, you cannot escape assessing the ethical soundness of your goals.

Be Fully Prepared for Each Speech

"A speech," as the American journalist Jenkin Lloyd Jones stated, "is a solemn responsibility." You have an obligation—to yourself and to your listeners—to prepare fully every time you stand in front of an audience.

The obligation to yourself is obvious: The better you prepare, the better your speech will be. But the obligation to your listeners is no less important. Think of it this way: The person who makes a bad 30-minute speech to an audience of 200 people wastes only a half hour of his or her own time. But that same speaker wastes 100 hours of the audience's time—more than four full days. This, Jones exclaimed, "should be a hanging offense!"

At this stage of your speaking career, you will probably not be facing many audiences of 200 people. But neither the size nor the composition of your audience changes your ethical responsibility to be fully prepared. Every audience—including your speech class—is worthy of your best effort.

Being prepared for a speech involves everything from analyzing your audience to creating visual aids, from organizing your ideas to rehearsing your delivery. Most crucial from an ethical standpoint, though, is making sure you do not communicate erroneous information or misleading advice. No matter what the occasion, you need to explore your speech topic as thoroughly as possible. Investigate the whole story; seek out competing viewpoints; get the facts right. Not only will you give a better speech, you will also fulfill one of your major ethical obligations.

Be Honest in What You Say

Nothing is more important to ethical speechmaking than honesty. Public speaking rests on the unspoken assumption that "words can be trusted and people will be truthful."[11]

Questions of ethics arise whenever a speaker faces an audience. Of all the ethical obligations facing speakers, none is more important than honesty in order to maintain the bond of trust with listeners.

Without this assumption, there is no basis for communication, no reason for one person to believe anything that another person says.

Blatant contempt for the truth is one kind of dishonesty in public speaking. But more subtle forms of dishonesty are just as unethical. They include juggling statistics, quoting out of context, misrepresenting sources, painting tentative findings as firm conclusions, portraying a few details as the whole story, citing unusual cases as typical examples, and substituting innuendo and half-truths for evidence and proof. All of these violate the speaker's duty to be accurate and fair in presenting information.

While on the subject of honesty in speechmaking, we should also note that ethically responsible speakers do not present other people's words as their own. They do not plagiarize their speeches. This subject is so important that we devote a separate section to it later in this chapter.

Put Ethical Principles into Practice

It is easy to pay lip service to the importance of ethics. It is much harder to act ethically. Yet that is just what the responsible public speaker must do. As one popular book on ethics states, "Being ethical means behaving ethically *all the time*—not only when it's convenient."[12]

As you work on your speeches, you will ask yourself such questions as "Is my choice of topic suitable for the audience?" "Are my supporting materials clear and convincing?" "How can I phrase my ideas to give them more impact?" These are *strategic* questions. As you answer them, you will try to make your speech as informative, as persuasive, or as entertaining as possible.

But you will also face moments of *ethical* decision. When those moments arrive, don't simply brush them aside and go on your way. Keep in mind the guidelines for ethical speechmaking we have discussed and do your best to follow them through thick and thin.

PLAGIARISM

plagiarism Presenting another person's language or ideas as one's own.

"Plagiarism" comes from *plagiarius*, the Latin word for kidnapper. To plagiarize means to present another person's language or ideas as your own—to give the impression you have written or thought something yourself when you have actually taken it from someone else.[13] We often think of plagiarism as an ethical issue in the classroom, but it can have repercussions in other situations:

> Joanne Calabro was in her second year as school superintendent in the U.S. town of Fort Lee, New Jersey. In May 2007, she spoke at a ceremony for students being inducted into the National Honor Society. It was a brief speech—only six minutes—but the repercussions would last much longer.
>
> One of the students at the ceremony recognized some of Calabro's passages and decided to check them online. He discovered that she had lifted the entire speech from a sample induction address posted on About.com. Further evidence came from a videotape of Calabro delivering the speech.
>
> When confronted with the facts, Calabro admitted to an error in judgment but insisted she had done nothing illegal. In fact, the speech on About.com was protected by copyright law, and Calabro might have been liable to legal action had the Web firm been so inclined. What she could not escape were the ethical consequences. Facing severe criticism within the school district and from the press, she had little choice but to resign her post as superintendent.

As this story shows, plagiarism is a serious matter. If you are caught plagiarizing a speech in class, the punishment can be severe. If you are caught plagiarizing outside the classroom, you stand to forfeit your good name or to damage your career. It is worth your while, then, to make sure you know what plagiarism is and how to avoid it.

Global Plagiarism

global plagiarism Stealing a speech entirely from a single source and passing it off as one's own.

Global plagiarism is stealing your speech entirely from another source and passing it off as your own. The most blatant—and unforgivable—kind of plagiarism, it is grossly unethical.

Global plagiarism in a college classroom usually occurs because a student puts off the assignment until the last minute. Then, in an act of desperation, the student downloads a speech from the Internet or gets one written by a friend and delivers it as his or her own.

The best way to avoid this, of course, is not to leave your speech until the last minute. By starting early, you will give yourself plenty of time to prepare a first-rate speech—a speech of your own.

Patchwork Plagiarism

patchwork plagiarism Stealing ideas or language from two or three sources and passing them off as one's own.

Unlike global plagiarism, in which a speaker pirates an entire speech from a single source, patchwork plagiarism occurs when a speaker cuts and pastes from two or three sources, without giving credit and without doing any additional research. This is no less plagiarism than is copying from a single source. When you give a speech, you declare that it is your work—the product of your thinking, your beliefs, your language. If your speech does not contain any of these, it stands open to the charge of plagiarism.

Ethical Public Speaking **Checklist**

	YES	NO
1. Have I examined my goals to make sure they are ethically sound?	☐	☐
2. Have I fulfilled my ethical obligation to prepare fully for the speech?	☐	☐
a. Have I done a thorough job of studying and researching the topic?	☐	☐
b. Have I prepared diligently so as not to communicate erroneous or misleading information?	☐	☐
3. Is the speech free of plagiarism?	☐	☐
a. Can I vouch that the speech represents my own work, my own thinking, my own language?	☐	☐
b. Do I cite the sources of all quotations and paraphrases?	☐	☐
4. Am I honest in what I say in the speech?	☐	☐
a. Is the speech free of any false or deliberately deceptive statements?	☐	☐
b. Does the speech present statistics, testimony, and other kinds of evidence fairly and accurately?	☐	☐
5. All in all, have I made a conscious effort to put ethical principles into practice in preparing my speech?	☐	☐

"But," you may be thinking, "not many students are experts on their speech topics. Why should they be expected to come up with new ideas that even the experts haven't thought of?" The answer is: They aren't. The key is not whether you have something absolutely original to say, but whether you do enough research and thinking to come up with your own slant on the topic.

As with global plagiarism, one key to averting patchwork plagiarism is to start working on your speech as soon as possible. The longer you work on it, the more apt you are to come up with your own approach. It is also vital to consult a large number of sources in your research. If you have only two or three sources, you are far more likely to fall into the trap of patchwork plagiarism than if you consult a wide range of research materials.

Incremental Plagiarism

In global plagiarism and patchwork plagiarism, the entire speech is cribbed more or less verbatim from a single source or a few sources. But plagiarism can exist even when the speech as a whole is not pirated. This is called incremental plagiarism. It occurs when the speaker fails to give credit for particular parts—increments—of the speech that are borrowed from other people. The most important of these increments are quotations and paraphrases.

incremental plagiarism
Failing to give credit for particular parts of a speech that are borrowed from other people.

Quotations

Whenever you quote someone directly, you must attribute the words to that person. Suppose you are giving a speech on Malcolm X, the famous African-American leader of the 1960s. While doing your research, you run across the following passage from Bruce Perry's acclaimed biography, *Malcolm: The Life of the Man Who Changed Black America:*

> Malcolm X fathered no legislation. He engineered no stunning Supreme Court victories or political campaigns. He scored no major electoral triumphs. Yet because of the way he articulated his followers' grievances and anger, the impact he had upon the body politics was enormous.[14]

This is a fine quotation that summarizes the nature and importance of Malcolm's impact on American politics. It would make a strong addition to your speech—as long as you acknowledge Perry as the author. The way to avoid plagiarism in this instance is to introduce Perry's statement by saying something like:

> In *Malcolm: The Life of the Man Who Changed Black America,* historian Bruce Perry says the following about Malcolm's impact on American politics. . . .

Or,

> According to historian Bruce Perry in his book *Malcolm: The Life of the Man Who Changed Black America*. . . .

Now you have clearly identified Perry and given him credit for his words rather than presenting them as your own.

Paraphrases

paraphrase
To restate or summarize an author's ideas in one's own words.

When you paraphrase an author, you restate or summarize his or her ideas in your own words. Suppose, once again, that your topic is Malcolm X. But this time you decide to paraphrase the statement from Bruce Perry's biography rather than quoting it. You might say:

> Malcolm X was not a politician. He did not pass any laws, or win any Supreme Court victories, or get elected to any office. But he stated the grievances and anger of his followers so powerfully that the whole nation took notice.

Even though you do not quote Perry directly, you still appropriate the structure of his ideas and a fair amount of his language. Thus you need to give him credit—just as if you were repeating his words verbatim.

It is especially important in this case to acknowledge Perry because you are borrowing his opinion—his judgment—about Malcolm X. If you simply recount basic facts about Malcolm's life, you do not have to report the source of your information. The facts are well known and can be found in any standard reference work.

On the other hand, there is still considerable debate about Malcolm's views of other African-American leaders, the circumstances surrounding his death, and what he might have done had he lived. If you were to cite Perry's views on any of these matters—regardless of whether you quoted or paraphrased—you would need to acknowledge him as your source.

Speakers who begin work on their speeches early and consult a wide range of sources are less likely to fall into the trap of plagiarism than are speakers who procrastinate and rely on a limited number of sources.

There are two ways to guard against incremental plagiarism. The first is to be careful when taking research notes to distinguish among direct quotations, paraphrased material, and your own comments. The second way to avoid incremental plagiarism is to err on the side of caution. In other words, when in doubt, cite your source.

Plagiarism and the Internet

When it comes to plagiarism, no subject poses more confusion—or more temptation—than the Internet. Because it's so easy to copy information from the Web, many people are not aware of the need to cite sources when they use Internet materials in their speeches. If you don't cite Internet sources, you are just as guilty of plagiarism as if you take information from print sources without proper citation.

One way to avoid patchwork plagiarism or incremental plagiarism when working with the Internet is to take careful research notes. Make sure you keep a record of the following:

- The title of the Internet document.
- The author or organization responsible for the document.
- The date on which the document was published, posted, or last updated.
- The date on which you accessed the document.

You will need all this information for your speech bibliography (see Chapter 9).

You will also need to identify your Internet sources when you present the speech. It is not enough to say "As I found on the Web," or "As the Internet states." If you are citing a specific person, you should identify him or her and the Web site on which you found the information. If you are citing an organization, rather than an individual, you need to provide the name of the organization.

Another issue with regard to the Internet is the large number of Web sites that sell entire speeches or papers. In addition to being highly unethical, using material from one of these sites is extremely risky. The same technology that makes it easy to plagiarize from the Web makes it easy for teachers to locate material that has been plagiarized and the exact source from which it has been taken.

You should also know that almost all the speeches (and papers) offered for sale on the Web are of very low quality. If you are ever tempted to purchase one, keep in mind there is a good chance you will waste your money and get caught in the process. Here, as in other aspects of life, honesty is the best policy.

SUMMARY

Stage fright is an issue for public speakers in all countries. Rather than trying to eliminate every trace of stage fright, you should try to transform it into positive energy. To some extent, this will happen naturally as you gain experience as a speaker, but you should also think positively, prepare thoroughly, visualize yourself giving a successful speech, remember that most nervousness is not visible to the audience, and think of your speech as communication rather than as a performance in which you must do everything perfectly.

Because public speaking is a form of power, it carries with it heavy ethical responsibilities. There are four basic guidelines for ethical speechmaking. The first is to make sure your goals are ethically sound. The second is to be fully prepared for each speech. The third is to be honest in what you say. The fourth is to put ethical principles into practice at all times.

Of all the ethical lapses a speaker can commit, few are more serious than plagiarism. Global plagiarism is lifting a speech entirely from a single source. Patchwork plagiarism involves cutting and pasting a speech from a limited number of sources. Incremental plagiarism occurs when a speaker fails to give credit for specific quotations and paraphrases that are borrowed from other people.

Because it is so easy to copy information from the Internet, it poses special challenges with regard to plagiarism. If you don't cite Internet sources, you are just as guilty of plagiarism as if you take information from print sources without proper citation. As you research your speeches, be sure to take accurate notes of the Internet sources you use so you can identify them in your speech.

KEY TERMS

Key-Term Exercise

Check your knowledge with the Key-Term Exercise for this chapter.

stage fright *(17)*
adrenaline *(18)*
positive nervousness *(18)*
visualization *(20)*
ethics *(23)*
plagiarism *(26)*
global plagiarism *(26)*
patchwork plagiarism *(26)*
incremental plagiarism *(27)*
paraphrase *(28)*

EXERCISES FOR THINKING AND SPEAKING

1. What are your major anxieties about public speaking? Which of the tips presented in the chapter for dealing with nervousness do you find most helpful? Explain.

2. Experienced public speakers convey their confidence through a combination of their vocal and physical behaviors. Divide a sheet of paper into two columns: "Vocal Behaviors of a Confident Speaker" and "Physical Behaviors of a Confident Speaker." In each column, list and briefly explain three behaviors that, in your experience, reflect a confident public speaker. Be prepared to discuss your ideas in class.

3. Identify the ethical issues in each of the following situations and explain what your course of action would be.

   a. You are speaking on the topic of education reform. In your research, you run across two public opinion polls. One of them, an independent survey by a respected scholarly organization, shows that a majority of people in the province oppose your position. The other poll, suspect in its methods and conducted by a partisan organization, says a majority of people in the province support your position. Which poll do you cite in your speech? If you cite the second poll, do you point out its shortcomings?

   b. When listening to a speech by one of your classmates, you realize that much of it is plagiarized from an Internet article you read a couple weeks earlier. What do you do? Do you say something when your instructor asks for comments about the speech? Do you mention your concern to the instructor after class? Do you talk with the speaker? Do you remain silent?

   c. While researching your persuasive speech, you find a quotation from an article by a highly respected expert that will nail down one of your most important points. But as you read the rest of the article, you realize the author does not in fact support the policy you are advocating. Should you still include the quotation in your speech?

Public Speaking in Your Career

After working for several years at an English-language publishing company in Beijing, you have been promoted to marketing manager for a literature series. At your company's annual sales meeting, you will address the sales force about the company's new books and how to sell them to bookstores.

You are pleased to have this opportunity, but the closer you get to the speech, the harder it is to control the butterflies in your stomach. There will be 100 people in your audience, including all the company managers, in addition to the sales force. What strategies will you use to control your nerves and make them work for you?

3 Giving Your First Speech

You may be surprised to learn that one of your first assignments is to give a speech. You say to yourself, "What am I going to do? I have barely started this course, yet I'm supposed to stand up in front of the whole class and give a speech! I've only read a few pages in the textbook, and I don't know much about public speaking. Where do I begin?"

If these are your thoughts, you aren't alone. Most beginning speech students have a similar reaction. Fortunately, giving your first speech sounds a lot harder than it is. The purpose of this chapter is to help you get started on preparing and delivering your speech.

Preparing Your Speech

Usually a brief introductory presentation, the first assignment is often called an ice breaker speech because it is designed to "break the ice" by getting students up in front of the class as soon as possible. This is an important step because much of the anxiety associated with public speaking comes from lack of experience giving speeches. Once you have broken the ice by giving a speech, you will feel less anxious and will have taken the first step on the road to confidence.

DEVELOPING THE SPEECH

There are a number of possible assignments for the first speech. One is a speech of self-introduction that provides insight into the speaker's background, personality, beliefs, or goals. In other cases, students are asked to introduce a classmate, rather than themselves.

No matter which you are assigned, be sure to focus your presentation sharply so it conforms to the assigned time limit. One of the most common mistakes students make on their first speech is trying to cover too much material. You should select a limited number of points and illustrate them clearly.

It would be impossible, for example, to tell your audience everything about your life in a two-minute speech. A better approach would be to focus on one or two events that have helped define who you are—an incident from your childhood, the story behind a personal photograph, a few of your typical behaviors, or an important lesson you learned from someone you admire. This allows you to make a few well-developed points about a clearly defined subject.

Once you have a topic for your speech, be creative in developing it. Think of ways to make your presentation mysterious or suspenseful. Suppose you are telling the audience about meeting a celebrity. Rather than identifying the celebrity at the outset, you might save his or her name for the end of your speech. As your story unfolds, provide clues about your celebrity's gender, physical characteristics, special talents, and the like, but keep the name secret until the last moment.

In addition to mystery and suspense, audiences are naturally interested in drama, adventure, and danger. Suppose you are introducing a fellow student and you learn that he or she was caught in a flood or spent a summer working with the stage crew for CoCo Lee. The details would provide excellent material for a speech.

You can also make your speech interesting by using colorful, descriptive language. One speaker used this technique when introducing a fellow student, named Alexa, to the class. The speaker began by saying:

Video 3.1

View the introduction from "Gotta Dance."

> The spotlight shines. The music blares. The crowd cheers. The colors, bright and vibrant, bleed together as Alexa and her partner sail around the dance floor. Her partner touches her hand and her waist, but only briefly. He then spins her away, and she glides across the floor in what seems like a single motion. Alexa has worked many weeks for this moment. Alexa, you see, is a championship ballroom dancer.

Word pictures like this are always more interesting than dull language and abstract generalizations.

You might wonder whether you should use humor to make your first speech entertaining. Audiences love witty remarks, jokes, and funny situations, but like anything else, humor is effective only when done well. It should flow naturally out of the speech content rather than being contrived. If you are not normally a funny person, you are better off giving a sincere, enthusiastic speech and leaving out the jokes.

ORGANIZING THE SPEECH

Regardless of your topic, your speech will have three main parts—an introduction, a body, and a conclusion. Your first job in the introduction is to get the attention and interest of the audience. You can do this by posing a question, telling a story, making a startling statement, or opening with a quotation. The purpose of all these methods is to create a dramatic, colorful opening that will make your audience want to hear more.

Here, for example, is how one student from India began a narrative about a significant experience in her life:

Video 3.2

View the beginning of "Kiyomi and Me."

> Her name was Kiyomi. She was a mysterious Japanese dancer. Last autumn I got to meet her. How, you ask. Well, actually, she was a character in a play. I met her the day I became her. That day was one of the happiest days of my life. I wanted that part so desperately it was all I could think about. Being Kiyomi was one of the most memorable experiences of my life.

After this introduction, the speaker's listeners were eager to hear more about Kiyomi and her role in the speaker's life.

In addition to gaining attention and interest, the introduction should orient your listeners toward the subject matter of your speech. In the longer speeches you will give later in the term, you will usually need to provide an explicit preview statement that identifies the main points to be discussed in the body of your speech. (For example, "Today I will inform you about the symptoms, causes, and treatment of high blood pressure.")

preview statement
A statement in the introduction of a speech that identifies the main points to be discussed in the body.

Because your introductory speech is so short, you may not need a detailed preview statement. But you still need to give your audience a clear sense of your topic and purpose. Look back for a moment at the introduction about Kiyomi quoted earlier. Notice how it moves from arousing curiosity to letting the audience know what the rest of the speech will focus on. By the end of the introduction, there is no doubt about the topic of the speech.

After getting the audience's attention and revealing your topic, you are ready to move into the body of your speech. In some speeches, the body seems to organize itself. If you are telling a story about a significant experience in your life, you will relate the events chronologically, in the order they occurred.

chronological order
A method of speech organization in which the main points follow a time pattern.

But not all speeches follow such a format. Suppose you are giving a presentation introducing a classmate. You could organize the most important biographical facts about your subject in chronological order, but this might result in a dull, superficial speech: "Jinjin was born in Beijing in 1991, attended Beijing 2nd Primary School from 1997 to 2003, and graduated from Beijing No. 4 High School in 2009."

A better way of structuring your remarks might be to discuss three of the most important aspects of Jinjin's life, such as hobbies, career goals, and family. This is called the topical method of organization, which subdivides the speech topic into its natural, logical, or conventional parts. Although there are many other ways to organize a speech, your first presentation will probably use either chronological or topical order.

topical order
A method of speech organization in which the main points divide the topic into logical and consistent subtopics.

Regardless of the method of organization you use, remember to limit the number of main points in the body of your speech. In a two-minute presentation, you won't have time to develop more than two or three main points.

Once you have selected those points, make sure each one focuses on a single aspect of the topic. For example, if your first point concerns your classmate's hometown, don't introduce irrelevant information about her job or favorite music. Save this material for a separate point, or cut it.

Try to make your main points stand out by introducing each with a transition statement. In a speech introducing a classmate, you might begin the first main point by saying:

transition
A word or phrase that indicates when the speaker has finished one thought and is moving on to another.

> Rico's family moved a great deal throughout his childhood.

When you reach the second point, you might introduce it like this:

> Moving a lot led to Rico's outgoing nature and confidence in making friends. In fact, he has friends all around the world with whom he corresponds regularly by e-mail.

You have now let your audience know that the first main point is over and that you are starting the second one. The third main point might begin as follows:

> Corresponding with people all over the world is more than just a hobby for Rico, since he is majoring in international relations.

Transition statements such as these will help your audience keep track of your main ideas.

When you finish discussing your final point, you will be ready to move into your conclusion. You need to accomplish two tasks in this part of the speech: let the audience know you are about to finish and reinforce your major theme.

If possible, end on a dramatic, clever, or thought-provoking note. For example, in the presentation about Kiyomi, the speaker devoted the body of her talk to explaining how she won the role and what happened when she performed it on stage. Then, in her conclusion, she wrapped up by saying:

Video 3.3

View the ending of "Kiyomi and Me."

> I needed this experience to appreciate who I was. I realized that I should be myself and not long to be someone else. So what if I'm not the most graceful or feminine person? So what if I don't possess all the wonderful characteristics of Kiyomi? I am still me—not a character in a play. Yet by playing that character, I learned one of the most important lessons of my life. I learned that by becoming a woman who never was, I became proud of who I am.

The final lines bring the speech to a dramatic close and underscore why the experience of playing Kiyomi was so important to the speaker.

Delivering Your Speech

Once you have selected a subject and organized the content into a clear structure, it is time to work on the delivery of your speech. Because this is your first speech of the term, no one expects you to give a perfectly polished presentation. Your aim is to do as well as possible while also laying a foundation you can build upon in later speeches. With this in mind, we'll look briefly at the extemporaneous method of speech delivery, the importance of rehearsing your speech, and some of the major factors to consider when speech day arrives.

SPEAKING EXTEMPORANEOUSLY

extemporaneous delivery
A method of delivery in which the speech is carefully prepared and rehearsed but is presented from a brief set of notes.

You might be inclined, as are many beginning speakers, to write out your speech like an essay and read it word for word to your listeners. The other extreme is to prepare very little for the speech—to wing it by trusting to your wits and the inspiration of the moment. Neither approach is appropriate. Reading from a manuscript runs the risk of poor eye contact with the audience and a stiff, unenthusiastic delivery. On the other hand, ad-libbing is a recipe for disaster. The outcome is usually an aimless talk that is either embarrassingly short or rambles on far too long.

Most experts recommend speaking extemporaneously, which combines the careful preparation and structure of a manuscript presentation with the spontaneity and enthusiasm of an unrehearsed talk. Your aim in an extemporaneous speech is to plan your major points and supporting material without trying to memorize the precise language you will use on the day of the speech.

The extemporaneous method requires you to know the content of your speech quite well. In fact, when you use this method properly, you become so familiar with the substance of your talk that you need only a few brief notes to remind you of the points you intend to cover. The notes should consist of key words or phrases, rather than complete sentences and paragraphs. This way, when you are in front of the audience, you will tell them what you know about the topic in your own words.

Although it can be challenging, work on presenting your first speech extemporaneously. This will provide a strong foundation upon which you can build in later speeches.

Prepare your notes by writing or printing key terms and phrases on note cards or sheets of paper. In either case, your notes should be large enough to read clearly at arm's length. Many experienced speakers double- or triple-space their notes because this makes them easier to see at a glance. Write or print on only one side of the note card or paper, and use the fewest notes you can manage and still present the speech fluently and confidently.

At first, it may seem very demanding to deliver a speech extemporaneously. In fact, though, you use the extemporaneous method in everyday conversation. Do you read from a manuscript when you tell your friends an amusing story? Of course not. You feel relaxed and confident with your friends, so you just tell them what is on your mind in a conversational tone. Try to do the same thing in your speech.

REHEARSING THE SPEECH

When you watch a truly effective extemporaneous speaker, the speech comes out so smoothly that it seems almost effortless. In fact, that smooth delivery is the result of a great deal of practice. As your speech course progresses, you will gain more experience and will become more comfortable delivering your speeches extemporaneously.

The first time you rehearse your introductory speech, however, you will probably struggle. Words may not come easily, and you may forget some things you planned to say. Don't become discouraged. Keep going and complete the speech as well as you can. Concentrate on gaining control of the ideas rather than on trying to learn the speech word for word. You will improve every time you practice.

For this approach to work, you must rehearse the speech out loud. Looking silently over your notes is not enough. Speaking the words aloud will help you master the content and length of your talk. Once you have a fairly good grasp of the speech, ask friends or family members to listen and to give constructive feedback. Don't be shy about asking. Most people love to give their opinion about something, and it's crucial that you rehearse with a live audience before presenting the speech in class.

PRESENTING THE SPEECH

When it is your turn to speak, move to the front of the room and face the audience. Assume a relaxed but upright posture. Plant your feet a bit less than shoulder-width apart and allow your arms to hang loosely by your side. Arrange your notes before you start to speak. Then take a moment to look over your audience and to smile. This will help you establish rapport with your listeners from the start.

Once you are into the speech, feel free to use your hands to gesture, but don't try to plan all your gestures ahead of time. If you don't normally use your hands expressively during informal conversation, then you shouldn't feel compelled to gesture a lot during your speech. Whatever gestures you do use should flow naturally from your feelings.

Above all, don't let your gestures or bodily actions distract listeners from your message. Do your best to avoid nervous mannerisms such as twisting your hair, wringing your hands, shifting your weight from one foot to the other, rocking back and forth, or tapping your fingers on the lectern. No matter how nervous you feel, try to appear calm and relaxed.

During your talk, look at your audience as often as you can. One of the major reasons for speaking extemporaneously is to maintain eye contact with listeners. Be sure to look to the left and right of the room, as well as the center, and avoid the temptation to speak exclusively to one or two sympathetic individuals. When you are finished speaking, your listeners should have the impression that you established a personal connection with each of them.

Try to use your voice as expressively as you would in normal conversation. Concentrate on projecting to the back of the room and, despite your nerves, fight the temptation to race through your speech. If you make a conscious effort to speak up, slow down, and project clearly, you will be on the right track to an effective presentation.

Sample Speeches with Commentary

Videos 3.4–3.6
View "Pot, Soil, Water," "Rhymes with Orange," and "Confronting Myself: Color of the Wind."

The following three speeches provide excellent models of introductory speeches. All are clearly organized and creatively developed. Two were presented by students at the University of Wisconsin. The first is a speech of self-introduction; the second is a speech introducing a classmate. The third was presented by Xia Peng, a student at Nanjing University, during the final round of the 2004 CCTV Cup.

Pot, Soil, Water

COMMENTARY	SPEECH
The introduction captures attention and reveals the topic. By comparing herself to a houseplant and the elements it needs to grow, the speaker provides a creative touch that runs through the entire speech.	Those of you with a green thumb know that a healthy houseplant like this one needs a number of things to grow, including a good pot, rich soil, and adequate water. The pot is the plant's home, the comforting place where it grows up. The soil gives the plant nutrients and helps its roots expand. Water is the basis of all life and allows the plant to thrive. Like this plant and the pot, soil, and water it requires to grow, you can get a sense of my growth by looking at my family, my friends, and my interests.
Each main point in the body is clearly stated and discussed. As you can see from the video, the speaker communicates sincerely and with excellent eye contact.	The pot represents my family. A pot holds the plant together just like my family holds me together. My mom and dad not only gave me life but a loving home to grow up in. If I ever had a bad day, they kept me from falling apart. As the plant protects the roots and the soil, my family protected me as I grew through my childhood.
The assignment for this speech required students to use an object to introduce themselves to the class. As the speech proceeds, notice how the speaker does not focus on describing the object—in this case, her houseplant—but on how the plant provides insight into the speaker herself.	The soil represents my friends, who have supported me as I branched out into new experiences. Here on campus, my three best friends have helped me adjust to college by showing me around, by introducing me to new people, and by helping me with my assignments. They encourage me to follow my dreams and are always willing to offer advice. As the nutrients from the soil feed the plant, my friends have helped me grow and develop.
The speaker completes the body by mentioning some of her personal interests and weaving them into the overall theme of the speech.	The water represents my interests. Without water, this plant would turn brown and dull, but with water, the plant is bright and full of life. Like water for this plant, my interests help me flourish rather than wilt. I have a broad range of interests, including music, art, swimming, and watching movies. My interests make my personal colors more vibrant and allow me to bloom.
The speaker provides a harmonious conclusion that ends on a positive note and completes the comparison with her houseplant.	I wouldn't be who I am today without my family, my friends, and my interests. But like this plant, I still have some growing to do—more things to learn and more things to experience. Luckily, because of my own pot, soil, and water, I'm confident I will blossom into the person I want to be.

Rhymes with Orange

COMMENTARY	SPEECH
The opening sentence of this introduction gains attention; the second identifies the central idea of the speech.	Paul Madsen's first memory in life was sitting on his grandmother's lap and being fed his favorite food—an orange. Surprisingly, there are actually many similarities between Paul and his favorite food.
The body of this speech contains three main points. In the first, the speaker creatively uses a comparison with the tough skin of an orange to discuss Paul's major hobby, playing rugby.	Much like an orange has tough skin, so does Paul, which is evident by his choice of a major hobby—playing rugby. Paul started playing rugby while he was growing up near London, England. Rugby is described by many as the roughest sport in the world, a fact Paul can attest to since he has broken two ribs, two bones in his foot, and fractured his jaw while playing the sport. But rugby's brutal nature hasn't stopped Paul from pursuing the sport to its highest level, including leading his local team to the European championship game for its age group.
Now the speaker moves from the tough skin of an orange to its softer inside as a way to discuss Paul's humanitarian activities. The ideas are clear and concise, and the speaker has excellent vocal variety and eye contact.	But like an orange, Paul's tough skin can be misleading. Just as an orange has a softer inside, so does Paul. He is both a caring person and a humanitarian. He has done lots of charity work throughout his life, and this past summer he went to Namibia in Southern Africa and helped build schools so the local children could have a chance to be educated. Paul also helped teach some of the children English and distributed basic health products that the children had been lacking. Paul views it as an obligation to give back to those less fortunate than him because he has been so blessed in life—especially by his loving family, which includes his mother, father, and three younger brothers.
The speaker develops his third main point by comparing Paul to an orange about to be picked from a tree. All in all, this speech provides a good example of creativity in an introductory presentation.	Like an orange about to be picked from the tree, Paul has absolutely no idea where he will end up. After growing up in England, he's spending his first full year away from his homeland and is just starting to adjust to American culture. So far he's enjoying his new home immensely and is very much looking forward to furthering his education here at the university. As for a profession, Paul is not sure yet what he wants to do. He thinks he would like to have a job doing some sort of charity-related work, or he might want to coach rugby back in England.
The speaker concludes by adding a light touch of humor.	But no matter where life takes him, one thing is for sure—Paul will eat lots of oranges along the way.

Confronting Myself: Color of the Wind

COMMENTARY	SPEECH
The opening story gains attention and interest. By using dialogue, the speaker heightens the personal tone of his story.	When I was in kindergarten, I once showed off my painting to the class. To my surprise, they all burst into laughter. "Why did you paint the sky green?" one asked. Unable to seek a valid answer, I replied dryly, "Well, that's the color of wind."
The speaker states the moral of his opening story and indicates that the rest of his speech will focus on his colorblindness.	Though at that time I didn't realize that I was colorblind, my sensitivity told me something was missing. My confidence wavered, and from then on I tried to avoid every occasion that called for the use of colors.
The body of the speech revolves around the speaker's senior-high photography class, in which he progressed from shame about his colorblindness to pride in his skills of photographic composition.	However, there is something in life that I can never avoid. In my senior high, I had to choose photography to meet curricular requirements. Still suffering from color phobia, I only used black-and-white film to take pictures. Yet my works turned out to be good ones. They say I have a special sense of light and shade, and by the use of simple picture composition, I can fully convey the theme of the photo.
	"Why not try some color films?" my photography teacher asked.
	"I am colorblind."
As in the introduction, the speaker's use of dialogue gives vitality to his narrative.	"So what?" he patted on my shoulder, "It is your colorblindness that gives you the stronger sense of light and shade and helps you to grasp the theme of the photo without distractions of colors."
The speaker concludes by celebrating his colorblindness as a blessing in disguise. His penultimate sentence ties back to the introduction, while his final sentence ends on a poignant note.	My teacher's words struck me. Later, I found out that the incidence of colorblindness is one in a thousand. To me, it is a blessing in disguise. With that in mind, I put a roll of color film in my camera and set out to take pictures. With the snapping sound of the shutter, I could not help but paint the color of wind in my own pictures. The colors lie in my heart.

SUMMARY

Videos 3.7–3.8

View more sample introductory speeches.

One of your first assignments will be to present an introductory speech, either a speech of self-introduction or a speech introducing a classmate. Focus the speech on a limited number of ideas and be creative in developing them. Use interesting supporting materials and present them in colorful, descriptive language.

When organizing the speech, make sure you have a clear introduction, body, and conclusion. Most introductory speeches fall naturally into chronological or topical order. Using clear transitions will help your audience follow you from point to point.

Although you will write a complete manuscript or outline of your speech when preparing it, you should deliver it extemporaneously. This means you have rehearsed fully and can present your talk from a brief set of speaking notes. Concentrate on establishing eye contact with the audience and on speaking in a dynamic, engaged tone of voice.

KEY TERMS

Key-Term Exercise

Check your knowledge with the Key-Term Exercise for this chapter.

preview statement *(34)*
chronological order *(35)*
topical order *(35)*
transition *(35)*
extemporaneous delivery *(36)*

EXERCISES FOR THINKING AND SPEAKING

1. Carefully examine the three sample speeches with commentary on pages 39–41. Answer the following questions about them.

   a. How does the opening paragraph in each speech gain the attention of the audience?

   b. How clearly is each speech organized? What does the speaker do to help listeners follow the progression of ideas?

   c. What are the similarities and differences among the conclusions in the three speeches?

   d. Which speech do you find most effective? Least effective? Why?

2. Are there occasions outside the classroom on which you might give a speech of self-introduction? Identify two such occasions and explain how you might apply in each the principles of self-introductory speeches discussed in this chapter.

3. Prepare a 2-minute speech of self-introduction that you will present in class. Follow the principles of speech preparation and delivery discussed in this chapter. Develop your ideas by writing a manuscript or a full-sentence outline. Deliver the speech extemporaneously from a brief set of speaking notes.

4. As an alternative to the preceding exercise, prepare a 2-minute speech introducing one of your classmates. Arrange a time outside class when you and your classmate can interview each other to gain information for your speeches. Plan your questions in advance. In addition to asking about basic biographical information, try to develop creative questions that will give your speech color, detail, and interest.

   Prepare the speech by following the principles of speech development and delivery discussed in this chapter. Work out your ideas by writing a manuscript or a full-sentence outline. Deliver the speech extemporaneously from a brief set of speaking notes.

Public Speaking in Your Career

As a college senior, you are preparing for your job interviews. In your interviews, you will be asked to present a 1–2 minute speech of self-introduction that provides information about your background and explains why you will be an excellent person for the company to hire. Prepare a draft of your speech.

4 Selecting a Topic and a Purpose

As you read through this book, you will find examples of hundreds of speeches that were delivered in classrooms, in the political arena, in community and business situations. Here is a very small sample of the topics they cover:

acupuncture	Neo-Confucianism
breast cancer	Olympic Math
cloisonné	Peking Opera
Du Fu	Qiu Jin
environment	robots
free trade	study abroad
genetic engineering	Temple of Heaven
Hainan Island	United Nations
Internet fraud	volunteering
jade	women's gymnastics
kites	Xuankong Si
Leonardo da Vinci	yoga
Mount Tai	zoos

Undoubtedly you noticed that the list runs from A to Z. This array of topics wasn't planned. It happened naturally in the course of presenting many different kinds of speeches. The list is given here simply to show you that there are literally endless possibilities for speech topics—from A to Z.

Choosing a Topic

The first step in speechmaking is choosing a topic. For speeches outside the classroom this is seldom a problem. Usually the speech topic is determined by the occasion, the audience, and the speaker's qualifications. When Margaret Chan Fung Fu-chun lectures on a college campus, she is invited to speak about issues of world health. Ieoh Ming Pei will discuss architecture. Ang Lee might share his views about developments in filmmaking. The same is true of ordinary citizens. The head of a travel agency is asked to talk about sight-seeing tours; the middle-school principal speaks about curriculum and textbooks; the real estate agent discusses housing costs and availability.

topic
The subject of a speech.

In a public speaking class, the situation is different. Most of your speech assignments will not come with a designated topic. You need to select the topic yourself. There are two broad categories of potential topics: (1) subjects you know a lot about and (2) subjects you want to know more about. Let's start with the first.

TOPICS YOU KNOW A LOT ABOUT

Most people speak best about subjects with which they are most familiar. When thinking about a topic, draw on your own knowledge and experience. Everyone knows things or has done things that can be used in a speech. Think for a moment about unusual experiences you may have had or special expertise you may have acquired. You are bound to come up with something.

Here are a few examples of topics based largely on the speaker's personal knowledge and experience:

How to Have a Successful Job Interview

Shanghai: The Fashion Capital of Asia

Behind the Scenes at CCTV

A Tour of Qinghai Lake

Migraine Headache: You Can Live with It

TOPICS YOU WANT TO KNOW MORE ABOUT

On the other hand, you may decide to make your speech a learning experience for yourself as well as for your audience. You may choose a subject about which you already have some knowledge or expertise but not enough to prepare a speech without doing additional research. You may even select a topic that you want to explore for the first time. Say, for example, you've always been interested in Xuankong Si but never knew much about it. This would be a perfect opportunity to research a fascinating subject and turn it into a fascinating speech.

Another possibility—especially for persuasive speeches—is to think of subjects about which you hold strong opinions and beliefs. They may include national or international concerns such as global warming, media violence, or stock-market regulations. But not all such topics need be "political." They can deal with anything from dormitory regulations to helping people with disabilities, from vegetarianism to preserving a nature sanctuary.

BRAINSTORMING FOR TOPICS

brainstorming
A method of generating ideas for speech topics by free association of words and ideas.

After all this, you may still be thinking, "I *don't* care about vegetarianism. I've *never* worked at CCTV. I'm *not* active in campus affairs. WHAT am I going to talk about?" If you are having trouble selecting a topic, there are a number of brainstorming procedures you can follow to get started.

Personal Inventory

First, make a quick inventory of your experiences, interests, hobbies, skills, beliefs, and so forth. Jot down anything that comes to mind, no matter how silly or irrelevant it may seem. From this list may come a general subject area out of which you can fashion a specific topic.

When you look for a speech topic, keep in mind special expertise you may have or sports, hobbies, travel, and other personal experiences that would make for an interesting presentation.

Clustering

If personal inventory doesn't work, try a technique called clustering. Take a sheet of paper and divide it into nine columns as follows: People, Places, Things, Events, Processes, Concepts, Natural Phenomena, Problems, and Plans and Policies. Then list in each column the first four or five items that come to mind. The result might look like this:

People	**Places**	**Things**
my family	my hometown	cell phones
Mao Zedong	my province	MP3 players
Yang Liwei	Three Gorges	movies
Guo Jingjing	Dujiangyan	cartoons

Events	**Processes**
graduation	dreaming
marriage	taking photographs
Olympic Games	cooking Yunnan food
World Cup	carving jade

Concepts	**Natural Phenomena**
Buddhism	earthquakes
multiculturalism	tsunami
medical ethics	glaciers
feminism	ice age

Problems	Plans and Policies
cyber crime	developing solar power
childhood obesity	changing graduation requirements
college entrance exam	building a new computer center
divorce	recycling

Very likely, a number of items on your lists will strike you as potential topics. If not, take the items you find most intriguing and compose sublists for each. Try to free-associate. Write down a word or idea. What does that trigger in your mind? Whatever it is, write that down next and keep going until you have several ideas. For example, working from the lists printed above, one speaker composed sublists for movies, Three Gorges, and Yang Liwei:

Movies	Three Gorges	Yang Liwei
Academy Awards	Yangtze River	astronauts
prizes	Chongqing	space program
lotteries	mountains	moon
gambling	flooding	aliens

Can you follow her trail of association? In the first column, movies made her think of the Academy Awards. The Academy Awards are prizes. Prizes reminded her of lotteries. Lotteries are a form of gambling. Suddenly, this speaker remembered an article she had read on the problem of gambling addiction. The idea clicked in her mind. After considerable research, she developed an excellent speech titled "Gambling Addiction: Why You Can't Beat the Odds."

That's a far cry from movies! If you started out free-associating from movies, you would doubtless end up somewhere completely different. This is what clustering is all about.

Internet Search

Yet another possibility is to connect to a subject-based Web site such as Baidu Baike (baike.baidu.com), Yahoo! Directory (dir.yahoo.com) or the Librarians' Index to the Internet (www.lii.org). All three begin with a dozen or so major categories, such as Media, Education, Science, Recreation, Business, Government, and Society and Culture. If you click on one of the categories, you will see a group of subcategories, any of which might strike your fancy as a potential speech topic. If none of them appeal to you, click on one of the subcategories for additional possibilities. You can continue this process until you find just the right topic.

Whatever the means you use for selecting a topic, *start early*. Pay attention to interesting subjects in conversation, on television and the Internet, in newspapers and magazines. Jot down ideas for topics as they occur to you. If you get an early start on choosing a topic, you will have plenty of time to pick just the right one and prepare a first-rate speech.

Having trouble choosing a speech topic? Try browsing through the subject categories at the Librarians' Index to the Internet (www.lii.org). You'll find a wealth of high-quality materials to get your creative juices flowing.

The Creativity and Innovation Library (www.jpb.com/creative/index.php) has an excellent guide to brainstorming, as well as a number of links on creative thinking.

Internet Connection

Determining the General Purpose

general purpose
The broad goal of a speech.

Along with choosing a topic, you need to determine the general purpose of your speech. Usually it will fall into one of two overlapping categories—to inform or to persuade.

When your general purpose is to inform, you act as a teacher or lecturer. If you demonstrate how to perform folk dances, explain how the Great Pyramids were built, or report on your business's quarterly returns, you are speaking to inform. Your aim is to enhance the knowledge and understanding of your listeners—to give them information they did not have before.

When your general purpose is to persuade, you act as an advocate or a partisan. You go beyond giving information to espousing a cause. You want to *change* or *structure* the attitudes or actions of your audience. If you try to convince your listeners that they should join a folk dance club or that your business should adopt a new sales strategy, then you are speaking to persuade. In doing so, you cannot help but give information; but your primary goal is to win over your listeners to your point of view—to get them to believe something or do something as a result of your speech.

Determining the Specific Purpose

specific purpose
A single infinitive phrase that states precisely what a speaker hopes to accomplish in his or her speech.

Once you have chosen a topic and a general purpose, you must narrow your choices to determine the specific purpose of your speech. The specific purpose should focus on one aspect of a topic. You should be able to state your specific purpose in a single infinitive phrase that indicates *precisely* what you hope to accomplish with your speech. For example:

> To inform my audience about recent discoveries of dinosaur fossils.
>
> To inform my audience about the benefits of music therapy for people with psychological disabilities.
>
> To persuade my audience that personal happiness is more important than financial success.
>
> To persuade my audience that the nationwide college entrance examination is the best way to select qualified students.

Notice how clear these specific purpose statements are. Notice also how they relate the topic directly to the audience. That is, they state not only what the *speaker* wants to *say* but also what the speaker wants the *audience* to *know* as a result of the speech. This is very important, for it helps keep the audience at the center of your attention as you prepare your speech.

TIPS FOR THE SPECIFIC PURPOSE STATEMENT

Formulating a specific purpose is the most important early step in developing a successful speech. When writing your purpose statement, follow the principles outlined on the following pages.

Write the Purpose Statement as a Full Infinitive Phrase

Ineffective: Calendars.

More Effective: To inform my audience about the four major kinds of calendars used in the world today.

The ineffective statement is adequate as an announcement of the speech topic, but it is not thought out fully enough to indicate the specific purpose.

Express Your Purpose as a Statement, Not as a Question

Ineffective: What is Halloween?

More Effective: To inform my audience about the history of Halloween festivities.

The question might arouse the curiosity of an audience, but it is not effective as a specific purpose statement. It gives no indication about what direction the speech will take or what the speaker hopes to accomplish.

Avoid Figurative Language in Your Purpose Statement

Ineffective: To inform my audience that yoga is extremely cool.

More Effective: To inform my audience how yoga can improve their health.

Although the ineffective statement indicates something of the speaker's viewpoint, it does not state concisely what he or she hopes to achieve. Figurative language can reinforce ideas within a speech, but it is too ambiguous for a specific purpose statement.

Make Sure Your Specific Purpose Is Not Too Vague or General

Ineffective: To persuade my audience that something should be done about fraudulent land developers.

More Effective: To persuade my audience that harsher penalties are needed to prevent the practices of fraudulent land developers.

The ineffective purpose statement falls into one of the most common traps—it is too broad and ill-defined. It gives no clues about what the speaker believes should be done

When looking for speech topics, think of opinions you hold. One speaker selected "To persuade my audience that stronger measures should be taken to protect African elephants."

about fraudulent land developers. The more effective purpose statement reveals clearly what the speaker plans to discuss.

The more precise your specific purpose, the easier it is to prepare your speech. Consider this topic and specific purpose:

Topic: Hot-air balloons.

Specific Purpose: To inform my audience about hot-air balloons.

With such a hazy purpose, you have no systematic way of limiting your research or of deciding what to include in the speech and what to exclude. The origins of hot-air balloons, how they work, their current popularity—all could be equally relevant to a speech designed "to inform my audience about hot-air balloons."

In contrast, look at this topic and specific purpose:

Topic: Hot-air balloons.

Specific Purpose: To inform my audience about the scientific uses of hot-air balloons.

Now it is easy to decide what is germane and what is not. You can focus your research specifically on the scientific uses of hot-air balloons.

Choose a Specific Purpose That Is Appropriate for Your Audience

The price of retirement homes in Hangzhou might be an engrossing topic for older citizens who are in the market for such homes. Similarly, the quality of hot lunches in primary schools is of great concern to the students who eat them and the parents who pay for them. But if you reverse the audiences, the topics will not have nearly the same

Checklist Specific Purpose

YES	NO	
☐	☐	1. Is the specific purpose written as a full infinitive phrase?
☐	☐	2. Is the specific purpose phrased as a statement rather than a question?
☐	☐	3. Is the specific purpose free of figurative language?
☐	☐	4. Does the specific purpose indicate precisely what I plan to accomplish in the speech?
☐	☐	5. Is the specific purpose suitable for my audience?
☐	☐	6. Can the specific purpose be accomplished in the time allotted for the speech?

relevance. No matter how well you construct your speeches, they are likely to fall flat unless you speak about matters of interest to your listeners.

You also want to make sure that your specific purpose is not too technical for your audience. Although you may be perfectly familiar with the principles and vocabulary of molecular biology, international finance, or linguistic theory, your audience may not be. There are aspects of these and similar subjects that can be treated clearly, with a minimum of jargon. But if you find that you can't fulfill your specific purpose without relying on technical words and concepts, you should reconsider your purpose.

Choose a Specific Purpose You Can Achieve in the Allotted Time

Classroom speeches are usually quite short, ranging from two to eight minutes. Most speakers of English talk at a rate of 120 to 150 words a minute. This means that a six-minute speech will consist of roughly 720 to 900 words. That is not long enough to develop a highly complex topic. For example, none of the following specific purpose statements can be handled well in the time allotted for classroom speeches:

To inform my audience about the role of technology in Chinese history.

To inform my audience about the rise and fall of ancient Rome.

To persuade my audience to convert to vegetarianism.

You also need to be aware of time constraints outside the classroom. You might have up to one hour to make a business presentation, but you could just as likely have twenty minutes—or less. No matter what the audience or occasion, make sure you have a specific purpose that you can reasonably hope to achieve in the allotted time.

Unlike the specific purpose, which you need to settle on early in the speech preparation process, the central idea usually takes shape later, as a result of your research and analysis of the topic.

Phrasing the Central Idea

The specific purpose of a speech is what you hope to accomplish. The central idea is a concise statement of what you *expect to say*. Sometimes it is called the thesis statement, the subject sentence, or the major thought. Whatever the term, the central idea is usually expressed as a simple, declarative sentence that refines and sharpens the specific purpose statement.

central idea
A one-sentence statement that sums up or encapsulates the major ideas of a speech.

Imagine that you run into a friend. She says, "I hear you're giving a speech today. Can you tell me the gist of it in one sentence?" "Sure," you reply, "the three major tourist attractions in Washington, D.C., are the White House, the Washington Monument, and the U.S. Capitol." By stating exactly what the three major tourist attractions are, the central idea sums up your speech in a single sentence.

Another way to think of your central idea is as your residual message—what you want your audience to remember after they have forgotten everything else in the speech. Most of the time the central idea will encapsulate the main points to be developed in the body of the speech. For example:

residual message
What a speaker wants the audience to remember after it has forgotten everything else in a speech.

Topic:	Qipao.
General Purpose:	To inform.
Specific Purpose:	To inform my audience of the history, styles, and cultural impact of qipao.
Central Idea:	Qipao was created in the 1920s, comes in a number of styles, and has exerted significant cultural impact on Chinese women.

Checklist Central Idea

YES	NO	
☐	☐	1. Is the central idea written as a complete sentence?
☐	☐	2. Is the central idea phrased as a statement rather than a question?
☐	☐	3. Is the central idea free of figurative language?
☐	☐	4. Does the central idea clearly encapsulate the main points to be discussed in the body of the speech?
☐	☐	5. Can the central idea be adequately discussed in the time allotted for the speech?
☐	☐	6. Is the central idea suitable for my audience?

The speaker starts with a broad subject (qipao) that becomes narrower and narrower as the speaker moves from the general purpose to the specific purpose to the central idea. From the central idea, we can expect the speaker to address three main points: the first summarizing the history of qipao, the second looking at different styles of qipao, and the third exploring the impact of qipao on Chinese women.

This sharpening of focus as one proceeds to the central idea is crucial. Often you can settle on a specific purpose early in preparing your speech. The central idea, however, usually emerges later, after you have done your research and have decided on the main points.

TIPS FOR THE CENTRAL IDEA

What makes a well-worded central idea? Essentially the same things that make a well-worded specific purpose statement. The central idea should not be too general, should be expressed as a full sentence, should not be in the form of a question, and should avoid figurative language.

Make Sure the Central Idea Is Not Too General

Ineffective: Banning violent content on television is a good idea.

More Effective: Because violent content on television increases antisocial behavior in young children, it should be banned on weekends and before 9:00 p.m. on school nights.

The first central idea is too general. Saying that banning violent content on television is a "good idea" does not convey the speaker's viewpoint sharply and clearly. What does the speaker mean by a "good idea"? The more effective central idea reveals exactly what the speaker thinks should be done, and why.

Express the Central Idea as a Full Sentence

Ineffective: Green tea versus black tea.

More Effective: Despite different methods of preparation, green tea and black tea are both made from the leaves of *Camellia sinensis* and both have their own health benefits.

The phrase "green tea versus black tea" does not reveal enough about the content of the speech to serve as the central idea. The more effective central idea identifies with precision the similarities and differences of green tea and black tea.

State the Central Idea as a Declarative Sentence, Not as a Question

Ineffective: What are nanorobots?

More Effective: Microscopic in size, nanorobots are being developed for use in medicine, weaponry, and daily life.

Asking "What are nanorobots?" might be a good way to attract the attention of listeners, but posing a question does not identify the main points to be developed in the speech. The central idea should always be expressed as a full declarative sentence.

Avoid Figurative Language in the Central Idea

Ineffective: Hainan Island is an awesome place for a vacation.

More Effective: Hainan Island has many attractions for vacationers, including a warm climate, excellent food, and ethnic villages.

To describe Hainan Island as an "awesome" place for a vacation is perfectly appropriate for informal conversation, but not for the central idea of a speech. The more effective central idea avoids figurative language and specifies the major attractions of Hainan Island.

SUMMARY

The first step in speechmaking is choosing a topic. If you have trouble picking a topic, you can use clustering, a personal inventory, or an Internet search to come up with something that is right for you.

The general purpose of your speech will usually be to inform or to persuade. When your general purpose is to inform, your goal is to communicate information clearly, accurately, and interestingly. When your general purpose is to persuade, your goal is to win listeners over to your point of view.

Once you know your topic and general purpose, you must focus on a specific purpose statement that indicates precisely what your speech seeks to achieve. The specific purpose statement should (1) be a full infinitive phrase; (2) be worded as a statement, not a question;

(3) avoid figurative language; (4) not be vague or general; (5) be appropriate for your audience; and (6) be achievable in the allotted time.

The central idea is a concise statement of what you will say in your speech, and it usually crystallizes in your thinking after you have done your research and have decided on the main points. In most cases, it encapsulates the main points in a single declarative sentence.

KEY TERMS

Key-Term Exercise

Check your knowledge with the Key-Term Exercise for this chapter.

topic *(45)*

brainstorming *(46)*

general purpose *(49)*

specific purpose *(49)*

central idea *(53)*

residual message *(53)*

EXERCISES FOR THINKING AND SPEAKING

1. Using one of the brainstorming methods described in this chapter, come up with three topics you might like to deal with in your next speech. Devise a specific purpose statement for each topic.
2. Here are several specific purpose statements. Identify the problem with each, and rewrite the statement to correct the problem.

   Donate blood.

   To inform my audience about Guilin.

   To inform my audience about the history of Western civilization.

   To persuade my audience that something has to be done about traffic jams.

   To inform my audience how to use the subway system in Berlin, Germany.

   What is shuimo hua?
3. Below are two sets of main points for speeches. For each set, supply the general purpose, specific purpose, and central idea.

   General Purpose:

   Specific Purpose:

   Central Idea:

   Main Points:
   I. You should study abroad because it will enhance your personal development.
   II. You should study abroad because it will enhance your academic development.
   III. You should study abroad because it will enhance your career development.

General Purpose:

Specific Purpose:

Central Idea:

Main Points:

I. The first event in triathlon is swimming.

II. The second event in triathlon is cycling.

III. The third event in triathlon is running.

Public Speaking in Your Career

Your communication degree has helped you land a job as spokesperson for the mayor of a medium-size coastal city. A year after starting the job, you are selected to organize an information campaign explaining the benefits of a new public park proposed by the mayor.

To launch this campaign, you will hold a news briefing at the end of the week. To open the briefing, you will present a short set of comments on the mayor's initiative. You decide to focus on three benefits of the park: (1) It will provide green space in the middle of the city; (2) It will provide a location for healthy social activities; (3) It will be free and open to everyone.

Following the format used in this chapter, state the general purpose, specific purpose, central idea, and main points of your comments.

5 Analyzing the Audience

Audience-Centeredness

The Psychology of Audiences

Factors in Audience Analysis

- Size
- Physical Setting
- Demographic Traits
- Disposition Toward the Topic
- Disposition Toward the Speaker
- Disposition Toward the Occasion

Getting Information About the Audience

Adapting to the Audience

- Audience Adaptation Before the Speech
- Audience Adaptation During the Speech
- Audience Adaptation After the Speech

In the midst of the heated 2008 campaign for the U.S. Democratic presidential nomination, Barack Obama faced one of the biggest challenges of his political career. His former minister, Jeremiah Wright, had made controversial, racially charged comments that circulated widely in the national media. Suddenly, Obama was forced to deal with Wright's remarks, the issue of race in America, and the future of his presidential campaign. In doing so, he had to address multiple audiences, including the white community, the black community, his supporters, backers of rival Hillary Clinton, undecided voters, and the nation in general.

On March 18, 2008, Obama spoke on national television from Philadelphia, the birthplace of the American republic. Well aware of the situation he faced, he crafted a speech that dealt thoughtfully with the concerns of his various audiences while stressing the fundamental unity of the American people. Only by working together, he said, can we "move beyond some of our old racial wounds and . . . continue on the path of a more perfect union."

The speech garnered almost universal praise across the political spectrum. Obama was hailed for his capacity to "lead public opinion" by explaining issues "so both sides can see each other's point of view." He pushed the nation "to move beyond race and gender, beyond Democrat and Republican, beyond politics and into reviving the spirit of the nation itself." It was, by any measure, a striking achievement.

Audience-Centeredness

Obama's speech points up an important fact: Good public speakers are *audience-centered.* They know the primary purpose of speechmaking is not to browbeat the audience or to blow off steam. Rather, it is to gain a desired response from listeners. Barack Obama's purpose in his speech was to gain a favorable response from the major groups in his audience. He did that by presenting himself and his ideas in ways that connected with the audience's goals, values, and beliefs.

audience-centeredness
Keeping the audience foremost in mind at every step of speech preparation and presentation.

Being audience-centered does not involve compromising your beliefs to get a favorable response. Nor does it mean using devious, unethical tactics to achieve your goal. As did Barack Obama, you can remain true to yourself and speak ethically while adapting your message to the needs of your listeners.

To be audience-centered, you need to keep several questions in mind when you work on your speeches:

To whom am I speaking?

What do I want them to know, believe, or do as a result of my speech?

What is the most effective way of composing and presenting my speech to accomplish that aim?

This chapter will introduce the basic principles of audience analysis and adaptation. Chapters 13–14 will deal with those features of audience analysis unique to informative and persuasive speaking.

The Psychology of Audiences

What do you do when you listen to a speech? Sometimes you pay close attention; at other times you let your thoughts wander. People may be compelled to attend a speech, but no one can make them listen. The speaker must make the audience *choose* to pay attention.

Even when people do pay attention, they don't process a speaker's message exactly as the speaker intends. Auditory perception is always selective. Every speech contains two messages—the one sent by the speaker and the one received by the listener. As we saw in Chapter 1, what a speaker says is filtered through a listener's frame of reference—the sum of his or her needs, interests, expectations, knowledge, and experience. As a result, we listen and respond to speeches not as they are, but as we are.

egocentrism
The tendency of people to be concerned above all with their own values, beliefs, and well-being.

People are *egocentric.* They pay closest attention to messages that affect their own values, beliefs, and well-being. Harry Emerson Fosdick, the great American preacher, once said: "There is nothing that people are so interested in as themselves, their own problems, and the way to solve them. That fact is . . . the primary starting point of all successful public speaking."[1]

What do these psychological principles mean to you as a speaker? First, they mean your listeners will hear and judge what you say on the basis of what they already know and believe. Second, they mean you must relate your message to your listeners—show how it pertains to them, explain why they should care about it as much as you do. As Saul Alinksy, the noted community organizer, advises, "People only understand things in terms of their experience," which means that to communicate with them, "you must get inside their experience."[2]

Of course, you can't actually get inside another person's experience. But you can learn enough about your audience to know what you should do to make your ideas clear and meaningful. How you can do this is our next topic.

Factors in Audience Analysis

Anything characteristic of a given audience is potentially important to a speaker addressing that audience. In most cases, however, your audience analysis will proceed in light of six broad categories: size, physical setting, demographic traits, disposition toward the topic, disposition toward the speaker, and disposition toward the occasion. Let us look at each in turn.

SIZE

With the aid of television and the Internet, audiences can range in size from a few people to thousands or even millions of people. At this stage of your speaking career, you may be terrified at the prospect of addressing a huge crowd, but as you gain more experience, you may welcome the challenge of facing a big group. Some speakers actually prefer a large audience to a small one.

Good speakers are audience-centered. Whether speaking formally or informally, they look for creative ways to communicate their ideas and keep their audience's attention.

No matter what size group you are addressing, bear in mind one basic principle: The larger your audience, the more formal your presentation must be. Audience size may also affect your language, choice of appeals, and use of visual aids.

PHYSICAL SETTING

Which of the following would you rather address?

> An audience assembled immediately after lunch, crammed into an overheated room with inadequate seating
>
> An audience assembled at 10:00 in the morning, comfortably seated in an airy, well-lighted room

Undoubtedly you chose the second option. Any of the adverse conditions listed in the first option could seriously impair your audience's willingness to accept your ideas or even listen to you at all.

When you face any speaking situation, it is important to know in advance if there will be any difficulties with the physical setting. When you are invited to speak, don't be shy about asking questions of the person who arranged the speech. If possible, look over the room a few days in advance, or else arrive early on the day of your speech to inspect the room. If it is too warm or too cold, see about adjusting the thermostat. Check the seating arrangements and the location of the lectern to be sure your audience can see you. In short, do everything you can to control the influence of physical setting on your audience.

Internet Connection

The Internet is rich in resources that can help speakers with demographic audience analysis. A good starting point is Yahoo! Directory: Regional (http://dir.yahoo.com/Regional/Countries/), which provides links to countries around the world.

Do you want to learn more about using surveys for audience analysis? You can find a number of helpful tips at InfoPoll (www.accesswave.ca/~infopoll/tips.htm).

What about circumstances you can't control? Your speech *is* scheduled directly after lunch or dinner. The room *is* too small for the audience expected. The heat *cannot* be regulated. Then you are simply going to have to work harder to adapt to these aspects of your listeners' discomfort. Above all, don't be influenced *yourself* by the poor physical setting. If your audience sees that you are energetic, alert, and involved with your topic, chances are they will forget their discomfort and come right along with you.

DEMOGRAPHIC TRAITS

demographic traits
Audience characteristics such as age, gender, education, economic standing, cultural background, and the like.

The receptivity of listeners is strongly influenced by demographic traits such as age, gender, education, economic standing, cultural background, and the like. Ideas that attract younger listeners may offend older listeners. Topics that are appealing to women may be of less interest to men. People who are prosperous usually view the world differently than do those who are mired in poverty. And nothing affects an audience more than cultural background. Speakers who fail to take such factors into account when planning a talk are almost surely doomed to failure.

Keep in mind, however, that there can be a great deal of diversity among listeners with similar demographic characteristics. Not all young people think alike; nor do all older people. Men and women often have different personal interests, yet they can be of one mind on political and economic issues. Europeans have many common beliefs, but each country in Europe has its own national identity, values, and interests. The importance of any given demographic factor will vary from audience to audience depending on the occasion and the speech topic.

The most important thing to keep in mind about demographic audience analysis is that it is not an end in itself. Your aim is not just to list the major traits of your listeners, but to find in those traits clues about how your listeners will respond to your speech. When used sensibly and responsibly, demographic audience analysis can be of great benefit to a speaker.

DISPOSITION TOWARD THE TOPIC

As we saw in Chapter 4, you should keep your audience in mind when choosing a topic. Ideally, you will pick a topic that suits them as well as it suits you. Once you have your topic, however, you must consider in more detail how your listeners will react to it. In particular, you need to assess their interest in the topic, their knowledge about it, and their attitudes toward it.

Demographic audience analysis is vital to successful public speaking in any situation. Of all demographic traits, none is more important than cultural background.

Interest

People do not usually expend the time and effort to attend a speech unless they have some interest in the topic. Yet some listeners will inevitably have a higher interest level than will others. One of your tasks as a speaker is to assess their interest in advance and to adjust your speech accordingly.

Most important, if you think your topic is not likely to generate great interest, you must take special steps to get your listeners involved. In the chapters that follow, we'll look at ways you can develop interest in your topic—by an arresting introduction, provocative supporting materials, vivid language, dynamic delivery, and so forth.

Knowledge

There is often a strong correlation between interest in a topic and knowledge about it. People tend to be interested in what they know about. Likewise, they are inclined to learn about subjects that interest them. But there are exceptions. Few people know much about handwriting analysis, yet most would find it an interesting topic. On the other hand, almost all know a lot about going to the supermarket, but few would find it a fascinating subject for a speech.

Why is it important to gauge your listeners' knowledge about your topic? Quite simply, because it will to a large extent determine what you can say in your speech. If your listeners know little about your topic—whether or not they find it interesting—you will have to talk at a more elementary level. If they are reasonably well informed, you can take a more technical and detailed approach.

Attitude

attitude
A frame of mind in favor of or opposed to a person, policy, belief, institution, etc.

The attitude of listeners toward your topic can be extremely important in determining how you handle the material. If you know in advance the prevailing attitude among members of your audience, you can adjust your speech to address their concerns or to answer their objections.[3]

Audience attitudes are most important in persuasive speeches. If your audience is skeptical about or hostile toward your position, you will need to take special steps to overcome their skepticism or hostility. Above all, you will need to provide supporting materials—examples, statistics, or testimony—in support of your position. In the next chapter, we will discuss ways you can accomplish this.

DISPOSITION TOWARD THE SPEAKER

An audience's response to a message is invariably colored by their perception of the speaker. The more competent listeners believe a speaker to be, the more likely they are to accept what he or she says. Likewise, the more listeners believe that a speaker has their best interests at heart, the more likely they are to respond positively to the speaker's message.

We will come back to this subject in detail when we deal with strategies for persuasive speaking in Chapter 14. For now, keep in mind that your listeners will always have *some* set of attitudes toward you as a speaker. Estimating what those attitudes are and how they will affect your speech is a crucial part of audience analysis.

DISPOSITION TOWARD THE OCCASION

No matter what the situation, listeners have fairly definite ideas about the speeches they consider appropriate. They expect to hear graduation speeches on college campuses, political speeches in provincial legislatures, toasts to the bride and groom at weddings, and so forth. Speakers who seriously violate these expectations can almost always count on infuriating the audience.

Perhaps most important, the occasion will dictate how long a speech should be. When you are invited to speak, the chairperson will usually say how much time you have for your talk. If not, be sure to ask. And once you know, pare down your speech so it fits easily within the allotted time. Do not exceed that time under any circumstance, for you are likely to see your audience dwindle as you drone on.

Getting Information About the Audience

Now that you know *what* to learn about an audience, the next question is, *how* do you learn it? A political leader or a CEO can rely on hired professional pollsters. If you are invited to address a particular group, the person who invites you can usually provide a good sketch of the audience. Ask your contact where you can find out more about the group's history and mission. If you know someone who has spoken to the same group, be sure to sound out that person.

What about your classmates as an audience? You can learn a lot about them by observation and conversation, but you may want to know more about their knowledge and attitudes on specific speech topics. Some teachers encourage students to conduct a formal audience-analysis questionnaire for at least one of their speeches. In addition to providing information about your classroom listeners, such a questionnaire gives you practice in developing the skills of audience analysis you will need for speeches after your class is over.

There are three major kinds of questions to choose from when developing an audience-analysis questionnaire: fixed-alternative questions, scale questions, and open-ended questions.

Fixed-alternative questions, as their name implies, offer a fixed choice between two or more responses. For example:

fixed-alternative questions
Questions that offer a fixed choice between two or more alternatives.

Are you a fan of TV reality shows?

Yes ______________

No ______________

By limiting the possible responses, such questions produce clear, unambiguous answers. They also tend to yield superficial answers. Other techniques are needed to get beneath the surface.

Scale questions resemble fixed-alternative questions, but they allow more leeway in responding. For example:

scale questions
Questions that require responses at fixed intervals along a scale of answers.

Do you agree or disagree with the following? Reality shows have improved the quality of TV programs in China.

Strongly agree	Mildly agree	Undecided	Mildly disagree	Strongly disagree

Questions like these are especially useful for getting at the strength of a respondent's attitudes.

Open-ended questions give maximum leeway in responding. For example:

open-ended questions
Questions that allow respondents to answer however they want.

Why, in your opinion, are TV reality shows so popular?

What is the proper balance in TV programming between profits for broadcasters and the cultural and moral enlightenment of viewers?

Although open-ended questions invite more detailed responses than the other two types of questions, they also increase the likelihood of getting answers that do not give the kind of information you need.

Because each type of question has its advantages and disadvantages, many questionnaires contain all three types. Figure 5.1 shows a questionnaire that was distributed before a speech on volunteering. By using all three types of questions, the speaker

Two fixed-alternative questions establish the listeners' level of knowledge about and degree of involvement with the topic.

1. Have you ever engaged in volunteer work for a community or charitable organization?

   Yes ____________________
   No ____________________

2. Have you or anyone close to you ever benefited from the volunteer work of a community or charitable organization?

   Yes ____________________
   No ____________________
   Not sure ____________________

This scale question is designed to show the attitudes of listeners who have participated in volunteer work.

3. If you have engaged in volunteer work, how would you rate the experience?

   ☐ Very rewarding
   ☐ Somewhat rewarding
   ☐ Neutral
   ☐ Somewhat unrewarding
   ☐ Very unrewarding

Another scale question gauges the listeners' sense of social obligation.

4. Do you agree or disagree with the following statement? To the extent possible, people have an obligation to help those in less fortunate circumstances.

   ☐ Strongly agree
   ☐ Mildly agree
   ☐ Undecided
   ☐ Mildly disagree
   ☐ Strongly disagree

Two open-ended questions ask about the listeners' disposition toward volunteer work. The last question is especially important. It probes specific issues the speaker needs to address for listeners who have not engaged in volunteer work.

5. If you have worked as a volunteer, do you plan to do so again? Why or why not?

6. If you have not worked as a volunteer, what is your major reason for not doing so? Please explain.

• FIGURE 5.1 Sample Questionnaire.

did two things—elicited specific information about the audience and probed more deeply into their attitudes toward the speech topic.

When putting together your own questionnaire, keep the following principles in mind:

1. Plan the questionnaire carefully to elicit precisely the information you need.
2. Use all three types of questions: fixed-alternative, scale, and open-ended.
3. Make sure the questions are clear and unambiguous.
4. Keep the questionnaire relatively brief.

In marketing, poll-taking helps companies chart consumer preferences. For classroom speeches, you can use an audience-analysis questionnaire to gauge the knowledge and opinions of your listeners.

Adapting to the Audience

Once you have completed the audience analysis, you should have a pretty clear picture of your listeners. But this does not guarantee a successful speech. The key is how well you *use* what you know in preparing and presenting the speech.

AUDIENCE ADAPTATION BEFORE THE SPEECH

As we have seen, you must keep your audience in mind at every stage of speech preparation. This involves more than simply remembering who your listeners will be. Above all, it means two things: (1) assessing how your audience is likely to respond to what you say in your speech, and (2) adjusting what you say to make it as clear, appropriate, and convincing as possible.

You must submerge your own views so completely that you can adopt, temporarily, those of your listeners. When you do this, you will begin to hear your speech through the ears of your audience and to adjust it accordingly. Try to imagine what they will like, what they will dislike, where they will have doubts or questions, whether they will need more details here or fewer there, what will interest them and what will not. At every point you must *anticipate* how your audience will respond.

Here is how one speaker worked out his problems of audience adaptation:

A visiting scholar from the Academy of Traditional Chinese Medicine, in Beijing, Pan Weifang was invited to give a public lecture at an American university on "Traditional Chinese Medicine: Principles and Practice." The organizers told him to expect a diverse audience. In addition to students

Checklist Audience Analysis and Adaptation

YES	NO	
☐	☐	1. Have I approached my speech from an audience-centered frame of mind?
☐	☐	2. Have I considered all of the following in my audience analysis:
☐	☐	Size
☐	☐	Physical setting
☐	☐	Demographic traits
☐	☐	Disposition toward the topic
☐	☐	Disposition toward the speaker
☐	☐	Disposition toward the occasion
☐	☐	3. If I have been invited to speak, have I learned about the history and mission of the group I will be addressing?
☐	☐	4. If I am using an audience-analysis questionnaire, have I included all three question types:
☐	☐	Fixed-alternative
☐	☐	Scale
☐	☐	Open-ended
☐	☐	5. When preparing the speech, have I adapted to the audience so my ideas will be as clear and convincing as possible?

and faculty from the medical school, there would be attendees from other parts of the university, as well as people from the community at large.

Pan knew he could count on a high level of interest in his topic, but he also knew most listeners would not be versed in the details of traditional Chinese medicine. Some might be skeptical about its methods and effectiveness.

As Pan prepared the speech, he kept asking himself, "How can I make this topic clear and meaningful to someone who knows little about the history and methods of traditional Chinese medicine?" He worked diligently to explain key concepts such as qi, yin and yang, the five phases, and wu xing in ways that connected with Western listeners. He also developed an excellent set of PowerPoint slides to help bridge the gap in language and culture.

To be perfectly safe, he asked a faculty member who practiced Western medicine to listen to a few sections of the speech. "Stop me," Pan said, "any time I say something that seems unclear or questionable." His colleague stopped him four times, and at each point Pan worked out a better explanation. Finally, he had a speech that was perfectly adapted to his audience.

As you work on your speeches, try to keep your listeners constantly in mind. Anticipate how they will respond to your ideas and be creative in thinking about ways to adapt your message to them.

AUDIENCE ADAPTATION DURING THE SPEECH

No matter how hard you prepare ahead of time, things may not go exactly as planned on the day of your speech. You may find that the room for your speech has been changed, that the audience will be much larger (or smaller) than you had anticipated, or even that the time for your speech has been reduced because the previous speaker has talked too long.

If something like this happens to you, don't panic. Adjust your delivery to the changed room and audience size. If you have less time for your speech than you had planned, condense your speech to its most essential points and present them in the time available. Your listeners will sympathize with your predicament and will appreciate your efforts to adjust. This will more than compensate for your lost speaking time.

Finally, be sure to keep an eye out during your speech for audience feedback. If you find your listeners frowning or responding with quizzical looks, you may need to back up and go over your point again, as in the following example:

> Kang Ping, an economics major, had worked hard to make sure her speech on the stock market was not too technical for her audience, most of whom were humanities students. She explained everything from the ground up, prepared two excellent visual aids, and practiced giving the speech to her best friend, a literature major with no training in economics.
>
> On the day of Kang Ping's speech, everything went well until she got to her second main point, when she noticed that several listeners seemed confused by the relationship between common stock and preferred stock. Knowing they would be lost for the rest of the speech if they didn't understand that relationship, Kang Ping paused and said, "I can see some of you are confused by my explanation. Let me try it again from a different angle."
>
> As Kang Ping went through the material a second time, she saw her listeners nodding their heads in understanding. She could now go on with her speech, confident that her audience was ready to go with her.

AUDIENCE ADAPTATION AFTER THE SPEECH

It may seem strange to think of audience adaptation after a speech, but reflecting on your audience's response is an important part of skill development. For example, if you are presenting a workshop in a business or educational setting, the workshop organizers may distribute a survey afterward to gather data about the audience's response. You can use the survey to learn what kinds of changes you should make the next time you present the workshop.

But even in the absence of such a survey, you should think after every speech about how the audience reacted and how you might modify the speech if you were to present it again. Some speakers keep a journal of their speeches, audiences, and responses. This kind of systematic post-speech analysis is an important part of preparing for your next presentation and of becoming a more effective speaker in general.

SUMMARY

Good speakers are audience-centered. When working on your speeches, keep three questions in mind: To whom am I speaking? What do I want them to know, believe, or do as a result of my speech? What is the most effective way of composing and presenting my speech to accomplish that aim?

People are egocentric. They typically approach speeches with one question uppermost in mind: "Why is this important to *me*?" Therefore, you need to study your audience and adapt your speech to their beliefs and interests.

The major factors to consider in audience analysis are size, physical setting, demographic traits, disposition toward the topic, disposition toward the speaker, and disposition toward the occasion. For speeches outside the classroom, you can get information about the audience by asking the person who invites you to speak. For classroom speeches, you can circulate an audience-analysis questionnaire.

Once you complete the audience analysis, you must adapt your speech so it will be clear and convincing. Try to hear the speech as your listeners will. Anticipate questions and objections, and try to answer them in advance. When you deliver the speech, keep an eye out for audience feedback, and adjust your remarks in response. After the speech, think about your audience's response and about changes you would make if you were delivering the speech again.

KEY TERMS

Key-Term Exercise
Check your knowledge with the Key-Term Exercise for this chapter.

audience-centeredness *(59)*
egocentrism *(60)*
demographic traits *(62)*
attitude *(64)*
fixed-alternative questions *(65)*
scale questions *(65)*
open-ended questions *(65)*

EXERCISES FOR THINKING AND SPEAKING

1. Analyze three advertisements from a recent issue of a magazine such as *China Today* or *Beijing Review*. Try to determine the audience being appealed to in each advertisement and analyze the appeals (verbal and visual) used to persuade buyers. How might the appeals differ if the ads were designed to persuade a different audience?

2. For your next speech, design and circulate among your classmates an audience-analysis questionnaire like that discussed on pages 65–66. Use all three kinds of questions discussed in the chapter: fixed-alternative, scale, and open-ended. After you have tabulated results of the questionnaire, write an analysis explaining what the questionnaire reveals about your audience and what steps you should take to adapt your speech to the audience.

3. Read Barbara Bush's "Choices and Change" in the appendix of speeches for appreciation and analysis at the end of the book. Focus on how Bush adapts her message to her audience's gender, to their attitudes about the speaker, and to their attitudes about the topic. Be prepared to share your ideas in class.

Public Speaking in Your Career

As a university professor with a specialization in gender communication, you have been asked to address the managers of a major international accounting and consulting firm on the topic of male and female communication in the workplace. The firm has eleven offices in China; all the managers from each office will attend your speech.

In preparation, you have scheduled a conversation with the firm's human resource director who invited you. List the three most important questions you want to ask the human resource director about your audience. Be specific in your questions, and be prepared to explain your choice of questions.

6 Supporting Your Ideas

Good speeches are not composed of hot air and generalizations. They need strong supporting materials to answer the three questions listeners always ask of a speaker: "What do you mean?" "Why should I believe you?" "So what?" Consider, for example, the following statements:

General	Less General	Specific
Tea is very popular.	Large quantities of tea are consumed by people around the globe.	Tea is second only to water as the world's most consumed beverage. More tea is consumed each year than all other manufactured drinks in the world put together, including coffee, chocolate, soft drinks, and alcohol. Total tea consumption is 4 billion kilograms annually.

supporting materials
The materials used to support a speaker's ideas. The three major kinds of supporting materials are examples, statistics, and testimony.

Which statement do you find most interesting? Most convincing? Chances are you prefer that in the right-hand column. It is sharp and specific, clear and credible—just what a speech needs to come alive.

The skillful use of supporting materials often makes the difference between a poor speech and a good one. In Chapters 13 and 14, we will look at special uses of supporting materials in informative and persuasive speeches. In this chapter, we focus on the basic kinds of supporting materials—examples, statistics, and testimony—and on general principles for using them effectively and responsibly.

Examples

Research has shown that vivid, concrete examples have strong impact on listeners' beliefs and actions. Without examples, ideas often seem vague, impersonal, and lifeless. With examples, ideas become specific, personal, and lively. One social psychologist has concluded that "most people are more deeply influenced by one clear, vivid, personal example than by an abundance of statistical data."[1] Examples are so important that many experienced speakers consider them "the very life of the speech."[2] In addition to clarifying, personalizing, and reinforcing a speaker's ideas, they often appeal powerfully to our emotions.

example
A specific case used to illustrate or to represent a group of people, ideas, conditions, experiences, or the like.

BRIEF EXAMPLES

Brief examples—also called specific instances—may be referred to in passing to illustrate a point. The following excerpt uses a brief example to illustrate the miraculous nature of recent advances in creating artificial limbs for accident victims:

Changes in technology have made it possible for doctors to work wonders that once seemed impossible. Roger Charter, for example, lost both his feet when they were crushed in a truck accident. Now he has new feet—made of a springy plastic alloy that duplicates a normal arch. Not only can he walk normally, but he can run and play sports again!

brief example
A specific case referred to in passing to illustrate a point.

Another way to use brief examples is to pile them one upon the other until you create the desired impression. Here is how the technique was used by Wang Zhiyu, from Shenzhen University, during the 21st Century Cup National English Speaking Competition to support her claim that China's traditional culture has vigor and vitality in today's globalized world:

Japanese businessmen have already applied Confucian ethics in their business management, and the American military academy, West Point, has taken Sunzi's *The Art of War* as one of their textbooks. In these years, the cream of our culture, such as traditional medical science and medicine, acupuncture, Tai Chi, and paper cutting, has won popularity in the world.

EXTENDED EXAMPLES

extended example
A story, narrative, or anecdote developed at some length to illustrate a point.

Extended examples are often called narratives, illustrations, or anecdotes. By telling a story vividly and dramatically, they pull listeners into the speech. Here is such an example, from a speech by Sun Yan, a student at Fudan University. She used an extended example to illustrate the spirit of the Olympic Games:

In the history of the Olympic Games, there have been many shining stars. Among them was a European girl. With the lapse of time, her name has faded from memory, yet her unbending spirit shall never perish. It was she who highlighted the Olympic Creed.

In lead though she had been, she stumbled near the terminus and her leg was injured. Competitors passed her from behind in succession until finally only her weak and lonely figure remained on the track. Doctors came and offered to take her away. Yet she refused. With the only strength left in her, she managed to get up and shuffled feebly to the endpoint with drops of blood along her trail.

Video 6.1
View this excerpt from "The Olympic Spirit."

But cheers broke out. Though she failed in the race, the girl won applause from people all over the world. It was she who elucidated the Olympic creed of participation. It was she who instilled perseverance in our minds.

This long example captures vividly the courage of the Olympic runner and her personification of the Olympic spirit. The speaker could merely have said, "Olympic athletes often display great fortitude," but the story makes the point far more vividly.

HYPOTHETICAL EXAMPLES

hypothetical example
An example that describes an imaginary or fictitious situation.

All the examples presented up to now have been factual; the incidents they refer to really happened. Sometimes, however, speakers will use a hypothetical example—one that describes an imaginary situation. Usually such examples are brief stories that relate a general principle.

Here is how one speaker used a hypothetical example in a speech about the new organ donation system announced by the Red Cross Society of China and the Ministry of Health:

Using Examples **Checklist**

	YES	NO
1. Do I use examples to clarify my ideas?	☐	☐
2. Do I use examples to reinforce my ideas?	☐	☐
3. Do I use examples to personalize my ideas?	☐	☐
4. Are my examples representative of what they are supposed to illustrate or prove?	☐	☐
5. Do I reinforce my examples with statistics or testimony?	☐	☐
6. Are my extended examples vivid and richly textured?	☐	☐
7. Have I practiced the delivery of my extended examples to give them dramatic effect?	☐	☐

> Imagine this: Your father has been stricken with serious heart disease. At the hospital, you learn he has a chance to survive—if he can receive a heart transplant. But there are no heart donors available. Your father is one of the 1.5 million Chinese each year who need an organ transplant but cannot get one because of a shortage of donors.

This hypothetical example is especially effective. The speaker creates a realistic scenario, relates it directly to his listeners, and gets them involved in the speech.

TIPS FOR USING EXAMPLES

Make Examples Vivid and Richly Textured

The richly textured example supplies everyday details that bring the example to life. Recall the example of the Olympic runner earlier in this chapter. The speaker provided many details about the runner's bravery in the face of adverse conditions. The runner stumbles and injures her leg near the end of the race. She is passed by other competitors until she alone is left on the track. Doctors offer to help, but she refuses their assistance and shuffles to the finish line with drops of blood along her trail.

How much less compelling the example would have been if the speaker had merely said:

> One Olympic runner courageously completed her race despite being injured and exhausted.

Instead, the details let us *see* the runner as she battles through her pain and misfortune. The more vivid your examples, the more impact they are likely to have on your audience.

Reinforce Examples with Statistics or Testimony

Examples can bring an issue alive and dramatize it in personal terms. But listeners may still wonder how many people the issue actually affects. In such a situation, you should reinforce your examples with statistics or testimony. Research has shown that the impact of examples is enhanced when they are combined with other supporting materials that show the examples to be typical.[4]

Consider the case of a speaker discussing the misuse of powerful prescription medications in the United States. The speaker could cite a number of recent deaths from such misuse, including Heath Ledger and Michael Jackson. These examples help make the case persuasive, but a listener could dismiss them as sensational and atypical. To prevent this, the speaker might go on and say:

> According to the Centers for Disease Control, reactions to prescription drugs take 20,000 lives each year in the U.S., making it the second leading cause of accidental death, right behind automobile accidents. "Judged by any measure," says Leonard Paulozzi, a medical scientist at the CDC, "the prescription drug problem is a crisis that is steadily worsening."

With this backup material, not even a skeptical listener could reject the examples as atypical.

Statistics

statistics
Numerical data.

We live in an age of statistics. Day in and day out we are bombarded with a staggering array of numbers: China uses 45 billion pairs of disposable chopsticks each year; J. K. Rowling has sold more than 400 million Harry Potter books worldwide; the United States consumes 24 billion litres of beer annually; 1.2 million people a year are killed globally in traffic accidents.

What do all these numbers mean? Most of us would be hard-pressed to say. Yet we feel more secure in our knowledge when we can express it numerically. According to Lord Kelvin, the 19th-century physicist, "When you can measure what you are speaking about, and express it in numbers, you know something about it. But when you cannot measure it, when you cannot express it in numbers, your knowledge is . . . meager and unsatisfactory." It is this widely shared belief that makes statistics, when used properly, such an effective way to clarify and support ideas.[3]

SINGLE STATISTICS

Like brief examples, statistics are often cited in passing to clarify or strengthen a speaker's point. For instance:

> To document different saving rates in China and the United States: "Last year China's saving rate was 54 percent of GDP, according to *China Daily*. The U.S. rate, including households and corporations, was a mere 12 percent of GDP."

> To illustrate the growing popularity of electric bicycles: "The Associated Press reports that China produced 22 million electric bicycles last year. There are now more than 70 million e-bikes on Chinese roads."

A speech that is supported by statistics is usually more persuasive than an undocumented presentation. Here John Chambers, CEO of Cisco Systems, uses economic data when addressing the Boston Chamber of Commerce.

MULTIPLE STATISTICS

Statistics can also be used in combination to show the magnitude or seriousness of an issue. We find a good example of this technique in a speech about international tourism:

> Tourism is a huge global industry. According to the World Tourism Organization, last year there were 922 million international tourist arrivals, with total receipts of almost U.S.$1 trillion. France is the leading tourist nation, with 80 million visitors each year. China, with 50 million visitors, is closing in on the U.S. as the world's third most popular destination.

TIPS FOR USING STATISTICS

Use Representative Statistics

Suppose you choose ten people at random in a shopping mall and ask them whether they favor or oppose resuming excavation of the Terracotta Army at Xi'an. Suppose also that six approve of resuming the excavation and four do not. Would you then be accurate in claiming that 60 percent of the population in your city favors resuming the excavation?

Of course not. Ten people is not a big enough sample. But even if it were, other problems would arise. Do the ten people interviewed accurately reflect your city's proportion of men and women? Do they mirror different age groups? Diverse occupations? Socio-economic levels? In short, make sure your statistics are representative of what they claim to measure.

Identify the Sources of Statistics

Statistics are easy to manipulate. This is why careful listeners keep an ear out for the sources of a speaker's numbers. Rather than saying "Statistics show," or "My figures demonstrate," tell your audience where you got your statistics. Look back at the statistics cited earlier in this section. In each case, the speaker identifies the source of his or her figures (*China Daily*, Associated Press, World Tourism Organization). You should do the same in your speeches.[5]

Use Statistics from Reliable Sources

Which is the more reliable estimate of the dangers of using a mobile phone while driving: One from China Association for Road Traffic Safety or one from China Mobile? Easy—the estimate by China Association for Road Traffic Safety, which does not have a vested interest in what the figures look like. What about nutritional ratings for fast foods offered by Pizza Hut or by Consumers Union, a highly respected nonprofit organization? That's easy too—Consumers Union.

As a speaker, you must be aware of possible bias in the use of numbers. Because statistics can be interpreted in so many ways and put to so many uses, you should seek figures gathered by reliable, nonpartisan sources.

Round Off Complicated Statistics

Mount Kilimanjaro is 5,895.14 meters high; the world land speed record is 1,228.03 kilometers per hour; the population of Saudi Arabia is 28,686,633 people; Lake Poyang has a surface area of 3,585 square kilometers.

These are intriguing figures, but they are too complicated to be readily understood by listeners. Unless there is an important reason to give exact numbers, you should round off most statistics. You might say that Mount Kilimanjaro is 5,900 meters high; the world land speed record is 1,228 kilometers per hour; the population of Saudi Arabia is approaching 29 million; and Lake Poyang has a surface area of almost 3,600 square kilometers.

Explain Statistics

Statistics don't speak for themselves. They need to be interpreted and related to your listeners. Notice how effectively one speaker did this in a talk about Chinese culture in the United States:

> According to Jennifer Lee's *The Fortune Cookie Chronicles*, there are some 43,000 Chinese restaurants in the U.S. That's more than all the McDonalds, Burger Kings, and KFCs combined.

Explaining what statistics mean is particularly important when you deal with large numbers, because they are hard to visualize. How, for example, can we comprehend the four trillion yuan stimulus package implemented by the central government in 2009? We could explain that a trillion is a thousand billion and a billion is a thousand million. But that doesn't do much good, since millions and billions are almost as hard to visualize as are trillions. Suppose, instead, that we translate the huge numbers into terms a listener can relate to. Here is one solution:

> How much money is a trillion yuan? Think of it this way. If you had 1 million yuan and spent it at the rate of 1,000 yuan a day, you would run out of money in less than three years. If you had 1 billion yuan and spent it at the rate of 1,000 yuan a day, you would not run out of money

Using Statistics **Checklist**

	YES	NO
1. Do I use statistics to quantify my ideas?	☐	☐
2. Are my statistics representative of what they purport to measure?	☐	☐
3. Are my statistics from reliable sources?	☐	☐
4. Do I cite the sources of my statistics?	☐	☐
5. Do I round off complicated statistics?	☐	☐
6. Do I use visual aids to clarify statistical trends?	☐	☐
7. Do I explain my statistics and relate them to the audience?	☐	☐

for almost 3,000 years. And if you had 1 trillion yuan and spent it at the rate of 1,000 yuan a day, you would not run out of money for nearly 3 million years!

Be creative in thinking of ways to relate statistics to your audience. This is one of the most important steps you can take to make statistics work in your speeches.

Use Visual Aids to Clarify Statistics

In addition to explaining statistics verbally, you can use visual aids to give them clarity and meaning. This is especially crucial when you are discussing statistical trends, patterns, and other large blocks of information. Rather than drowning your audience in a sea of numbers, you can use a graph or chart to represent the numbers visually. We shall discuss this subject in detail in Chapter 12. For the moment, keep in mind that visual aids can significantly increase the impact of your statistics.

Testimony

Imagine you are talking with a friend about the classes you plan to take next term. You are not sure whether to sign up for interpretation or linguistics. Your friend says, "I took those classes last year. They're both good, but Professor Gao was excellent in linguistics. I'd take it for sure." You check the timetable and find that Professor Gao is indeed scheduled to teach linguistics. You sign up for her course.

As this story illustrates, we are often influenced by the *testimony* of other people. Just as you are likely to be swayed by your friend's recommendation about which class to take, so audiences tend to respect the opinions of people who have special knowledge or experience on the topic at hand. By quoting or paraphrasing such people, you can give your ideas greater strength and impact. The two major kinds of testimony are expert testimony and peer testimony.

testimony
Quotations or paraphrases used to support a point.

EXPERT TESTIMONY

expert testimony Testimony from people who are recognized experts in their fields.

In most speeches you will probably rely on expert testimony—testimony from people who are acknowledged authorities in their fields. Citing the views of people who are experts is a good way to lend credibility to your speeches. It shows that you are not just mouthing your own opinions, but that your position is supported by people who are knowledgeable about the topic.[6]

Suppose you are talking about mental health services in China. Surely you would cite statistics showing the number of people who need such services. You might also dramatize the issue with an example or two. But you should also buttress your position with expert testimony such as the following:

> According to Fan Li, deputy director of the PLA General Hospital, China is experiencing a surge in the number of people with anxiety, depression, and other forms of mental illness. Fan also noted that mental health service users are getting younger and younger, with the youngest reported case just eight years old.

PEER TESTIMONY

peer testimony Testimony from ordinary people with firsthand experience or insight on a topic.

Another type of testimony often used in speeches is peer testimony—opinions of people like ourselves; not prominent figures, but ordinary citizens who have firsthand experience on the topic. This kind of testimony is especially valuable because it gives a more personal viewpoint on issues than can be gained from expert testimony.

For example, if you were speaking about the barriers faced by people with physical disabilities, you would surely include testimony from doctors and other medical authorities. But in this case, the expert testimony would be limited because it cannot communicate what it really means to have a physical disability. To communicate that, you need a statement from someone who can speak with the voice of genuine experience—as in the following case:

> Itzhak Perlman, the world-renowned violinist whose legs are paralyzed, once said: "When you are in a wheelchair, people don't talk to you. Perhaps they think it is contagious, or perhaps they think crippled legs mean a crippled mind. But whatever the reason, they treat you like a thing."

There is no way expert testimony can express these ideas with the same authenticity and emotional impact.

TIPS FOR USING TESTIMONY

Decide Whether to Quote or Paraphrase

direct quotation Testimony that is presented word for word.

The statement above from Itzhak Perlman is presented as a direct quotation. Testimony can also be presented by paraphrasing. Rather than quoting someone verbatim, you present the gist of that person's ideas in your own words.

When should you use a direct quotation as opposed to paraphrasing? The standard rule is that quotations are most effective when they are brief, when they convey your meaning better than you can, and when they are particularly eloquent, witty, or compelling. If you find a quotation that fits these criteria, then recite the quotation word for word.

Citing expert testimony is an excellent way for students to lend credibility to their speeches. It shows that the speaker's views are shared by people who have special knowledge on the topic.

Paraphrasing is better than direct quotation in two situations: (1) when the wording of a quotation is obscure or cumbersome; (2) when a quotation is longer than two or three sentences. Audiences often tune out partway through lengthy quotations, which tend to interrupt the flow of a speaker's ideas.

paraphrase
To restate or summarize a source's ideas in one's own words.

Quote or Paraphrase Accurately

Accurate quotation involves three things: making sure you do not misquote someone; making sure you do not violate the meaning of statements you paraphrase; making sure you do not quote out of context.

Of these, the last is the most subtle—and the most dangerous. By quoting out of context, you can twist someone's remarks so as to prove almost anything. Take movie advertisements. A critic pans a movie with these words:

quoting out of context
Quoting a statement in such a way as to distort its meaning by removing the statement from the words and phrases surrounding it.

> This movie is a colossal bore. From beginning to end it is a disaster. What is meant to be brilliant dialogue is about as fascinating as the stuff you clean out of your kitchen drain.

But when the movie is advertised in the newspapers, what appears in huge letters over the critic's name? "COLOSSAL! FROM BEGINNING TO END—BRILLIANT! FASCINATING!"

This is so flagrant as to be humorous. But quoting out of context can have serious consequences, especially when it is used to create a false impression of someone's words or ideas. Be sure, when you quote or paraphrase someone, that you represent their words and ideas with complete accuracy.

Checklist Using Testimony

YES	NO	
☐	☐	1. Do I use testimony to support my ideas?
☐	☐	2. Do I use testimony from qualified sources?
☐	☐	3. Do I use testimony from unbiased sources?
☐	☐	4. Do I distinguish between expert testimony and peer testimony?
☐	☐	5. Do I identify the sources of all testimony?
☐	☐	6. Do I quote and paraphrase all sources of testimony with complete accuracy?

Use Testimony from Qualified Sources

We have all become accustomed to the celebrity testimonial in television and magazine advertising. The Olympic diver praises a brand of swimsuit. The badminton player recommends a racquet. So far, so good. These are the tools of the trade for the people who endorse them.

But what happens when a movie star endorses a milk powder? A singer represents a mobile phone company? Do they know more about these products than you or I? Probably not.

Listeners will find your speeches much more credible if you use testimony from sources qualified *on the subject at hand*. As we have seen, this may include either recognized experts or ordinary citizens with special experience on the speech topic.

Use Testimony from Unbiased Sources

Talking about pesticide residue in bottled water from India, one speaker said:

> A Pepsi-Cola spokesperson said there are no problems with India-bottled Aquafina water, which is "produced to meet WHO-prescribed standards and follows a stringent seven-step process of purification." We can conclude, therefore, that Aquafina is perfectly safe for consumers.

As you might expect, the speaker's audience was not persuaded. After all, what would you expect spokespersons for bottled water producers to say—that their products are unsafe and should be recalled?

Careful listeners are suspicious of testimony from biased or self-interested sources. Be sure to use testimony from credible, objective authorities.

Identify the People You Quote or Paraphrase

The usual way to identify your source is to name the person and sketch his or her qualifications before presenting the testimony. For example:

There are a multitude of Web sites you can consult to find supporting materials for your speeches. For current events, they include *Xinhua News* (www.xinhuanews.com/english2010/), *China Daily* (www.chinadaily.com.cn/), and *Global Times* (www.globaltimes.cn/). For more encyclopedic information, try the Internet Public Library's Subject Collection (www.ipl.org/div/subject/), which provides links to a wide range of high-quality resources.

Internet Connection

> According to Zheng Hongbo, professor at the School of Ocean and Earth Science at Tongji University, the rise of global sea levels is indisputable. "We could search for the exact causes for a long time," he says, "but in terms of the dangers it poses to Shanghai, we have little time. We have to take it very seriously."

Had the speaker not identified Professor Zheng, listeners would not have known who he is or why his opinion should be heeded.

As we saw in Chapter 2, identifying the source of testimony is also an important ethical responsibility. If you use another person's words or ideas without giving credit to that person, you will be guilty of plagiarism. This is true whether you paraphrase the original source or quote it verbatim.

Sample Speech with Commentary

The following speech was given in the United States; its subject is the need to eliminate pennies from the U.S. money supply. Worth 1/100 of a dollar, the penny is similar to the fen in China. As you read the speech, which is organized in problem-solution order, notice how the speaker uses supporting materials to reinforce her argument and to answer potential objections from the audience.

The Problem with Pennies

COMMENTARY	SPEECH
The speaker captures attention with clever variations on traditional sayings.	"A nickel for your thoughts." "A nickel saved is a nickel earned." "Nickels from heaven."
The contrast between the original sayings and the variations in the first paragraph is a witty way for the speaker to introduce the topic of her speech.	Okay, maybe these phrases don't have quite the same ring as the original sayings—"A penny for your thoughts," "A penny saved is a penny earned," and "Pennies from heaven." But it's a fact of our nation's economic life that the penny is becoming obsolete. It's time to let this dinosaur of our economy go extinct.

The speaker relates the topic directly to her audience, establishes her credibility, and previews the main points to be covered in the body of her speech.	Sure, most of you say, pennies can be annoying. But why do we have to get rid of them? And what would we do without pennies? I had the same questions when I started work on this speech. But as a result of my research, I'm convinced that the continued use of pennies is a costly problem and that we can get along just fine without them. Today, I hope to convince you of the same thing.
The speaker begins her first main point, which deals with the problems caused by pennies.	We can begin by noting that pennies cause problems for individuals, for businesses, and for the nation as a whole.
A series of brief examples illustrates the annoyance caused by pennies. The speaker then quantifies her point with figures from a survey by the U.S. Mint.	Many Americans consider pennies a useless annoyance. Pennies take up space and add weight to your pockets, wallets, and purses. They get in the way when you're trying to find other coins. They slow down checkout lines when you have to search for exact change. In fact, many people don't use pennies. A survey by the U.S. Mint showed that only half of the 12,000 people questioned use pennies on a daily basis. Most of the other half collect pennies around the house, waiting until they have enough to cash in at the bank.
The speaker uses statistics to support her claim that pennies are a problem for the business community.	Pennies are a nuisance for businesses as well as for individuals. The National Association of Convenience Stores estimates that an average of two seconds is spent handling pennies during each of its members' 33 billion annual cash transactions. That totals more than 18 million hours spent handling pennies—at an annual cost of $600 million.
The supporting materials in this paragraph are especially effective. Notice how the speaker identifies her sources as she proceeds.	Keeping pennies in circulation also costs the nation as a whole. To keep an adequate supply of pennies in circulation, the U.S. Mint creates 6 billion new pennies each year. According to U.S. Mint director Ed Moy, the cost of manufacturing these new pennies is 1.66 cents apiece, which adds up to $100 million a year. Why keep pennies when making them costs more than they are worth?
A transition moves the speaker into the solution section of her speech.	You can now see the magnitude of the problem with pennies. Fortunately, it's a problem that can be easily solved.
The speaker establishes credibility for her plan by linking it with the Coin Coalition. Later in the paragraph, she cites research from economist Robert Whaples to show that her plan will not harm consumers.	The solution I recommend is similar to a plan supported by the Coin Coalition, a group working to eliminate pennies from the U.S. economy. The plan has three basic steps. First, the national government should legalize and standardize the rounding off of all purchases—including sales tax—to the nearest nickel. Because the number of purchases rounded up would roughly equal the number rounded down, this would not cause any increased cost to consumers, as has been shown in research by economist Robert Whaples of Wake Forest University.

Second, with the need for pennies eliminated, the U.S. Mint should stop making new pennies. As we have seen, this will save taxpayers some $100 million a year in minting costs alone.

Third, people should cash in the pennies already in circulation, thereby removing pennies entirely from the money supply.

The speaker cites the example of phasing out the half-penny coin in 1857 to show that the penny can be eliminated today without problem. Testimony from James Benfield provides additional support, as do the examples of Australia, New Zealand, and the Netherlands.

I admit that it may be hard to imagine a world without pennies, but there is plenty of evidence that this plan will work. James Benfield, former executive director of the Coin Coalition, notes that when the U.S. stopped minting half-cent coins in 1857, a similar procedure of rounding off purchases and phasing out the coins worked extremely well. None of us misses the half-cent, and none of us will miss the penny. Australia, New Zealand, and the Netherlands have all successfully eliminated penny coins in recent years.

The conclusion reinforces the speaker's central idea and provides unity by echoing language used in the introduction.

In conclusion, we have seen the problems pennies create for individuals, for businesses, and for the U.S. as a whole. We have also seen that eliminating pennies is a practical solution. Just as America adjusted to life without the half-penny, so will it adjust to life without the penny. Given time, we will even get used to the phrase "A nickel saved is a nickel earned."

SUMMARY

Good speeches need strong supporting materials to bolster the speaker's point of view. The three basic types of supporting materials are examples, statistics, and testimony.

In the course of a speech you may use brief examples—specific instances referred to in passing—and sometimes you may want to give several brief examples in a row to create a stronger impression. Extended examples are longer and more detailed. Hypothetical examples describe imaginary situations and can be quite effective for relating ideas to the audience.

Statistics can help convey your message as long as you make them meaningful to the audience. Make sure statistics come from reliable sources and are representative of what they claim to measure. Usually, you should round off complicated statistics so they are easier to understand and recall.

Citing the testimony of experts is a good way to make your ideas more credible. You can also use peer testimony, from ordinary people who have firsthand experience on the topic. Be sure to quote or paraphrase accurately, to use testimony from qualified, unbiased sources, and to identify the people you quote or paraphrase.

KEY TERMS

Key-Term Exercise

Check your knowledge with the Key-Term Exercise for this chapter.

supporting materials *(73)*
example *(73)*
brief example *(74)*
extended example *(74)*
hypothetical example *(74)*
statistics *(76)*
testimony *(79)*
expert testimony *(80)*
peer testimony *(80)*
direct quotation *(80)*
paraphrase *(81)*
quoting out of context *(81)*

EXERCISES FOR THINKING AND SPEAKING

1. Each of the following statements violates at least one of the criteria for effective supporting materials discussed in this chapter. Identify the flaw (or flaws) in each statement.
   a. In the words of one expert, "Despite the popularity of bilingual education, there is little evidence that it produces better learning by students."
   b. At its closest point, Jupiter is 628,743,036 kilometers from Earth; at its most distant point, it is 928,081,020 kilometers from Earth.
   c. As Jackie Chan noted in a recent interview, the International Monetary Fund should rethink its criteria for Flexible Credit Lines, given current global economic conditions.
   d. A recent study shows that the use of mobile phones by automobile drivers increases traffic accidents by 37 percent.
   e. I don't see why doctors keep warning people about heavy salt intake. My parents and grandparents use lots of salt, and they are all very healthy.
   f. According to a spokesperson for the video game industry, gaming is beneficial because it develops physical coordination in young children.
2. Read "The Problem with Pennies," the sample speech with commentary at the end of this chapter. Think about how you would construct a speech for or against eliminating small coins such as the fen in China. What sources might you consult in your research, and what kinds of supporting materials might you use?
3. Prepare and deliver a one-point speech in which you state your point, back it up with three pieces of supporting material, and then summarize the point. Be sure to follow the tips for supporting materials presented in this chapter. The speech should be one to two minutes in length.

The provincial department of education you work for has developed a new program for children from poor rural areas. You have been asked to help publicize the program and to build support for it. You want to prepare a talk that makes good use of statistics and expert testimony to demonstrate the value of early childhood education programs, especially for poor children.

As part of your research, you decide to search the Web for supporting materials. List three Web sites that provide useful statistics or testimony on the value of early childhood education. Explain why each Web site is reputable, and list one statistic or expert quotation you obtain from each source.

7 Organizing of the Spee

Main Points
- Strategic Orde
- Tips for Prepar

Supporting Mat

Connectives
- Transitions
- Internal Previe
- Internal Summ
- Signposts

Listeners demand coherence. Unlike readers, they cannot flip back to a previous page if they have trouble grasping a speaker's ideas. In this respect a speech is much like a movie. Just as a director must be sure viewers can follow the plot of a film from beginning to end, so must a speaker be sure listeners can follow the progression of ideas in a speech from beginning to end. This requires that speeches be organized *strategically*. They should be put together in particular ways to achieve particular results with particular audiences.

strategic organization
Putting a speech together in a particular way to achieve a particular result with a particular audience.

Speech organization is important for other reasons as well. As we saw in Chapter 1, it is closely connected to critical thinking. When you work to organize your speeches, you gain practice in the general skill of establishing clear relationships among your ideas. In addition, using a clear, specific method of speech organization can boost your credibility, your confidence, and your ability to deliver a message fluently.

The first step in developing a strong sense of speech organization is to gain command of the three basic parts of a speech—introduction, body, and conclusion—and the strategic role of each. In this chapter, we deal with the body of the speech. The next chapter will take up the introduction and conclusion.

There are good reasons for talking first about the body of the speech. The body is the longest and most important part. Also, you will usually prepare the body first. It is easier to create an effective introduction after you know exactly what you will say in the body.

The process of organizing the body of a speech begins when you determine the main points.

Main Points

The main points are the central features of your speech. You should select them carefully, phrase them precisely, and arrange them strategically. Here are the main points of a speech about the events in women's gymnastics:

main points
The major points developed in the body of a speech. Most speeches contain from two to five main points.

Specific Purpose: To inform my audience about the four events in women's gymnastics.

Central Idea: The four events in women's gymnastics are floor exercise, vault, balance beam, and uneven parallel bars.

Main Points:
I. Floor exercise combines dancing, acrobatics, and tumbling.
II. Vault features explosive power and dramatic midair maneuvers.
III. Balance beam requires precise routines and perfect coordination.
IV. Uneven parallel bars demand strength, flexibility, and agility.

These four main points form the skeleton of the speech. If there are four events in women's gymnastics, then logically there can be four main points in the speech.

How do you choose your main points? Sometimes they will be evident from your specific purpose statement. Suppose your specific purpose is "To inform my audience about the goals, structure, and member states of the United Nations." Obviously, your speech will have three main points. The first will deal with the goals of the United

Nations, the second with the organization's structure, and the third with its member states. Written in outline form, the main points will be:

Specific Purpose: To inform my audience about the goals, structure, and member states of the United Nations.

Central Idea: Composed of five administrative bodies and 192 member states, the United Nations is devoted to facilitating international cooperation.

Main Points:

I. The overarching goal of the United Nations is to facilitate international cooperation.

II. The United Nations is divided into five administrative bodies.

III. The United Nations is made up of 192 member states.

Even if your main points are not stated expressly in your specific purpose, they may be easy to project from it. Let's say your specific purpose is "To inform my audience of the basic steps in making a cloisonné object." You know each of your main points will correspond to a step in the cloisonné-making process. They might look like this in outline form:

Specific Purpose: To inform my audience of the steps in making a cloisonné object.

Central Idea: There are five basic steps in making a cloisonné object.

Main Points:

I. The first step is shaping the metal into the form of the finished object.

II. The second step is creating a design by soldering fine wire to the surface of the object.

III. The third step is filling the design with colored enamel.

IV. The fourth step is polishing the object.

V. The final step is gilding the object with fluid gold.

STRATEGIC ORDER OF MAIN POINTS

Once you establish your main points, you need to decide the order in which you will present them. The most effective order depends on three things—your topic, your purpose, and your audience. Chapters 13 and 14 will cover special aspects of organizing informative speeches and persuasive speeches. Here we look briefly at the four basic patterns of organization used most often by public speakers.

Chronological Order

chronological order
A method of speech organization in which the main points follow a time pattern.

Speeches arranged chronologically follow a time pattern. They may narrate a series of events in the sequence in which they happened. For example:

Specific Purpose: To inform my audience how the Great Wall of China was built.

Central Idea: The Great Wall of China was built in three major stages.

Main Points:

I. Building of the Great Wall began during the Qin Dynasty of 221–206 B.C.

Research studies confirm that clear organization is vital to effective public speaking. Listeners must be able to follow the progression of ideas in a speech from beginning to end.

II. New sections of the Great Wall were added during the Han Dynasty of 206 B.C.–220 A.D.
III. The Great Wall was completed during the Ming Dynasty of 1368–1644.

Video 7.1
View an excerpt from "The Great Wall of China."

Chronological order is also used in speeches explaining a process or demonstrating how to do something. For example:

Specific Purpose: To inform my audience of the steps in laser-assisted corrective eye surgery.

Central Idea: There are three main steps in laser-assisted corrective eye surgery.

Main Points:
I. First, a thin layer is sliced off the surface of the eye to expose the cornea.
II. Second, an ultraviolet laser is used to reshape the cornea.
III. Third, the thin layer sliced off at the beginning of the surgery is reaffixed to the eye.

As you can see from this outline, chronological order is especially useful for informative speeches.

Spatial Order

Speeches arranged in spatial order follow a directional pattern. That is, the main points proceed from top to bottom, left to right, front to back, inside to outside, east to west, or some other route. For example:

Specific Purpose: To inform my audience about the structure of a typhoon.

spatial order
A method of speech organization in which the main points follow a directional pattern.

Central Idea: A typhoon is made up of three parts going from inside to outside.

Main Points:
I. At the center of a typhoon is the calm, cloud-free eye.
II. Surrounding the eye is the eyewall, a dense ring of clouds that produces the most intense wind and rainfall.
III. Rotating around the eyewall are large bands of clouds and precipitation called spiral rain bands.

Or:

Specific Purpose: To inform my audience about the three major regions in Italy.

Central Idea: Northern, central, and southern Italy have their own identities and attractions.

Main Points:
I. Northern Italy is home to Venice and its world-famous canals.
II. Central Italy is home to Rome and its historical treasures.
III. Southern Italy is home to Sicily and its culinary traditions.

Spatial order, like chronological order, is used most often in informative speeches.

Problem-Solution Order

problem-solution order
A method of speech organization in which the first main point deals with the existence of a problem and the second main point presents a solution to the problem.

Speeches arranged in problem-solution order are divided into two main parts. The first shows the existence and seriousness of a problem. The second presents a workable solution to the problem. For example:

Specific Purpose: To persuade my audience that tougher measures are needed to control illegal selling of antiques.

Central Idea: Illegal selling of antiques is a serious problem that requires a combination of government action and individual awareness.

Main Points:
I. Illegal selling of antiques is a serious problem in parts of China.
II. The problem can be solved by a combination of government action and individual awareness.

As this example indicates, problem-solution order is most appropriate for persuasive speeches.

Topical Order

Topical order results when you divide the speech topic into *subtopics,* each of which becomes a main point in the speech.

Suppose your speech topic is Leonardo da Vinci, who was born in the 1400s and is regarded by many people as the greatest genius in Western history. Your specific purpose is "To inform my audience about the achievements of Leonardo da Vinci." You could organize your speech chronologically—by discussing Leonardo's achievements during each stage of his career. On the other hand, you could arrange the

The main points of a speech should be organized to communicate the speaker's message. Chronological order would work very well for a speech on the history of space exploration.

speech topically—by dividing Leonardo's achievements into categories. Then your central idea and main points might be:

topical order

A method of speech organization in which the main points divide the topic into logical and consistent subtopics.

Specific Purpose: To inform my audience about the achievements of Leonardo da Vinci.

Central Idea: Leonardo da Vinci was accomplished as a painter, an inventor, and an astronomer.

Main Points:

I. As a painter, Leonardo produced the *Mona Lisa*, the *Last Supper*, and other masterpieces.

II. As an inventor, Leonardo drew plans for a parachute and a flying machine.

III. As an astronomer, Leonardo concluded that the earth revolves around the sun.

Notice how the main points subdivide the speech topic logically and consistently. Suppose, however, that the main points looked like this:

I. As a painter, Leonardo produced the *Mona Lisa*, the *Last Supper* and other masterpieces.

II. As an inventor, Leonardo drew plans for a parachute and a flying machine.

III. During the final years of his life, Leonardo lived in France.

This would *not* be a good topical order, since main point III is inconsistent with the rest of the main points. It deals with a time period in Leonardo's career, whereas main points I and II deal with fields of achievement.

Checklist Main Points

YES	NO	
☐	☐	1. Are my main points organized according to one of the following methods of organization?
☐	☐	Chronological order
☐	☐	Spatial order
☐	☐	Topical order
☐	☐	Problem-solution order
☐	☐	2. Does the body of my speech contain two to five main points?
☐	☐	3. Are my main points clearly separate from one another?
☐	☐	4. As much as possible, have I used the same pattern of wording for all my main points?
☐	☐	5. Have I roughly balanced the amount of time devoted to each main point?
☐	☐	6. Is each main point backed up with strong, credible supporting materials?
☐	☐	7. Do I use connectives to make sure my audience knows when I am moving from one main point to another?

The da Vinci example refers to an informative speech. But topical order also works for persuasive speeches. Usually the topical subdivisions are the *reasons* why a speaker believes in a certain point of view. Here, for example, are the main points for a speech on why China should continue its program of space exploration:

Specific Purpose: To persuade my audience that China should continue its program of space exploration.

Central Idea: China should continue its program of space exploration because it produces scientific knowledge, opens access to natural resources, and furthers the search for extraterrestrial life.

Main Points:

I. Space exploration produces scientific knowledge that benefits life on Earth.

II. Space exploration opens access to natural resources that are in limited supply on Earth.

III. Space exploration furthers the search for extraterrestrial life.

Because it is applicable to almost any subject and to any kind of speech, topical order is used more often than any other method of speech organization.

TIPS FOR PREPARING MAIN POINTS

Limit the Number of Main Points

Theoretically, a long speech can develop many more main points than can a short speech. In fact, however, listeners will have trouble sorting things out if a speaker has too many main points—regardless of the length of the speech. In most cases, a speech will contain from two to five main points.

If, when you list your main points, you find that you have too many, you may be able to condense them into categories. Here is a set of main points for a speech about yoga:

Specific Purpose: To inform my audience about the practice of yoga.

Central Idea: Yoga is an ancient practice that involves the whole body.

Main Points:

I. Yoga breathing starts with deep inhalation.
II. Yoga breathing requires slow exhalation.
III. Yoga breathing includes prolonged pauses.
IV. Yoga postures involve all parts of the body.
V. Yoga postures increase flexibility.
VI. Yoga postures strengthen muscle tone.
VII. Yoga postures demand precise movements.

You have seven main points—which is too many. But if you look at the list, you see that the seven points fall into two broad categories: yoga breathing and yoga postures. You might, therefore, restate your main points this way:

I. One part of practicing yoga involves proper breathing.
II. Another part of yoga involves body postures.

Video 7.2
View an excerpt from "Yoga: Uniting Mind, Body, and Spirit."

Keep Main Points Separate

Each main point in a speech should be clearly independent of the others. Compare these two sets of main points for a speech about the process of producing a Broadway play:

Ineffective

I. The first step is choosing the play.
II. The second step is selecting the cast.
III. The third step is conducting rehearsals and then performing the play.

More Effective

I. The first step is choosing the play.
II. The second step is selecting the cast.
III. The third step is conducting the rehearsals.
IV. The fourth step is performing the play.

The problem with the left-hand list is that Point III contains two main points. It should be divided, as shown in the right-hand list.

Try to Use the Same Pattern of Wording for Main Points

Consider the following main points for an informative speech about the benefits of exercise.

Ineffective	More Effective
I. Regular exercise increases your endurance.	I. Regular exercise increases your endurance.
II. Your sleeping pattern is improved by regular exercise.	II. Regular exercise improves your sleeping pattern.
III. It is possible to help control your weight by regular exercise.	III. Regular exercise helps control your weight.

The main points on the right follow a consistent pattern of wording. As a result, they are easier to understand and easier to remember than the main points on the left.

You will find that it is not always possible to use this kind of parallel wording. Some speeches just don't lend themselves to such a tidy arrangement. But try to keep the wording parallel when you can, for it is a good way to make your main points stand out from the details surrounding them.

Balance the Amount of Time Devoted to Main Points

Because your main points are so important, you want to be sure they all receive enough emphasis to be clear and convincing. You need to allow sufficient time to develop each main point.

This is not to say that all main points must receive exactly equal emphasis, but only that they should be roughly balanced. For example, either of the following would be fine:

I. 30 percent	I. 20 percent
II. 40 percent	II. 30 percent
III. 30 percent	III. 50 percent

The amount of time spent on each main point depends on the amount and complexity of supporting material for each point.

Supporting Materials

By themselves, main points are only assertions. As we saw in Chapter 6, listeners need supporting materials to accept what a speaker says. Here, for example, are the main points for a speech on the growing use of acupuncture in Western medicine:

I. Acupuncture is used in the West for pain management.
II. Acupuncture is used in the West to help break physical addictions.
III. Acupuncture is used in the West to treat anxiety and depression.

When supporting materials are added, the outline looks like the following:

I. Acupuncture is used in the West for pain management.
  A. Millions of Westerners rely on acupuncture to reduce pain from arthritis, back sprains, and even some forms of cancer.
  B. The value of acupuncture for pain management is well documented.
    1. Testimony from Pain Management Center in Toronto, Canada.
    2. Example of Jurgen Streck, from Hamburg, Germany.
II. Acupuncture is used in the West to help break physical addictions.
  A. Acupuncture is gaining popularity as a way to help people stop smoking.
    1. Story of Linda Chang.
    2. Statistics from *New York Times*.
  B. Acupuncture is also being used in the battle against alcoholism.
    1. Long-term success rates are not yet available.
    2. Short-term evidence, though, is promising.
III. Acupuncture is used in the West to treat anxiety and depression.
  A. Many Westerners are turning to acupuncture to deal with anxiety and depression.
    1. Statistics from *Psychiatric Times Online*.
    2. Testimony from Radcliffe Hospital in Oxford, England.
  B. This trend is part of a movement toward natural remedies.
    1. By restoring the flow of qi, acupuncture can help the body heal itself.
    2. Acupuncture avoids the harmful side effects of anti-anxiety and anti-depression medicines.

supporting materials
The materials used to support a speaker's ideas. The three major kinds of supporting materials are examples, statistics, and testimony.

In Chapter 6, we discussed the major kinds of supporting materials and how to use them. Here, we need stress only the importance of organizing your supporting materials so they are directly relevant to the main points they are supposed to support.

Once you have organized your main points and supporting points, you must give attention to the third element in the body of a speech—connectives.

Connectives

Connectives are words or phrases that join one thought to another and indicate the relationship between them. Without connectives, a speech is disjointed and uncoordinated—much as a person would be without ligaments and tendons to join the bones and hold the organs in place. Four types of speech connectives are transitions, internal previews, internal summaries, and signposts.

connective
A word or phrase that connects the ideas of a speech and indicates the relationship between them.

TRANSITIONS

Transitions are words or phrases that indicate when a speaker has completed one thought and is moving on to another. Technically, transitions state both the idea the speaker is leaving and the idea he or she is coming up to. In the following examples, the transitional phrases are underlined:

transition
A word or phrase that indicates when a speaker has finished one thought and is moving on to another.

Now that we have a clear understanding of the problem, let me share the solution with you.

We have spoken so far of Guan Yu's skill as a warrior, but above all it is his honor and righteousness that make him a mythic figure in Chinese history.

Keeping these points in mind about sign language, let's return to the sentence I started with and see if we can learn the signs for "You are my friend."

Notice how these phrases remind the listener of the thought just completed and reveal the thought about to be developed.

INTERNAL PREVIEWS

internal preview
A statement in the body of the speech that lets the audience know what the speaker is going to discuss next.

Internal previews let the audience know what the speaker will take up next, but they are more detailed than transitions. In effect, an internal preview works just like the preview statement in a speech introduction, except that it comes in the body of the speech—usually as the speaker is starting to discuss a main point. For example:

In discussing how China has been stereotyped in the Western media, we'll look first at the origins of the problem and second at its continuing impact today.

After hearing this, the audience knows exactly what to listen for as the speaker develops the "problem" main point.

Internal previews are often combined with transitions. For example:

[*Transition*]: Now that we have seen how serious the problem of faulty credit reports is, let's look at some solutions. [*Internal Preview*]: I will focus on three solutions—instituting tighter regulation of credit bureaus, holding credit bureaus financially responsible for their mistakes, and giving individuals easier access to their credit reports.

You will seldom need an internal preview for each main point in your speech, but be sure to use one whenever you think it will help listeners keep track of your ideas.

INTERNAL SUMMARIES

internal summary
A statement in the body of the speech that summarizes the speaker's preceding point or points.

Internal summaries are the reverse of internal previews. Rather than letting listeners know what is coming up next, internal summaries remind listeners of what they have just heard. Such summaries are usually used when a speaker finishes a complicated or particularly important main point or set of main points. For example:

In short, regular walking at a brisk pace strengthens the heart, increases lung capacity, improves blood circulation, and burns calories—all without the strain on the knees and ankles caused by running.

Internal summaries are an excellent way to clarify and reinforce ideas. By combining them with transitions, you can also lead listeners into your next main point:

[*Internal Summary*]: Let's sum up what we have discussed so far. First, we have seen that Li Shizhen's classic work *Bencao Gangmu* divides the substances from minerals into four categories. Second, we have seen that it divides the substances from animals into six categories. [*Transition*]: Now let us see how it divides the substances from plants.

Experienced speakers include transitions and other connectives to help listeners keep track of their ideas. The result is a crisp presentation that moves clearly from point to point.

SIGNPOSTS

Signposts are very brief statements that indicate exactly where you are in the speech. Frequently they are just numbers. Here is how one speaker used simple numerical signposts when discussing the causes of famine in Africa:

signpost
A very brief statement that indicates where a speaker is in the speech or that focuses attention on key ideas.

The first cause of this problem is inefficient agricultural production.

The second cause is recurrent drought in the affected countries.

The third cause is mismanagement of available food resources by local leaders.

Another way to accomplish the same thing is to introduce your main points with a question, as did one speaker on the topic of Internet fraud. His first main point explored the problem of Internet fraud. He introduced it this way:

So just how serious is the problem of Internet fraud? Is it a few isolated cases, or is it widespread enough to require serious measures to protect consumers?

His second main point dealt with ways to curb Internet fraud. He introduced it by saying:

So how can we solve this problem? Is there a way to protect the rights of legitimate businesses while attacking the fraudulent ones?

Questions are particularly effective as signposts because they invite subliminal answers and thereby get the audience more involved with the speech.

Besides using signposts to indicate where you are in the speech, you can use them to focus attention on key ideas. You can do this with a simple phrase, as in the following example:

The most important thing to remember about abstract art is that it is always based on forms in the natural world.

The underlined words alert the audience to the fact that an especially significant point is coming up. So do phrases such as these:

Be sure to keep this in mind . . .

Above all, you need to know . . .

SUMMARY

Listeners get only one chance to grasp a speaker's ideas, and they have little patience for speakers who ramble aimlessly from one idea to another. A well-organized speech will enhance your credibility and make it easier for the audience to understand your message.

The process of planning the body of a speech begins when you determine the main points. Because listeners cannot keep track of a multitude of main points, most speeches contain from two to five. Each should focus on a single idea, should be worded concisely, and should receive enough emphasis to be clear and convincing.

You can organize main points in various ways, depending on your topic, purpose, and audience. Chronological order follows a time pattern, whereas spatial order follows a directional pattern. Topical order results when you divide your main topic into subtopics. Problem-solution order breaks the body of the speech into two main parts—the first showing a problem, the second giving a solution.

Supporting materials are the backup ideas for your main points. When organizing supporting materials, make sure they are relevant to the main points they are supposed to support.

Connectives help tie a speech together. The four major types of speech connectives are transitions, internal previews, internal summaries, and signposts. Using them effectively will make your speeches more unified and coherent.

KEY TERMS

Check your knowledge with the Key-Term Exercise for this chapter.

strategic organization *(89)*
main points *(89)*
chronological order *(90)*
spatial order *(92)*
problem-solution order *(92)*
topical order *(93)*
supporting materials *(97)*
connective *(97)*
transition *(98)*
internal preview *(98)*
internal summary *(98)*
signpost *(99)*

EXERCISES FOR THINKING AND SPEAKING

1. What organizational method (or methods) might you use to arrange main points for speeches with the following specific purpose statements?

   To inform my audience of the symptoms, causes, and treatment of Parkinson's disease.

   To inform my audience about the major stages of the May Fourth Movement.

   To persuade my audience that the United Nations should take stronger measures to deal with the problem of endangered species.

   To inform my audience about the geographical regions of Canada.

2. Turn to the outline of main points and supporting materials for the speech about acupuncture on page 97. Create appropriate transitions, internal previews, internal summaries, and signposts for the speech.

3. Identify the organizational method used in each of the following sets of main points.

   I. The first major cause of airplane crashes is pilot error.
   II. The second major cause of airplane crashes is weather.
   III. The third major cause of airplane crashes is mechanical failure.

   I. The peak of Mount Kilimanjaro has an arctic climate with snow, ice, and violent winds.
   II. The middle of Mount Kilimanjaro has a rain forest climate with lush vegetation and diverse animal species.
   III. The base of Mount Kilimanjaro has a bushland climate with grassy pastures and farming communities.

   I. The Chinese film industry began in the early 20th century.
   II. The first golden period of Chinese cinema occurred during the 1930s.
   III. The second golden period occurred in the years after World War II.
   IV. The Chinese film industry was scaled back during the 1960s and 1970s.
   V. Today Chinese films are in another golden period of international acclaim.

Public Speaking in Your Career

You work in the purchasing department of a large clothing manufacturer. The company's design team has come up with an idea for a new shirt requiring a lightweight, stretchable fabric. Because the fabric cannot be provided by your company's usual suppliers, you were assigned to research other suppliers and to evaluate their products for quality, availability, and cost.

You have just returned from a 10-day trip during which you visited textile firms in Turkey, Italy, India, and Japan. You will present your findings and recommendations to the purchasing and design departments, but you are not sure how best to organize your talk. Your major choices are chronological order, problem-solution order, and topical order. What might be the main points of your speech with each of these methods of organization? Explain which method you think will be most effective for your presentation.

8 Beginning and Ending the Speech

On the night of October 9, 1986, a conductor at Her Majesty's Theatre in London tapped his baton, raised his arms, and signaled the orchestra to play. Moments later the public first heard the unforgettable opening chords of the hit musical *The Phantom of the Opera*.

Like most musical stage plays, *The Phantom of the Opera* begins with an overture, an introduction that captures the audience's attention and gives them a preview of the music they are going to hear. Similarly, most musicals end with a finale, when the whole cast is onstage, the plot is resolved, and the music is brought to a dramatic climax. If there were no such conclusion, if the actors just stopped and walked offstage, the audience would be left unsatisfied.

Like musical plays, speeches need appropriate beginnings and endings. The beginning, or introduction, prepares listeners for what is to come. The conclusion ties up everything and alerts listeners that the speech is going to end. Ideally, it is a satisfying conclusion.

In this chapter we explore the roles played by an introduction and a conclusion in speechmaking. We also discuss techniques aimed at fulfilling those roles. If you apply these techniques imaginatively, you will take a big step toward elevating your speeches from the ordinary to the splendid.

The Introduction

First impressions are important. A poor beginning may so distract or alienate listeners that the speaker can never fully recover. Moreover, getting off on the right foot is vital to a speaker's self-confidence. What could be more encouraging than watching your listeners' faces begin to register interest, attention, and pleasure? A good introduction, you will find, is an excellent confidence booster.

In most speech situations, the introduction has four objectives:

- Get the attention and interest of your audience.
- Create a positive relationship with the audience.
- Establish your credibility.
- Preview the body of the speech.

We'll look at each of these objectives in turn.

GET ATTENTION AND INTEREST

Getting the initial attention of your audience is usually easy—even before you utter a single word. After you are introduced and step to the lectern, your audience will normally give you their attention. If they don't, wait patiently. Look directly at the audience without saying a word. In a few moments all talking and physical commotion will stop. Your listeners will be attentive. You will be ready to start speaking.

Keeping the attention of your audience once you start talking is more difficult. Here are the methods used most often. Employed individually or in combination, they will help get the audience caught up in your speech.

Relate the Topic to the Audience

People pay attention to things that affect them directly. If you can relate the topic to your listeners, they are much more likely to be interested in it.

Suppose, for example, that a speaker begins her speech like this:

> Today I am going to talk about collecting postcards—a hobby that is both fascinating and financially rewarding. I would like to explain the basic kinds of collectible postcards, why they are so valuable, and how collectors buy and sell their cards.

This is certainly a clear introduction, but it is not one to get you hooked on the speech. Now what if the speaker were to begin this way:

> It's Saturday morning, and you are helping clean out your grandmother's house. After working a while, you stumble upon a trunk, open it, and discover hundreds of old postcards. Thinking about getting to your driving lesson on time, you start tossing the cards into the trash can. Congratulations! You have just thrown away a year's tuition.

This time the speaker has used just the right bait. Chances are you will be hooked.

Even when you use other interest-arousing lures, you should *always* relate your topic to the audience. At times this will test your ingenuity, but it pays dividends. Here is an excellent example from a speech about dreams. The speaker began by saying:

Video 8.1
View the beginning of "In Your Dreams."

> You're being chased by an object of unspeakable horror, yet your legs can only move in slow motion. Each step takes unbearably long, and your frantic struggle to run faster is hopeless. Your pursuer gets closer, and your desperation turns to terror. You're completely helpless—eye to eye with death.
>
> Then you wake up, gasping for air, your heart pounding, your face clammy with sweat. It takes a few minutes for your heart and breathing to slow down. You reassure yourself that it was "just a dream." Soon you drift back to sleep.

By using vivid language to describe something all his listeners had experienced, the speaker made sure of an attentive audience.

State the Importance of Your Topic

Presumably, you think your speech is important. Tell your audience why they should think so too. Here is how one speaker used this method in a speech about the global economic cost of traffic jams:

> Traffic jams are more than a nuisance. They are a worldwide economic problem. In Guangzhou alone, they cost 12 billion yuan each year. In major U.S. cities, they are responsible for more than 21 billion liters of wasted fuel and 68 billion dollars in lost productivity. Traffic jams will soon cost the British economy more than 20 billion pounds sterling a year.

These are striking statistics. By citing them in her introduction, the speaker emphasized the importance of her topic and captured the attention of her audience.

A good introduction will get your speech off to a strong start. To be most effective, it should relate the topic to the audience and be delivered from a minimum of notes.

Startle the Audience

One surefire way to arouse interest quickly is to startle your listeners with an arresting or intriguing statement. Everyone in the audience paid close attention after this speaker's introduction:

> As I speak today, the silent killer is striking somewhere in China. Controllable but incurable, the silent killer is a symptomless disease. You can have it for years and never know until it fells you. As many as 300 million Chinese have this disease, and more than half a million will die from it this year. Odds are that one in five of us in this room have it.
>
> What is this silent killer? Not cancer. Not diabetes. Not heart disease. It is hypertension—high blood pressure.

This technique is highly effective and easy to use. Just be sure the startling introduction relates directly to the subject of your speech. If you choose a strong opening simply for its shock value and then go on to talk about something else, your audience will be confused and quite possibly annoyed.

Arouse the Curiosity of the Audience

People are curious. One way to draw them into your speech is with a series of statements that progressively whet their curiosity about the subject of the speech. For example:

> Every day, fierce battles take place in public parks throughout China. Generals move their soldiers against the enemy. Horses, chariots, cannons, even elephants are used in the pursuit of victory. No quarter is given when the losing general is captured.
>
> And yet, no lives are lost. No nations are conquered. The battles are fought on chessboards, and they reflect the Chinese people's love of Xiangqi.

Notice how much less effective the introduction would have been if the speaker had simply said, "Today I am going to talk about Xiangqi."

Question the Audience

rhetorical question
A question that the audience answers mentally rather than out loud.

Asking a *rhetorical question* is another way to get your listeners thinking about your speech. Sometimes a single question will do:

> What is your most valuable possession?
>
> Do you know how many township enterprises are started each year in China?

In other circumstances, you may want to pose a series of questions, each of which draws the audience deeper and deeper into the speech. Here is how one speaker used this method:

> Have you ever spent a sleepless night writing a report for your boss? Can you remember rushing to finish a project because you waited too long to start? Do you often feel overwhelmed by all the things you have to get done?
>
> If so, you may be the victim of poor time management. Fortunately, there are proven strategies you can follow to use your time effectively and to keep control of your life.

Like beginning with a startling statement, opening with a question works best when the question is meaningful to the audience and firmly related to the content of the speech. It also works most effectively when you pause for just a moment after each question. This adds dramatic impact and gives the question time to sink in. The audience, of course, will answer mentally—not out loud.

Begin with a Quotation

Another way to arouse the interest of your audience is to start with an attention-getting quotation. You might choose your quotation from Shakespeare or Confucius, from a poem, song, or film. Here is how one speaker used a quotation from Mark Twain to add a hint of humor to the introduction of a speech about the future of the stock market:

> Mark Twain once said: "Predictions are very difficult to make—especially when they involve the future."

You need not use a well-known or famous quotation. The following made an effective beginning for a speech about the growing popularity of bird watching in China:

> "It is a moment I will always cherish. I was at the mouth of the Minjiang River, when I saw a Chinese crested tern—one of the rarest birds on Earth. I was so excited I could barely keep my binoculars from shaking." These words come from my uncle, a member of the Fujian Bird Watching Society.

Notice that both the quotations used here as examples are relatively short. Opening your speech with a lengthy quotation is a sure way to set your audience yawning.

As you research your speeches, keep an eye out for quotations, stories, and other materials you can use to craft an introduction that will capture the attention of your listeners.

Tell a Story

We all enjoy stories—especially if they are provocative, amusing, dramatic, or suspenseful. To work well as introductions, they should also be clearly relevant to the topic of the speech. Used in this way, stories are perhaps the most effective way to begin a speech.

Consider the story told by one speaker at the start of his remarks on heroes of the Sichuan earthquake:

> Lin Hao was only 9 years old when the Sichuan earthquake struck Yingxiu Township. He was in school with 30 other students, but only 10 escaped from the building. Risking his own life, Lin Hao went back to the rubble and pulled two of his classmates to safety.
>
> For his bravery, Lin Hao was named a Heroic Child by the Chinese people. In August 2008, people all over the world saw him as he walked into Bird's Nest alongside Yao Ming in the opening ceremony of the Olympic Games.

Like many good introductions, this one does a double job—it arouses the interest of the audience and gets listeners emotionally involved in the speech.

You can also use stories based on your personal experience. Here is how one medical student used such a story. She began by recounting the first time she observed doctors performing surgery in the operating room:

> There I stood, wearing a surgical mask, in the middle of a large, brightly lit room. In the center of the room were five figures huddled over a table. I found it difficult to see since everything was draped in blue sheets, yet I didn't dare take a step toward the table.
>
> Then one of the figures called to me, "Angela, get over here and take a closer look." My knees buckled as I walked through the sterile environment. But eventually I was there, standing over an unconscious body in the operating room.

Video 8.2
View the beginning of "Hoping to Heal."

Internet Connection

Looking for a quotation to use in the introduction or conclusion of your speech? Visit Yahoo! Directory: Quotations (http://dir.yahoo.com/Reference/Quotations/) for a comprehensive roster of links to collected quotations on the Web.

To read introductions and conclusions from famous speeches, visit .American Rhetoric (www.americanrhetoric.com/).

The effectiveness of any story—especially a personal one—hinges on the speaker's delivery as well as on the content. If you begin your speech with a story, make sure you can deliver it with strong eye contact and expressive vocal variety.

The seven methods discussed above are the ones used most often by speakers to gain attention and interest. Other methods include referring to the occasion, inviting audience participation, using audio equipment or visual aids, relating to a previous speaker, and beginning with humor. For any given speech, try to choose the method that is most suitable for the topic, the audience, and the occasion.

CREATE A POSITIVE RELATIONSHIP WITH THE AUDIENCE

In addition to gaining attention and interest, the introduction should foster a positive relationship with the audience. This is especially important whenever the speaker is controversial or advocates an unpopular position. It is also crucial in cross-cultural communication when the speaker needs to reach out across national or linguistic borders to create a bond with listeners. Here is an excellent example, from former U.S. President Ronald Reagan, speaking at the Great Hall of the People, in Beijing, in April 1984:

> I'm honored to come before you today, the first American president ever to address your nation from the Great Hall of the People.
>
> My wife, Nancy, and I have looked forward to visiting the people and treasures of your great and historic land, one of the world's oldest civilizations. We have marveled at Beijing's sweeping vistas, and we have felt the warmth of your hospitality touch our hearts.
>
> We only regret that our visit will be so brief. I'm afraid it will be as a Tang Dynasty poet once wrote: "Looking at the flowers while riding on horseback." But you have another saying from *The Book of Han* which describes how Nancy and I feel: "To see a thing once is better than hearing about it a hundred times."

You can see from this excerpt why Reagan was known as the Great Communicator. Not only does he express great respect for China, but he finds exactly the right words from revered Chinese writings to generate positive sentiments on the part of his listeners.

ESTABLISH CREDIBILITY

Credibility is mostly a matter of being qualified to speak on a given topic—and of being *perceived* as qualified by your listeners. If, for example, Zhang Ziyi got up before an audience to speak on the topic of nuclear physics, she would have to take drastic steps to demonstrate her credibility on the subject.

Telling a story is an excellent way to gain attention in a speech introduction. The story should be clearly relevant to the topic and should be delivered expressively with strong eye contact.

Establishing credibility in the introduction is important for student speakers, because they are not usually recognized as experts on their speech topics. Here is how one student established her credibility during a speech about the Eiffel Tower:

credibility
The audience's perception of whether a speaker is qualified to speak on a given topic.

As a French major, I had an opportunity last summer to study in Paris and to spend time living with a French family. I was so impressed with the Eiffel Tower that I visited it four times and read everything I could find about it.

As this example shows, your credibility can be based on research, firsthand knowledge, or some combination of the two. Whatever the source of your expertise, be sure to let the audience know in your introduction.

PREVIEW THE BODY OF THE SPEECH

Many people are poor listeners, but even good listeners need all the help they can get in sorting out a speaker's ideas. One way to help listeners is to tell them in the introduction what they should listen for in the rest of the speech. Nearly always, you should include a preview statement such as the following:

preview statement
A statement in the introduction of a speech that identifies the main points to be discussed in the body.

Today I will talk with you about the causes of high blood pressure, the strain high blood pressure is putting on China's health care system, and what people can do to reduce the likelihood of having high blood pressure.

There are many fascinating aspects of Xiangqi. This afternoon, I will focus on two: the origins of Xiangqi and the relationship between Xiangqi and Western chess.

Preview statements such as these serve another purpose as well. Because they usually come at the very end of the introduction, they provide a smooth lead-in to the body of the speech. They signal that the body of the speech is about to begin.

Checklist Speech Introduction

YES	NO	
☐	☐	1. Do I gain the attention and interest of my audience by using one or more of the methods discussed in this chapter?
☐	☐	2. Do I relate the speech topic to my audience?
☐	☐	3. Do I establish my credibility to speak on the topic?
☐	☐	4. If my topic is controversial, do I create a positive relationship with my audience?
☐	☐	5. Do I provide a preview statement of the main points to be covered in the body of the speech?
☐	☐	6. Is the introduction limited to 10–20 percent of my entire speech?
☐	☐	7. Have I been creative in devising my introduction?
☐	☐	8. Have I worked out the language of my introduction in detail?
☐	☐	9. Have I practiced the delivery of my introduction so I can present it fluently, confidently, and with strong eye contact?

SAMPLE INTRODUCTION WITH COMMENTARY

So far we have seen many excerpts showing how to fulfill the various objectives of an introduction. Now here is a complete introduction. The side comments indicate the principles used in developing the introduction.

Keeping Hope Alive

COMMENTARY	SPEECH
The speaker begins by gaining attention and relating to the audience. The second sentence uses a rhetorical question to convey the importance of the topic, while the third sentence states the central idea.	I am sure most of you remember the anxious look of a big-eyed rural girl on the promotional poster of Project Hope. But do you know that every year in China, many children like the big-eyed girl are deprived of education because of poverty? By sponsoring a child through Project Hope, you can help him or her complete an elementary school education.
The speaker establishes credibility by mentioning her experience as a volunteer for Project Hope.	During the past three years, I have worked as a volunteer teacher for Project Hope, and I have visited a number of elementary schools in China's remote mountainous areas.
The speaker states the purpose of her speech and previews the main points she will discuss in the body.	Today, I will show you the need to help rural children with their education. Then I will explain the functions and accomplishments of Project Hope. I will conclude by encouraging all of you to become involved with this highly ethical public service project.

TIPS FOR THE INTRODUCTION

1. Keep the introduction relatively brief. Under normal circumstances it should not constitute more than 10–20 percent of your speech.

2. Be on the lookout for possible introductory materials as you do your research. File them with your notes so they will be handy when you are ready for them.

3. Be creative in devising your introduction. Experiment with two or three different openings and choose the one that seems most likely to get the audience interested in your speech.

Video 8.3
View Stephen E. Lucas for more guidance on creating introductions and conclusions.

4. Don't worry about the exact wording of your introduction until you have finished preparing the body of the speech. After you have determined your main points, it will be much easier to make final decisions about how to begin the speech.

5. Don't apologize in your introduction. Avoid statements such as "I'm sorry to be so nervous," or "I wish I had done a better job preparing." Such statements weaken your credibility and give the audience little reason to pay attention to the rest of your speech.

6. Work out your introduction in detail. Some teachers recommend that you write it out word for word; others prefer that you outline it. Whichever method you use, practice the introduction over and over until you can deliver it smoothly from a minimum of notes and with strong eye contact. This will get your speech off to a good start and give you a big boost of confidence.

7. Don't start talking too soon. Make sure the audience has quieted down and is focused on you before you begin. Establish eye contact with the audience, smile, and then launch into your opening words. Give yourself every chance to make sure your introduction has the desired impact.

The Conclusion

"Great is the art of beginning," said the American poet Longfellow, "but greater the art is of ending." Longfellow was thinking of poetry, but his insight is equally applicable to public speaking. Your closing remarks are your last chance to drive home your ideas. Moreover, your final impression will probably linger in your listeners' minds. Thus you need to craft your conclusion with as much care as your introduction.

No matter what kind of speech you are giving, the conclusion has two major functions:

- To let the audience know you are ending the speech.
- To reinforce the audience's understanding of, or commitment to, the central idea.

Let us look at each.

SIGNAL THE END OF THE SPEECH

It may seem obvious that you should let your audience know you are going to stop soon. However, you will sometimes hear speeches in which the speaker concludes so abruptly that you are taken by surprise. Too sudden an ending leaves the audience puzzled and unfulfilled.

How do you let an audience know your speech is ending? One way is through what you say. "In conclusion," "My purpose has been," "Let me end by saying"—these are all brief cues that you are getting ready to stop.

You can also let your audience know the end is in sight by your manner of delivery. The conclusion is the climax of a speech. A speaker who has carefully built to a peak of interest and involvement will not need to say "in conclusion." By use of the voice—its tone, pacing, intonation, and rhythm—a speaker can build the momentum of a speech so there is no doubt when it is over.

crescendo ending
A conclusion in which the speech builds to a zenith of power and intensity.

One method of doing this has been likened to a musical crescendo. As in a symphony, in which one instrument after another joins in until the entire orchestra is playing, the speech builds in force until it reaches a zenith of power and intensity.[1] (This does *not* mean simply getting louder and louder. It is a combination of many things, including vocal pitch, choice of words, dramatic content, gestures, pauses—and possibly loudness.)

A superb example of this method is the memorable conclusion to Martin Luther King's "I've Been to the Mountaintop," the speech he delivered the night before he was assassinated in April 1968. Speaking to an audience of 2,000 people in Memphis, Tennessee, he ended his speech with a stirring declaration that the civil rights movement would succeed despite the many threats on his life:

> Like anybody, I would like to live a long life. Longevity has its place, but I'm not concerned about that now. I just want to do God's will, and he's allowed me to go up to the mountain, and I've looked over and I've seen the Promised Land. I may not get there with you, but I want you to know tonight that we as a people will get to the Promised Land. So I'm happy tonight. I'm not worried about anything; I'm not fearing any man. Mine eyes have seen the glory of the coming of the Lord.

dissolve ending
A conclusion that generates emotional appeal by fading step by step to a dramatic final statement.

Another effective method might be compared to the dissolve ending of a concert song that evokes deep emotions: "The song seems to fade away while the light on the singer shrinks gradually to a smaller and smaller circle until it lights only the face, then the eyes. Finally, it is a pinpoint, and disappears with the last note of the song."[2] Here is a conclusion that does much the same thing. It was delivered at the 2004 CCTV Cup competition by Xia Peng, a student at Nanjing University.

In the body of his speech, Xia Peng explained that he is colorblind. Early in life, he said, he was ashamed of his colorblindness. But then he took a photography class in high school. His teacher told him that colorblindness made him a better photographer because he was more alert to theme, light, and shade without distraction from colors. In his conclusion, Xia Peng created a dissolve ending by evoking the emotions of his experience with photography:

> My teacher's words struck me. Later, I found out that the incidence of colorblindness is one in a thousand. To me, it is a blessing in disguise. With that in mind, I put a roll of color film in my

The conclusion is your last chance to drive home your ideas. Successful speakers craft their endings with great care to leave a strong final impression.

camera and set out to take pictures. With the snapping of the shutter, I could not help but to paint the color of wind in my own pictures. The colors lie in my heart.

Video 8.4
View the conclusion of Xia Peng, "Confronting Myself: Color of the Wind."

Both the crescendo and the dissolve endings must be worked out with great care. Practice until you get the words and the timing just right. The benefits will be well worth your time.

REINFORCE THE CENTRAL IDEA

The second major function of a conclusion is to reinforce the audience's understanding of, or commitment to, the central idea. There are many ways to do this. Here are the ones you are most likely to use.

Summarize Your Speech

Restating the main points is the easiest way to end a speech. One speaker used this technique effectively in talking about the AIDS epidemic in Africa:

In conclusion, we have seen that the AIDS epidemic is having a devastating effect on African society. An entire adult generation is slowly being wiped out. An entirely new generation of AIDS orphans is being created. Governments in the nations most afflicted have neither the resources nor the expertise to counter the epidemic. Many African economies are being crippled by the loss of people in the workplace.

Before it's too late, the United Nations and developed countries need to increase their efforts to halt the epidemic and bring it under control. The lives and well-being of tens of millions of people hang in the balance.

Video 8.5
View the conclusion of "AIDS in Africa: A World Crisis."

The value of a summary is that it explicitly restates the central idea and main points one last time. But as we shall see, there are more imaginative and compelling ways to end a speech. They can be used in combination with a summary or, at times, in place of it.

End with a Quotation

A quotation is one of the most common and effective devices to conclude a speech. Here is a fine example, from Vice Premier Li Lanqing's speech to the International Olympic Committee as part of Beijing's bid to host the 2008 Olympic Games. After explaining the reasons why Beijing should be awarded the role of host city, Vice Premier Li concluded with these words:

> Chinese sage Confucius says, "Is it not a delight after all to have friends come from afar!" Indeed, it is our delight to welcome all guests with open arms in Beijing in the year 2008. I am sure you will have a great Games in Beijing. Thank you!

The quotation from Confucius is particularly effective because it reinforces the personal tone of the speech. When you run across a *brief* quotation that so perfectly captures your central idea, keep it in mind as a possible conclusion.

Make a Dramatic Statement

Rather than using a quotation to give your conclusion force and vitality, you may want to devise your own dramatic statement. Some speeches have become famous because of their powerful closing lines. One is Patrick Henry's legendary "Liberty or Death" oration. It takes its name from the final sentences Henry uttered on March 23, 1775, as he exhorted his audience to resist British tyranny:

> Is life so dear, or peace so sweet, as to be purchased at the price of chains and slavery? Forbid it, Almighty God! I know not what course others may take; but as for me, give me liberty, or give me death.

Although your speeches may not become famous, you can still rivet your listeners with a dramatic concluding statement. What follows is a particularly striking example, from a speech on suicide prevention. Throughout her remarks, the speaker referred to a friend who had tried to commit suicide the previous year. Then, in the conclusion, she said:

> My friend is back in school, participating in activities she never did before—and enjoying it. I'm happy and proud to say that she's still fighting for her life and even happier that she failed to kill herself. Otherwise, I wouldn't be here today trying to help you. You see, I am my "friend," and I'm more than glad to say I've made it.

As you can imagine, the audience was stunned. The closing lines brought the speech to a dramatic conclusion. The speaker made it even more effective by pausing a moment before the last words and by using her voice to give them just the right inflection.

Refer to the Introduction

An excellent way to give your speech psychological unity is to conclude by referring to ideas in the introduction. Here is how Gu Qiubei, of Shanghai International Studies University, used the method in her prepared speech at the 2003 21st Century Cup. Her topic was the tension between international tourism and environmental protection:

Introduction: There was once a physical therapist who traveled all the way from America to Africa to do a census about mountain gorillas. These gorillas are a main attraction to tourists from all over the world. . . . She witnessed a scene, a scene taking us to a place we never imagined, where, in the very depth of the African rain forest, surrounded by trees, flowers, and butterflies, the mother gorillas cuddled their babies.

Yes, that's a memorable scene in one of my favorite movies, called *Gorillas in the Mist*, based on the true story of Dian Fossey, who spent most of her lifetime in Rwanda to protect the eco-environment there, until the very end of her life. To me, the movie not only presents an unforgettable scene, but also acts as a timeless reminder that we should not develop the tourist industry at the cost of our eco-environment.

Video 8.6
View the beginning and ending of Gu Qiubei, "A Scene to Remember."

In the body of her speech, Gu Qiubei explained the manner in which tourism is causing ecological damage in many parts of the globe. Then, in her conclusion, she tied the whole speech together by returning to the story presented in her introduction:

Conclusion: Once again, I have come to think of Dian Fossey, because it is with her spirit, passion, courage, and strong sense of our eco-environment that we are taking our next step into the world. And no matter who we are, what we do, and where we go, in our minds there's always a scene to remember, a scene worth our effort to protect and fight for.

Summarizing the speech, ending with a quotation, making a dramatic statement, referring to the introduction—all these techniques can be used separately. But you have probably noticed that speakers often combine two or more in their conclusions. Actually, all four techniques can be fused into one—for example, a dramatic quotation that summarizes the central idea while referring to the introduction.

One other concluding technique is making a direct appeal to your audience for action. This technique applies only to a particular type of persuasive speech, however, and will be discussed in Chapter 14. The four methods covered in this chapter are appropriate for all kinds of speeches and occasions.

SAMPLE CONCLUSION WITH COMMENTARY

How do you fit these methods together to make a conclusion? Here is an example, from the speech about Project Hope whose introduction we looked at earlier.

COMMENTARY	CONCLUSION
The speaker creates a full circle by referring back to her introduction. The use of repetition reinforces her ideas and lends rhythm to her prose.	Think back to the big-eyed little girl I mentioned at the beginning of this speech. Think about all the other children like her in rural areas throughout China. Remember what we saw about the educational needs of those children, and how you can make a difference in their lives by supporting Project Hope.
Referring to Project Hope's logo adds emotional appeal and ends the speech on a strong note.	The logo of Project Hope means that society cares for the development of young people like the ocean supports the rising sun. You can help all of China by being part of that ocean.

Checklist Speech Conclusion

YES	NO	
☐	☐	1. Do I signal that my speech is coming to an end?
☐	☐	2. Do I reinforce my central idea by (check all that apply):
☐	☐	Summarizing the main points of my speech
☐	☐	Ending with a quotation
☐	☐	Making a dramatic statement
☐	☐	Referring to the introduction
☐	☐	3. Is the conclusion limited to 5–10 percent of my entire speech?
☐	☐	4. Have I worked out the language of my conclusion in detail?
☐	☐	5. Have I practiced the delivery of my conclusion so I can present it fluently, confidently, and with strong eye contact?

TIPS FOR THE CONCLUSION

1. As with the introduction, keep an eye out for possible concluding materials as you research and develop the speech.

2. Conclude with a bang, not a whimper. Be creative in devising a conclusion that hits the hearts and minds of your audience. Work on several possible endings, and select the one that seems likely to have the greatest impact.

3. Don't be long-winded. The conclusion will normally make up no more than 5–10 percent of your speech.

4. Don't end with an apology. Statements such as "I'm sorry I didn't do a better job with my speech," or "I wish I had explained my ideas more clearly" are deadly to an effective conclusion. If you don't believe in your speech, your listeners won't either.

5. Don't leave anything in your conclusion to chance. Work it out in detail, and give yourself plenty of time to practice delivering it. Many speakers like to write out the conclusion word for word to guarantee it is just right. If you do this, make sure you can present it smoothly, confidently, and with feeling—without relying on your notes or sounding wooden. Make your last impression as forceful and as favorable as you can.

SUMMARY

In most speech situations, you need to accomplish four objectives with the introduction: gain the attention and interest of your audience, create a positive relationship with the audience, establish your credibility, and preview the body of the speech. Every aspect of the introduction should be worked out in detail so as to create a favorable first impression.

The first objective of a speech conclusion is to let the audience know you are ending, which you can do by your words or by your manner of delivery. The second objective of a conclusion is to reinforce your central idea. You can accomplish this by summarizing the speech, ending with a quotation, making a dramatic statement, or referring to the introduction. Be creative in devising a vivid, forceful conclusion.

KEY TERMS

rhetorical question *(106)*
credibility *(109)*
preview statement *(109)*
crescendo ending *(112)*
dissolve ending *(112)*

Key-Term Exercise
Check your knowledge with the Key-Term Exercise for this chapter.

EXERCISES FOR THINKING AND SPEAKING

1. Here are six speech topics. Explain how you might relate each to your audience in a speech introduction.

laughter	media violence	soccer
health care	historic preservation	climate change

2. Think of a speech topic (preferably one for your next speech in class). Create an introduction for your speech in which you gain the attention of the audience, establish your credibility, and preview the body of the speech.
3. Using the same topic as in Exercise 2, create a speech conclusion. Be sure to let your audience know the speech is ending, to reinforce the central idea, and to make the conclusion vivid and memorable.

Public Speaking in Your **Career**

As the public relations manager of a media corporation, you are assigned to deliver two fund-raising speeches for cancer research. First, you will speak to business executives at a high-profile dinner in Beijing. Second, you will address faculty at a local university. Create an introduction for each speech; be sure to adapt your remarks to the different audiences and occasions.

9 Outlining the Speech

Think what might happen if you tried to build an apartment without a floor plan or an architect's blueprint. You place the kitchen next to the door to make it easy for carrying in groceries. But the dining room turns up at the other end of the apartment. When you cook a meal, you have to run with the plates to keep the food from getting cold. You set up the bedroom so the bed will not be directly across from the door. But then you end up with a window right behind the bed. You think it's wonderful to have almost no interior walls. But when the snow comes, your (unsupported) roof collapses.

Just as plans and blueprints are essential to architecture, so are outlines essential to successful speeches. An outline is like a blueprint for your speech. It allows you to see the full scope and content of your speech at a glance. By outlining, you can judge whether each part of the speech is fully developed, whether you have adequate supporting materials for your main points, and whether the main points are properly balanced. An outline helps you make sure that related items are together, that ideas flow from one to another, that the structure of your speech will "stand up"—and not collapse.

In most cases, you will use two kinds of outlines for your speeches—one very detailed, for the planning stage, and one very brief, for the delivery of the speech.

The Preparation Outline

The preparation outline is just what its name implies—an outline that helps you prepare the speech. Writing a preparation outline means putting your speech together—deciding what you will say in the introduction, how you will organize the main points and supporting materials in the body, and what you will say in the conclusion.

preparation outline
A detailed outline developed during the process of speech preparation that includes the title, specific purpose, central idea, introduction, main points, subpoints, connectives, conclusion, and bibliography of a speech.

GUIDELINES FOR THE PREPARATION OUTLINE

Over the years, a relatively uniform system for preparation outlines has developed. It is explained below and is exemplified in the sample outline on pages 122–124.

State the Specific Purpose and Central Idea

The specific purpose statement and the central idea should be separate units that appear before the text of the outline itself. Including them with the outline makes it easier to assess how well you have constructed the speech to accomplish your purpose and to communicate your central idea.

Label the Introduction, Body, and Conclusion

If you label the parts of your speech, you will be sure that you indeed *have* an introduction and conclusion and have accomplished the essential objectives of each. Usually the names of the speech parts are placed in the middle of the page or in the far left margin. They are technical labels only and are not included in the system of symbolization used to identify main points and supporting materials.

Use a Consistent Pattern of Symbolization and Indentation

In the most common system of outlining, main points are identified by Roman numerals and are indented equally so as to be aligned down the page. Subpoints (components of the main points) are identified by capital letters and are also indented equally so as to be aligned with each other. Beyond this, there may be sub-subpoints and even sub-sub-subpoints. For example:

I. Main point
  A. Subpoint
  B. Subpoint
    1. Sub-subpoint
    2. Sub-subpoint
      a. Sub-sub-subpoint
      b. Sub-sub-subpoint
II. Main point
  A. Subpoint
    1. Sub-subpoint
    2. Sub-subpoint
  B. Subpoint
    1. Sub-subpoint
    2. Sub-subpoint

visual framework
The pattern of symbolization and indentation in a speech outline that shows the relationships among the speaker's ideas.

The clear *visual framework* of this outline immediately shows the relationships among the ideas of the speech. The most important ideas (main points) are farthest to the left. Less important ideas (subpoints, sub-subpoints, and so on) are progressively farther to the right. This pattern reveals the structure of your entire speech.

State Main Points and Subpoints in Full Sentences

Strictly speaking, your preparation outline should be a fully developed speech manuscript written in outline form. This means all your main points and subpoints should be expressed as full sentences. Your preparation outline should indicate clearly the content of the main points and subpoints.

It is important not to confuse the preparation outline with your speaking outline. You can't state main points or subpoints with a single word or a short phrase in your preparation outline. A skimpy preparation outline is of little value. Stating main points and subpoints in full sentences will ensure that you develop your ideas fully.

Label Transitions, Internal Summaries, and Internal Previews

One way to make sure you have strong transitions, internal summaries, and internal previews is to include them in your preparation outline. Usually they are not incorporated into the system of symbolization and indentation, but are labeled separately and are inserted in the outline where they will appear in the speech.

As blueprints are essential to architecture, so outlines are essential to speechmaking. Developing an outline helps ensure that the structure of your speech is clear and coherent.

Attach a Bibliography

You should include with the outline a bibliography that shows all the books, magazines, newspapers, and Internet sources you consulted, as well as any interviews or field research you conducted.

bibliography
A list of all the sources used in preparing a speech.

Two major bibliographic formats are those developed by the Modern Language Association (MLA) and the American Psychological Association (APA). No matter which you adopt, make sure your statement of sources is clear, accurate, and consistent. For help, check the Bibliography Formats on the CD-ROM, where you will find sample citations for a wide range of sources. For help formatting your bibliography, use the Bibliomaker on the CD-ROM.

Bibliography Formats
Check the Bibliography Formats for sample citations.

Give Your Speech a Title

There are three requirements for a good speech title. It should (1) be brief, (2) attract the attention of your audience, and (3) encapsulate the main thrust of your speech. Here are two groups of titles. Those on the left are straightforward and descriptive. Those on the right are figurative alternatives to the ones on the left.

Bibliomaker
Use Bibliomaker to format your bibliography automatically.

Group I	**Group II**
Unsafe Drinking Water	Toxins on Tap
Living with Deafness	The Sounds of Silence
The Rage to Diet	The Art of Wishful Shrinking

There is one other kind of title you should consider—the question. Phrasing your title as a question can be both descriptive and provocative. Using this method, we can construct a third set of titles combining the virtues of groups I and II:

Checklist Preparation Outline

YES	NO	
☐	☐	1. Does my speech have a title?
☐	☐	2. Do I state the specific purpose before the text of the outline itself?
☐	☐	3. Do I state the central idea before the text of the outline itself?
☐	☐	4. Are the introduction, body, and conclusion clearly labeled?
☐	☐	5. Are main points and subpoints written in full sentences?
☐	☐	6. Are transitions, internal summaries, and internal previews clearly labeled?
☐	☐	7. Does the outline follow a consistent pattern of symbolization and indentation?
☐	☐	8. Does the outline provide a clear visual framework that shows the relationships among the ideas of my speech?
☐	☐	9. Does the bibliography identify all the sources I consulted in preparing the outline?

Group III

Is Your Water Safe to Drink?

Can You See What I'm Saying?

Diets: How Effective Are They?

SAMPLE PREPARATION OUTLINE WITH COMMENTARY

The following preparation outline illustrates the principles of outlining just discussed. The commentary explains the procedures used in organizing the speech and writing the outline.

Harbin International Ice and Snow Festival

COMMENTARY	OUTLINE
Stating your specific purpose and central idea before the outline makes it easier to judge how well you have constructed the outline to achieve your purpose and to communicate your central idea.	*Specific Purpose:* To inform my audience about the history and major attractions of the Harbin International Ice and Snow Festival. *Central Idea:* The Harbin International Ice and Snow Festival has a long history and world-famous attractions.

The opening questions get attention and reveal the topic of the speech.

The speaker establishes her credibility and previews the main points to be discussed in the body.

Labeling the introduction, body, and conclusion marks each as a distinct part of the speech.

The three subpoints of main point I are shown by the capital letters A, B, and C and, like the main point, are written in full sentences to make sure the speaker has thought them out fully. Points below the level of subpoint are indicated by Arabic numerals.

Including transitions ensures that the speaker has worked out how to connect one idea with the next.

Throughout the outline, progressive indentation shows visually the relationships among main points, subpoints, and sub-subpoints.

Introduction

I. Looking for an exciting place for winter fun?
II. Why not consider the Harbin International Ice and Snow Festival?
III. The festival is world-famous for its spectacular ice lanterns and snow sculptures.
IV. As a native of Harbin, I have loved the ice and snow festival since I was a little child.
V. Today, I would like to share some highlights of the festival's history and attractions.

(*Transition:* Let's start with the history of the festival.)

Body

I. The history of the Harbin International Ice and Snow Festival goes back many years.
  A. Origins of the festival can be traced to the Qing Dynasty tradition of making ice lanterns during winter.
    1. They were first made by peasants as lights for hunting and fishing.
    2. Later, they were made for decoration.
  B. Harbin's first organized ice lantern show was held in 1963, but was suspended during the late 1960s and early 1970s.
  C. The festival as we know it today began in 1985.
    1. It opens every January 5 and runs for one month.
    2. It draws more than 800,000 spectators each year, says Jia Yan of the Harbin tourism bureau.

(*Transition:* Now that you know something about the history of the festival, let's look at its major attractions.)

II. The festival's three major attractions are the ice lantern show, the snow sculptures fair, and the ice sculptures exhibition.
  A. The ice lantern show is held at Zhaolin Park, in downtown Harbin.
    1. It is filled with exotic castles, bridges, flowers, and wild animals—all made of ice.
    2. It is also adorned with thousands of ice lanterns, which produce a dazzling display of lights.
  B. The snow sculptures fair is held at Sun Island Park, on the north bank of the Songhua River.
    1. The fair presents an impressive display of snow artworks.
    2. Most popular is the 50-meter-wide sculpture of Snow Maiden.
  C. The ice sculptures exhibition is also held at Sun Island Park.
    1. Each year the exhibition has a different theme.
    2. No matter what the theme, the ice sculptures are always massive in size and spectacular in design.

Labeling the conclusion marks it as a distinct part of the speech.	*Conclusion*
The conclusion reinforces the speaker's central idea, relates the topic to the audience one last time, and ends with a pleasing final line.	I. As we have seen, the Harbin International Ice and Snow Festival is a world-class event, with a long history and spectacular attractions. II. I hope you will be able one day to attend the festival. III. Just wrap up warm, and you will have a magical experience.
	Bibliography
This bibliography follows APA format. See if your instructor has a preferred format for your bibliography.	People's Daily Online. (2008, December 26). China builds world's largest ice Santa. Retrieved from http://english.peopledaily.com.cn/index.html. Kristof, N. (1990, January 22). In the city of ice, heat brings the biggest shivers. *New York Times*, section 1, p. 4. Li, X. (2009, February 12). Ice and snow gala: China's ice city Harbin is about to host the largest winter universiade in history. *Beijing Review*, 52, 44–45. Travel China Guide. (2009, April 15). Harbin ice festival. Retrieved from www.TravelChinaGuide.com.

The Speaking Outline

speaking outline
A brief outline used to jog a speaker's memory during the presentation of a speech.

The aim of a speaking outline is to help you remember what you want to say. In some ways, it is a condensed version of your preparation outline. It should contain key words or phrases to jog your memory, as well as essential statistics and quotations that you don't want to risk forgetting. But it should also include material *not* in your preparation outline—especially cues to direct and sharpen your delivery.

Most speakers develop their own variations on the speaking outline. As you acquire more experience, you, too, should feel free to experiment. But for now, your best bet is to follow the basic guidelines below and to use the sample speaking outline on pages 126–127 as your model.

GUIDELINES FOR THE SPEAKING OUTLINE

Follow the Visual Framework Used in the Preparation Outline

Your speaking outline should use the same visual framework—the same symbols and the same pattern of indentation—as your preparation outline. This will make it much easier to prepare the speaking outline. More important, it will allow you to see instantly where you are in the speech at any given moment while you are speaking. You will find this a great advantage. As you speak, you will look down at your outline periodically to make sure you are covering the right ideas in the right order.

Many experienced speakers are more comfortable with a brief set of notes, or no notes at all, which allows them to maintain eye contact and to communicate directly with the audience.

Make Sure the Outline Is Legible

Your speaking outline is all but worthless unless it is instantly readable at a distance. When you make your outline, use large lettering, leave extra space between lines, provide ample margins, and write or type on only one side of your paper or note cards.

Keep the Outline as Brief as Possible

If your notes are too detailed, you will have difficulty maintaining eye contact with your audience. To guard against having too many notes, keep your speaking outline as brief as possible. It should contain key words or phrases to help you remember major points, subpoints, and connectives. If you are citing statistics, you will probably want to include them in your notes. Unless you are good at memorizing quotations, write them out fully as well.

Finally, there may be two, three, or four key ideas whose wording is so important that you want to state them in simple complete sentences. The best rule is that your notes should be the minimum you need to jog your memory and keep you on track.

Give Yourself Cues for Delivering the Speech

A good speaking outline reminds you not only of *what* you want to say but also of *how* you want to say it. You can achieve this by including delivery cues—directions for delivering the speech. One way to do this is by underlining or otherwise highlighting key ideas that you want to be sure to emphasize. Then, when you reach them in the outline, you will be reminded to stress them. Another way is to jot down on the outline explicit cues such as "pause," "repeat," "slow down," "louder," and so forth. Both techniques are good aids for beginning speakers, but they are also used by experienced speakers.

delivery cues
Directions in a speaking outline to help a speaker remember how he or she wants to deliver key parts of the speech.

SAMPLE SPEAKING OUTLINE WITH COMMENTARY

Below is a sample speaking outline for an informative speech about the Harbin International Ice and Snow Festival. By comparing it with the preparation outline for the same speech on pages 122–124 in this chapter, you can see how a detailed preparation outline is turned into a concise speaking outline.

COMMENTARY	OUTLINE
These comments remind the speaker to establish eye contact and not to race through the speech.	*Eye Contact!!* *Slow Down* I. Looking for exciting winter fun?
The word "pause" reminds the speaker to pause after the opening sentence.	—*Pause*—
Including main ideas of the introduction gets the speaker off to a strong start.	II. Why not Harbin Ice and Snow Festival? III. World-famous ice lanterns and snow sculptures. IV. Native of Harbin—loved festival since childhood. V. Today, highlights of history and attractions. (Let's start with history.)
Pausing before the first main point helps signal the transition to the body of the speech.	—*Pause*—
Many speakers label the body in the speaking outline.	*Body*
The visual format of the outline makes it easy to read at a glance.	I. History goes back many years. A. Qing Dynasty tradition of ice lanterns. 1. Made by peasants for light. 2. Later used for decoration. B. First show in 1963; suspended during the late 1960s and early 1970s.
Including sources of statistics or testimony prompts the speaker to cite them during the speech.	C. Today's festival began in 1985. 1. Opens January 5—one month. 2. 800,000: Jia Yan of tourism bureau.
Inserting transitions makes sure the speaker doesn't forget them.	(Now you know history . . . look at attractions.) II. Three major attractions. A. Ice lantern show—Zhaolin Park.
Underlining reminds the speaker to stress important words or phrases.	1. Castles, bridges, flowers, wild animals—<u>all of ice</u>. 2. <u>Thousands</u> of ice lanterns. B. Snow sculptures fair—Sun Island Park. 1. Display of snow artworks. 2. Snow Maiden: <u>50 meters wide</u>.

C. Ice sculptures exhibition—also Sun Island Park.
   1. Different theme each year.
   2. Sculptures <u>always</u> massive and spectacular.

It is usually a good idea to pause before the conclusion.

—*Pause*—

Conclusion

Including key phrases from the conclusion cues the speaker's memory and ensures that the speech will end as planned.

I. As we have seen, festival has long history and spectacular attractions.
II. Hope you can attend one day.
III. Wrap up warm and have magical experience.

SUMMARY

Outlines are essential to effective speeches. By outlining, you make sure that related ideas are together, that your thoughts flow from one to another, and that the structure of your speech is coherent.

In the preparation outline, you state your specific purpose and central idea; label the introduction, body, and conclusion; write main points and subpoints in full sentences; and designate transitions, internal summaries, and internal previews. You should employ a consistent pattern of symbolization and indentation throughout the outline.

The speaking outline should contain key words or phrases to jog your memory, as well as essential statistics and quotations. Make sure your speaking outline is legible, follows the same visual framework as your preparation outline, and includes cues for delivering the speech.

KEY TERMS

preparation outline *(119)*
visual framework *(120)*
bibliography *(121)*
speaking outline *(124)*
delivery cues *(125)*

Key-Term Exercise
Check your knowledge with the Key-Term Exercise for this chapter.

EXERCISES FOR THINKING AND SPEAKING

Outline Exercises
Go to the Outline Exercises to complete this exercise.

1. In the left-hand column below is a partially blank outline from a speech about robots. In the right-hand column, arranged in random order, are subpoints to fill in the outline. Choose the appropriate subpoint for each blank in the outline.

   To complete this exercise on computer, go to the Outline Exercises on the CD-ROM. You will also find additional scrambled outlines that you can use to hone your outlining skills.

Outline

I. Robots have captured the human imagination for centuries.

   A.

   B.

   C.

II. Today robots are used in many fields, including space exploration and medicine.

   A.

      1.

      2.

   B.

      1.

      2.

Subpoints

Astronauts use robots to perform maintenance on the International Space Station.

In 1937, Westinghouse created a seven-foot robot that could walk, talk, blow up balloons, and smoke cigarettes.

They also allow surgeons to operate on patients from thousands of miles away.

Robots have become indispensable to space exploration.

In 1497, Leonardo da Vinci designed a mechanical suit of armor that could sit up and move its arms, neck, and jaw.

They can navigate hospital corridors to deliver pharmaceuticals, x-rays, and bandages.

In addition, NASA sends robotic spacecraft to explore distant planets.

Robots are becoming more and more important in medicine.

In 1773, Pierre and Henri Jaquet-Droz built dolls that could write, play music, and draw pictures.

2. From the preparation outline on robots you constructed in Exercise 1, create a speaking outline that you might use in delivering the speech. Follow the guidelines for a speaking outline discussed in this chapter.

Public Speaking in Your Career

As the defense attorney in a car theft case, you need to prepare your closing argument to the judge before a verdict is reached. After reviewing evidence from the trial, you decide to stress the following points to demonstrate the innocence of your client:

a. The stolen car was found abandoned three hours after the theft with the engine still warm; at the time the car was found, your client was at the airport to meet the flight of a friend who was flying into town.
b. Lab analysis of muddy shoe prints on the floor mat of the car indicates that the prints came from a size 27 shoe; your client wears a size 25.
c. Lab analysis shows the presence of cigarette smoke in the car, but your client does not smoke.
d. The only eyewitness to the crime, who was 20 meters from the car, said the thief "looked like" your client; yet the eyewitness admitted that at the time of the theft she was not wearing her contact lenses, which had been prescribed for improving distance vision.
e. The car was stolen at about 1 p.m.; your client testified that he was in a town 400 kilometers away at 11 a.m.
f. In a statement to police, the eyewitness described the thief as tall; your client is short.

As you work on the outline of your speech, you see that these points can be organized into three main points, each with two supporting points. Compose an outline that organizes the points in this manner.

10 Using Language

- Using Language Accurately
- Using Language Clearly
  - Use Familiar Words
  - Choose Concrete Words
  - Eliminate Clutter
- Using Language Vividly
  - Imagery
  - Rhythm
- Using Language Appropriately
  - Appropriateness to the Occasion
  - Appropriateness to the Audience
  - Appropriateness to the Topic
  - Appropriateness to the Speaker
- Using Language Inclusively

Words are the tools of a speaker's craft. They have special uses, just like the tools of any other profession. Have you ever watched a carpenter at work? The job that would take you or me a couple of hours is done by the carpenter in 10 minutes—with the right tools. You can't drive a nail with a screwdriver or turn a screw with a hammer. It is the same with public speaking. You must choose the right words for the job you want to do.

Good speakers know how to use language accurately, clearly, vividly, appropriately, and inclusively. This chapter will explore each of these areas.

Using Language Accurately

Using language accurately is as vital to a speaker as using numbers accurately is to an accountant. One study-abroad student found this out the hard way. Speaking to a meeting of host families in London, he stated that all the sightseeing had been "tiresome." What he meant was that visits to tourist attractions such as Windsor Castle and the Houses of Parliament had been "tiring"—that they had made him tired. But that is not the meaning of "tiresome." It means boring, annoying, dull, and uninteresting—hardly the message the speaker meant to communicate!

Every word has shades of meaning that distinguish it from every other word. As Mark Twain said, "The difference between the right word and the almost right word is the difference between lightning and the lightning bug."

If you look in a thesaurus, you will find that the following words are listed as synonyms:

thesaurus
A book of synonyms.

victory accomplishment success

All mean roughly the same thing—a favorable outcome. But all these words have different shades of meaning. See if you can fill in the best word to complete each of the sentences below:

1. My cousin's most important ____________ this year was getting an A in calculus.
2. Chen Xiaodan's business ____________ results from a combination of hard work and street smarts.
3. Yang Wei's ____________ on the high bar gave him the men's individual all-around gold medal in the 2008 Olympic Games.

The best answers for the three statements are:

1. accomplishment 2. success 3. victory

Each of the words means something a little different from the others, and each says something special to listeners.

As you prepare your speeches, ask yourself constantly, "What do I *really* want to say? What do I *really* mean?" When in doubt, consult a dictionary or thesaurus to make sure you have the best words to express your ideas.

Using Language Clearly

People are different. What makes perfect sense to some may be nonsense to others. You cannot assume that what is clear to you is clear to your audience. Listeners, unlike readers, cannot turn to a dictionary or reread an author's words to discover their meaning. A speaker's meaning must be *immediately* comprehensible; it must be so clear that there is no chance of misunderstanding. You can ensure this by using familiar words, by choosing concrete words over abstract words, and by eliminating verbal clutter.

USE FAMILIAR WORDS

One of the biggest barriers to clear speech is using big, bloated words where short, sharp ones will do the job better.[1] This is especially true when it comes to technical language that may be familiar to the speaker but not to the audience. Yet, if you work at it, you will almost always be able to translate even the most specialized topic into clear, familiar language.

Here, for instance, are two passages explaining the devastating effects of a pregnant woman's drinking on her unborn child. The first passage is technically accurate, but it contains too many obscure words:

> The deleterious effects of alcohol on the unborn child are very serious. When a pregnant woman consumes alcohol, the ethanol in the bloodstream easily crosses the placenta from mother to child and invades the amniotic fluid. This can produce a number of abnormal birth syndromes, including central-nervous-system dysfunctions, growth deficiencies, a cluster of facial aberrations, and variable major and minor malformations.

Well-informed listeners may be able to figure out "deleterious effects," "central-nervous-system dysfunctions," and "facial aberrations." But these terms don't create sharp mental images of what the speaker is trying to say.

Here, in contrast, is the second passage. It is utterly clear and shows what can be done with work, imagination, and a healthy respect for everyday words:

> When the expectant mother drinks, alcohol is absorbed into her bloodstream and distributed throughout her entire body. After a few beers or a couple martinis, she begins to feel tipsy and decides to sober up. She grabs a cup of coffee, two aspirin, and takes a little nap. After a while she'll be fine.
>
> But while she sleeps, the fetus is surrounded by the same alcoholic content as its mother had. After being drowned in alcohol, the fetus begins to feel the effect. But it can't sober up. It can't grab a cup of coffee. It can't take a couple aspirin. For the fetus's liver, the key organ in removing alcohol from the blood, is just not developed. The fetus is literally pickled in alcohol.[2]

This kind of plain talk is what listeners want. You cannot go wrong by following the advice of Winston Churchill to speak in "short, homely words of common usage." If you think big words (or a lot of words) are needed to impress listeners, bear in mind that Abraham Lincoln's Gettysburg Address—considered the finest speech in the English language—contains 271 words, of which 251 have only one or two syllables.

Words are the tools of the speaker's craft. Good speakers use them accurately and correctly. They also use language that will be clear, vivid, and appropriate for their listeners.

CHOOSE CONCRETE WORDS

concrete words Words that refer to tangible objects.

abstract words Words that refer to ideas or concepts.

Concrete words refer to tangible objects—people, places, and things. They differ from abstract words, which refer to general concepts, qualities, or attributes. "Carrot," "pencil," "nose," and "door" are concrete words. "Humility," "science," "progress," and "philosophy" are abstract words.

Of course, few words are completely abstract or concrete. "Great Wall" is concrete, but in China the phrase also has abstract values of patriotism and national spirit. Usually, the more specific a word, the more concrete it is. Let us say you are talking about basketball. Here are several words and phrases you might use:

physical activity	abstract/general
sports	
basketball	
NBA	↓
Yao Ming	concrete/specific

As you move down the list, the words become less abstract and more concrete. You begin with a general concept (physical activity), descend to one type of activity (sports), to a particular sport (basketball), to a division of that sport (NBA), to one specific professional basketball player (Yao Ming).

Although abstract words are necessary to express certain kinds of ideas, they are much easier to misinterpret than are concrete words. Also, concrete words are more likely to claim your listeners' attention. A speech dominated by concrete words will almost always be clearer, more interesting, and easier to recall than one dominated by abstract words.

Internet Connection

Looking for just the right word to express your ideas? There's a good chance you will find it at Merriam-Webster Online (www.merriam-webster.com). In addition to providing a dictionary and thesaurus, this site contains links to a number of language-related items from Merriam-Webster.

There are many resources on the Web for nonnative speakers of English. One of the best is Ohio University's Resources for ESL Learners (www.ohio.edu/linguistics/esl/), which provides dozens of links on subjects such as grammar, vocabulary, reading, writing, and speaking.

ELIMINATE CLUTTER

Cluttered speech has become an international epidemic. Whatever happened to such simple words as "before," "if," and "now"? When last seen they were being routed by their cluttered counterparts "prior to," "in the eventuality of," and "at this point in time." By the same token, why can't weather forecasters say, "It's raining," instead of saying, "It appears as if we are currently experiencing precipitation activity"?

clutter
Discourse that takes many more words than are necessary to express an idea.

This type of clutter forces listeners to hack through a tangle of words to discover the meaning. When you make a speech, keep your language lean and lively. Beware of using several words where one or two will do. Avoid flabby phrases. Let your ideas emerge sharply and firmly. Above all, watch out for redundant adjectives and adverbs. Inexperienced speakers (and writers) tend to string together two or three synonymous adjectives, such as "a learned and educated person" or "a hot, steamy, torrid day."

Here is part of a speech that has been revised to eliminate clutter:

> Born in Fujian Province in 1875, Qiu Jin is one of the most revered ~~and respected~~ Chinese ~~female~~ heroines. She was a ~~leader and a path breaking~~ pioneer of equal rights for women. In addition to ~~giving her support to~~ *supporting* women's ~~learning and~~ education, she opposed the ~~brutal, barbaric, and~~ cruel tradition of foot binding. Trained in classical literature, she ~~ended up becoming~~ *became* a talented poet, orator, and political writer. The first woman to ~~join and~~ be a member of Sun Yat-sen's Kuomintang, she was tortured and executed by Qing officials in ~~the year of~~ 1907. ~~In this day and age~~ *Today* she is enshrined beside West Lake in ~~the city of~~ Hangzhou.

Notice how much more concise the revised version is. No longer are the speaker's ideas hidden in a thicket of wasted words.

This kind of pruning is easy once you get the knack of it. The hardest part—and it is often very hard—is recognizing clutter and forcing yourself to throw away the unnecessary words. Watch for clutter when you write your speech outlines. Be prepared to revise the outline until your ideas emerge clearly and crisply.

Even when discussing technical subjects, effective speakers such as biologist Francis Collins look for ways to communicate their ideas in clear, familiar language.

You can also help eliminate clutter by practicing your speeches with a digital recorder. As you play the speech back, keep an ear out for flabby phrases and for verbal fillers such as "well," "you know," and "like." Practice delivering the speech again, this time making a special effort to trim it of wasted or distracting words. This will not only make you a better public speaker, but it will help you present ideas more effectively in meetings, conversations, and group discussions.

Using Language Vividly

Just as you can be accurate without being clear, so you can be both accurate and clear without being interesting. Here, for example, is what Barack Obama *might have* said in his famous "Yes, We Can" speech during the 2008 U.S. presidential election campaign:

> Giving up is something we cannot do. We must continue to persevere as Americans have always done historically. Only when we work hard, can we solve our problems. We must be positive.

Here is what Obama *actually* said:

> When we've been told that we're not ready, or that we shouldn't try, or that we can't, generations of Americans have responded with a simple creed that sums up the spirit of a people: Yes, we can.
>
> It was a creed written into the founding documents that declared the destiny of a nation. Yes, we can.
>
> It was whispered by slaves and abolitionists as they blazed a trail toward freedom through the darkest of nights. Yes, we can.

> It was sung by immigrants as they struck out from distant shores and pioneers who pushed westward against an unforgiving wilderness. Yes, we can. . . .
>
> Yes, we can to justice and equality. Yes, we can to opportunity and prosperity. Yes, we can heal this nation. Yes, we can repair this world. Yes, we can.

Much more stirring, isn't it? If you want to move people with your speeches, use vivid, animated language. Although there are several ways to do this, two of the most important are imagery and rhythm.

IMAGERY

imagery
The use of vivid language to create mental images of objects, actions, or ideas.

One sign of a good novelist is the ability to create word pictures that let you "see" the red chambers, or "hear" the birds chirping on a warm spring morning, or "taste" the hotpot at a Sichuan restaurant.

Speakers can use imagery in much the same way to make their ideas come alive. Three ways to generate imagery are by using concrete words, simile, and metaphor.

Concrete Words

As we saw earlier in this chapter, choosing concrete words over abstract words is one way to enhance the clarity of your speeches. Concrete words are also the key to effective imagery. Consider the following excerpt from Ronald Reagan's famous address commemorating the 40th anniversary of D-Day. Speaking at the scene of the battle, Reagan dramatically recounted the heroism of the U.S. Rangers who scaled the cliffs at Pointe du Hoc to help free Europe from Hitler's stranglehold:

> We stand on a lonely, windswept point on the northern shore of France. The air is soft, but 40 years ago at this moment, the air was dense with smoke and the cries of men, and the air was filled with the crack of rifle fire and the roar of cannon.
>
> At dawn, on the morning of the 6th of June, 1944, 225 Rangers jumped off the British landing craft and ran to the bottom of these cliffs. . . . The Rangers looked up and saw the enemy soldiers—at the edge of the cliffs shooting down at them with machine guns and throwing grenades. And the American Rangers began to climb. They shot rope ladders over the face of these cliffs and began to pull themselves up.
>
> When one Ranger fell, another would take his place. When one rope was cut, a Ranger would grab another and begin his climb again. They climbed, shot back, and held their footing. Soon, one by one, the Rangers pulled themselves over the top, and in seizing the firm land at the top of these cliffs, they began to seize back the continent of Europe.

Concrete words call up mental impressions of sights, sounds, touch, smell, and taste. In Reagan's speech, we do not merely learn that the U.S. Rangers helped win the battle of D-Day. We visualize the Rangers landing at the foot of the cliffs. We see them fighting their way up the cliffs in the face of enemy grenades and machine guns. We hear the crack of rifle fire and the cries of the soldiers. The concrete words create images that pull us irresistibly into the speech.

Simile

Another way to create imagery is through the use of simile. Simile is an explicit comparison between things that are essentially different yet have something in common. It always contains the word "like" or "as." Here are some examples:

> Virtue, like a strong and hardy plant, takes root in any place. (Plutarch)
>
> A word once spoken, like an arrow shot, can never be retracted. (The Talmud)
>
> The way of truth is like a great road; it is not hard to find. (Mencius)

simile
An explicit comparison, introduced with the word "like" or "as," between things that are essentially different yet have something in common.

Metaphor

You can also use metaphor to create imagery in your speeches. Metaphor is an implicit comparison between things that are essentially different yet have something in common. Unlike simile, metaphor does not contain the word "like" or "as." For example:

> Art is the torch of a nation's spirit. (Li Changchun)
>
> With globalization, the same sea washes all of humankind. We are all in the same boat. There are no safe islands. (Kofi Annan)

metaphor
An implicit comparison, not introduced with the word "like" or "as," between two things that are essentially different yet have something in common.

These are both brief metaphors. Sometimes, however, a speaker will develop a longer metaphor. Here is an excellent example, from Al Gore's speech accepting the 2007 Nobel Peace Prize for his efforts to help the world deal with climate change:

> The earth has a fever. And the fever is rising. The experts have told us it is not a passing affliction that will heal by itself. We asked for a second opinion. And a third. And a fourth. And the consistent conclusion, restated with increasing alarm, is that something basic is wrong.

When used effectively, metaphor—like simile—is an excellent way to bring color to a speech, to make abstract ideas concrete, to clarify the unknown, and to express feelings and emotions.

RHYTHM

Language has a rhythm created by the choice and arrangement of words. Speakers, like poets, sometimes seek to exploit the rhythm of language to enhance the impact of their words. Winston Churchill was a master at this. Here is a passage from one of his speeches during World War II. To emphasize its cadence, the passage has been printed as if it were poetry rather than prose:

rhythm
The pattern of sound in a speech created by the choice and arrangement of words.

> We cannot tell what the course
>   of this fell war will be. . . .
> We cannot yet see
>   how deliverance will come. . . .
> But nothing is more certain
>   than that every trace of Hitler's footsteps,

Clear, vivid, uncluttered language is a hallmark of Thomas Friedman's speeches. The Pulitzer-Prize-winning journalist gives a great deal of thought to finding just the right words to express his ideas.

every stain of his infected and corroding fingers,
will be sponged and purged
and, if need be,
blasted from the surface of the earth.

The impact of the passage was heightened by Churchill's superb delivery; but even by themselves the words take on an emphatic rhythm that reinforces the message. You can see why one observer said that Churchill "mobilized the English language and sent it into battle."[3]

A speech, however, is not a poem. You should never emphasize sound and rhythm at the expense of meaning. The aim is to think about ways you can use the rhythm and flow of language to enhance your meaning. Although you may never have paid much conscious attention to this subject, you can develop an ear for English vocal rhythms by study and practice. What's more, you can easily begin using four basic stylistic devices employed by Churchill and other fine speakers to improve the rhythm of their prose.

Parallelism

parallelism
The similar arrangement of a pair or series of related words, phrases, or sentences.

The first device is parallelism—the similar arrangement of a pair or series of related words, phrases, or sentences. For example:

> The battle is not to the strong alone; it is to *the vigilant, the active, the brave.* (Patrick Henry)

The effects of parallelism are perhaps best illustrated by seeing what happens when it is absent. For instance, compare this statement:

> I speak as a Republican. I speak as a woman. I speak as a United States Senator. I speak as an American. (Margaret Chase Smith)

with this one:

> I speak as a Republican. I speak as a woman. I speak as a United States Senator. And I am also addressing you as an American.

The first statement is clear, consistent, and compelling. The second is not. By violating the principle of parallel structure, its final sentence ("And I am also addressing you as an American") destroys the progression begun by the preceding three sentences. It turns a strong, lucid, harmonious statement into one that is fuzzy and jarring.

Repetition

Repetition means reiterating the same word or set of words at the beginning or end of successive clauses or sentences. For example:

If not now, when? *If not* us, who? *If not* together, how? (Gordon Brown)

We must imagine *greatly*, dare *greatly*, and act *greatly*. (Adlai Stevenson)

As you can see, repetition usually results in parallelism. In addition to building a strong cadence, it also unifies a sequence of ideas, emphasizes an idea by stating it more than once, and helps create a strong emotional effect.

repetition
Reiteration of the same word or set of words at the beginning or end of successive clauses or sentences.

Alliteration

The third device you can use to enhance the rhythm of your speeches is alliteration. The most common method of alliteration is repeating the initial consonant sound of close or adjoining words. For example:

alliteration
Repetition of the initial consonant sound of close or adjoining words.

*P*eace is essential for *p*rogress, but *p*rogress is no less essential for *p*eace. (Liaquat Ali Khan)

China endured many *t*rials and *t*ribulations because of the *d*ecadent and *d*eclining rule of feudalism. (Hu Jintao)

By highlighting the sounds of words, alliteration catches the attention of listeners and can make ideas easier to remember. Used sparingly, it is a marvelous way to spruce up your speeches. Used to excess, however, it can be laughable and draw too much attention, so that listeners get more involved in listening for the next alliteration than in absorbing the content of the speech.

Antithesis

Finally, you might try using antithesis—the juxtaposition of contrasting ideas, usually in parallel structure. For example:

antithesis
The juxtaposition of contrasting ideas, usually in parallel structure.

Ask not what your country can do for you; ask what you can do for your country. (John F. Kennedy)

Let us never negotiate out of fear. But let us never fear to negotiate. (John F. Kennedy)

It is no accident that both of these examples are from speeches by President Kennedy. Antithesis was one of his favorite language devices, and the one he used in his most memorable phrases. Because it nearly always produces a neatly turned phrase, it is a fine way to give your speeches a special touch of class.

Using Language Appropriately

In addition to being accurate, clear, and vivid, language should be appropriate—to the occasion, to the audience, to the topic, and to the speaker.

APPROPRIATENESS TO THE OCCASION

Language that is appropriate for some occasions may not be appropriate for others. As a simple example, a coach might address the soccer team as "you guys" (or worse!), whereas the speaker in a more formal situation would begin with "distinguished guests." Try reversing these two situations, and see how ridiculous they become. It's only common sense to adjust your language to different occasions.

APPROPRIATENESS TO THE AUDIENCE

Appropriateness also depends on the audience. If you keep this in mind, it will help you greatly when dealing with technical topics. When addressing an audience of physicians, you might use the words "fractured fibula." Your audience would know exactly what you meant. But when talking to a nonmedical audience, the appropriate phrase would be "broken leg."

Dealing with issues of appropriateness can be especially challenging when you are speaking in a second tongue and across cultural boundaries. As a general rule, you should avoid slang, jargon, technical terms, idioms, and other language that may confuse, annoy, or jar your audience.

The same is true when you are choosing between formal and informal modes of address. You will almost never offend an audience by using full names, official titles, and traditional standards of correctness, but you may create problems by being overly casual or colloquial. Remember, speakers are expected to elevate and polish their language when addressing an audience.

APPROPRIATENESS TO THE TOPIC

Language should also be appropriate to the topic. You would not use metaphor, antithesis, and alliteration when explaining how to change a bicycle tire. But you might use all three in a speech honoring Sichuan earthquake workers. The first topic calls for straightforward description and explanation. The second calls for special language skills to evoke emotion, admiration, and appreciation.

APPROPRIATENESS TO THE SPEAKER

No matter what the occasion, audience, or topic, language should be appropriate to the speaker. Every public speaker develops his or her own language style.

To say that language should be appropriate to the speaker, however, does not justify ignoring the other needs for appropriateness. There is a difference between one's everyday style and one's *developed* style as a public speaker. Accomplished speakers have developed their speaking styles over many years of trial, error, and practice. They have worked at using language effectively.

You can do the same if you become language-conscious. One way to develop this consciousness is to read and listen to effective English-language speakers. Study their techniques for achieving accuracy, clarity, and vividness, and try to adapt those techniques to your own speeches. But do not try to "become" someone else when you speak. Learn from other speakers, blend what you learn into your own language style, and seek to become the best possible you.

Language needs to be appropriate to a speaker's topic, as well as to the audience. A speech on beach volleyball would use more action-oriented words than a speech about theories of psychology.

Using Language Inclusively

As the English-speaking world has become more diverse, language usage has evolved to reflect that diversity. Regardless of the situation, audiences expect public speakers to use inclusive language that is respectful of the different cultures and ethnic groups that make up the global community. They also expect speakers to avoid stereotypes based on age, race, gender, disability, and other factors. Today, a number of principles for inclusive language have become so widespread in English-speaking countries that no speaker (or writer) can afford to ignore them. Here are a few of the most important:

inclusive language
Language that does not stereotype, demean, or patronize people on the basis of culture, gender, race, disability, or other factors.

Avoid the Generic "He"

Ineffective: Each time a surgeon walks into the operating room, *he* risks being sued for malpractice.

More Effective: Each time a surgeon walks into the operating room, *he or she* risks being sued for malpractice.

generic "he"
The use of "he" to refer to both women and men.

Often, a more graceful alternative is to pluralize. For example:

More Effective: Whenever surgeons walk into the operating room, *they* risk being sued for malpractice.

Avoid Using "Man" When Referring to Both Men and Women

Ineffective: If a large comet struck the earth, it could destroy all of mankind.

More Effective: If a large comet struck the earth, it could destroy all human life.

Checklist Using Language

YES	NO	
☐	☐	1. Have I consulted a dictionary or thesaurus to check the accuracy of my words?
☐	☐	2. Do I use familiar words that will make my meaning immediately clear?
☐	☐	3. Have I trimmed my speech of unnecessary or distracting words?
☐	☐	4. Do I use concrete words that create sharp, visual images?
☐	☐	5. Do I bring my ideas alive with simile and metaphor?
☐	☐	6. Do I employ repetition, parallelism, alliteration, or antithesis to enhance the rhythm of my speech?
☐	☐	7. Is my language appropriate to the occasion?
☐	☐	8. Is my language appropriate to the audience?
☐	☐	9. Is my language appropriate to the topic?
☐	☐	10. Am I language-conscious in an effort to develop my personal speaking style?
☐	☐	11. Do I use inclusive language that is respectful of cultural, racial, and gender differences?

Avoid Stereotyping Jobs and Social Roles by Gender

Ineffective: Being a small businessman in the current economic climate is not easy.

More Effective: Being a small businessperson in the current economic climate is not easy.

Sometimes you can solve this problem with a simple twist in sentence construction. For example:

More Effective: Owning a small business is not easy in the current economic climate.

Use Names That Groups Use to Identify Themselves

One of the most fundamental ways of showing respect for others is to refer to them by the names they use to identify themselves and to avoid names they consider offensive.

Ineffective: The Paralympics show what crippled people can accomplish in the athletic arena.

Ineffective: The Paralympics show what handicapped people can accomplish in the athletic arena.

More Effective: The Paralympics show what people with disabilities can accomplish in the athletic arena.

Like many other aspects of modern life, issues of inclusive language can be confusing. Although "steward" and "stewardess" gave way long ago to "flight attendant," most people—including those who bestow the Academy Awards—continue to distinguish between "actor" and "actress." Is this logical? Hardly. Language is alive and constantly evolving, so what is considered inclusive today may shift down the road. If you have questions in any particular case, check the Internet for the most up-to-date information.

SUMMARY

Good speakers respect language and how it works. As a speaker, you should use language accurately, clearly, vividly, appropriately, and inclusively.

Never use a word unless you are sure it is accurate. If you are not sure, look up the word in a dictionary. As you prepare your speeches, ask yourself constantly, "What do I *really* want to say? What do I *really* mean?"

Using language clearly allows listeners to grasp your meaning immediately. You can ensure this by using words that are known to the average person and require no specialized background, by choosing concrete words in preference to more abstract ones, and by eliminating verbal clutter.

Using language vividly helps bring your speech to life. One way to make your language more vivid is through imagery, which you can develop by using concrete language, simile, and metaphor. Another way to make your speeches vivid is by exploiting the rhythm of language with parallelism, repetition, alliteration, and antithesis.

Using language appropriately means adapting to the particular occasion, audience, and topic at hand. It also means developing your own language style instead of trying to copy someone else's.

Using language inclusively is an important element of intercultural communicative competence. Four strategies for inclusiveness are avoiding the generic "he," dropping the use of "man" when referring to both men and women, refraining from stereotyping jobs and social roles by gender, and using names that groups use to identify themselves.

KEY TERMS

thesaurus *(131)*
concrete words *(133)*
abstract words *(133)*
clutter *(134)*
imagery *(136)*
simile *(137)*
metaphor *(137)*
rhythm *(137)*
parallelism *(138)*
repetition *(139)*
alliteration *(139)*
antithesis *(139)*
inclusive language *(141)*
generic "he" *(141)*

Key-Term Exercise
Check your knowledge with the Key-Term Exercise for this chapter.

EXERCISES FOR THINKING AND SPEAKING

1. List the three major aspects of language usage that you most want to improve upon when giving speeches in English. Explain specific steps you can take to achieve each objective.
2. Write a 1–2 minute speech in which you use the resources of language discussed in this chapter to describe a scene or to capture an emotion. Present your speech in class. Possible topics include:

a scene at sunset	my happiest moment
walking in the mountains	my worst experience
life in the city	my favorite person
any special location	my greatest goal

3. Analyze Martin Luther King's "I Have a Dream" in the appendix of sample speeches that follows Chapter 16. Identify the methods King uses to make his language clear, vivid, and appropriate. Look particularly at King's use of familiar words, concrete words, imagery, and rhythm.

Public Speaking in Your Career

As a student counselor at a comprehensive university, you are scheduled to speak with new students during registration week for the upcoming semester. In the opening part of your speech, you want the audience to feel as you did when you began college. The best strategy, you decide, is to present two or three similes that complete the sentence, "Beginning college is like. . . ." Write your similes.

11 Delivering the Speech

- What Is Good Delivery?
- Methods of Delivery
  - Reading from a Manuscript
  - Reciting from Memory
  - Speaking Impromptu
  - Speaking Extemporaneously
- The Speaker's Voice
  - Volume
  - Pitch
  - Rate
  - Pauses
  - Vocal Variety
  - Pronunciation
  - Articulation
- The Speaker's Body
  - Personal Appearance
  - Eye Contact
  - Gestures
  - Movement
- Practicing Delivery

If you were to record one of Dashan's comedy routines, memorize it word for word, and stand up before your friends to recite it, would you get the same response Dashan does? Not very likely. And why not? Because you would not *deliver* the jokes as Dashan does. Of course, the jokes are basically funny. But Dashan brings something extra to the jokes—his manner of presentation, his vocal inflections, his perfectly timed pauses, his facial expressions, his gestures. All these are part of an expert delivery. It would take you years of practice—as it took Dashan—to duplicate his results.

This example demonstrates how important delivery can be to any public speaking situation. Even a mediocre speech will be more effective if it is presented well, whereas a wonderfully written speech can be ruined by poor delivery. You cannot make a good speech without having something to say. But having something to say is not enough. You must also know *how* to say it.

What Is Good Delivery?

Good delivery does not call attention to itself. It conveys the speaker's ideas clearly, interestingly, and without distracting the audience. Most audiences prefer delivery that combines a certain degree of formality with the best attributes of good conversation—directness, spontaneity, animation, vocal and facial expressiveness, and a lively sense of communication.

Speech delivery is an art, not a science. What works for one speaker may not work for another. And what succeeds with today's audience may fail with tomorrow's. You cannot become a skilled speaker just by following a set of rules in a textbook. In the long run, there is no substitute for experience. But take heart! A textbook *can* give you basic pointers to get you started in the right direction.

When you plan your first speech, you should concentrate on such basics as speaking intelligibly, avoiding distracting mannerisms, and establishing eye contact with your listeners. Once you get these elements under control and feel fairly comfortable in front of an audience, you can work on polishing your delivery to enhance the impact of your ideas. Eventually, you may find yourself able to control the timing and rhythm of a speech as skillfully as a conductor controls an orchestra.

Methods of Delivery

There are four basic methods of delivering a speech: (1) reading verbatim from a manuscript; (2) reciting a memorized text; (3) speaking impromptu; and (4) speaking extemporaneously. Let us look at each.

READING FROM A MANUSCRIPT

Certain speeches must be delivered word for word, according to a meticulously prepared manuscript. Examples include an engineer's report to a professional meeting or a prime minister's speech at the United Nations. In such situations, absolute accuracy is essential. Every word of the speech will be analyzed by the press, by colleagues, perhaps by enemies. In the case of the prime minister, a misstated phrase could cause an international incident.

manuscript speech
A speech that is written out word for word and read to the audience.

Although it looks easy, delivering a speech from manuscript requires great skill. Some people do it well. Others ruin it every time. Instead of sounding vibrant and conversational, they march through the speech without even glancing at their audience. In short, they come across as *reading to* their listeners, rather than as *talking with* them.

If you are in a situation where you must speak from a manuscript, practice aloud to make sure the speech sounds natural. Work on establishing eye contact with your listeners. Be certain the final manuscript is legible at a glance. Above all, reach out to your audience with the same directness and sincerity that you would if you were speaking extemporaneously.

RECITING FROM MEMORY

Presenting a speech entirely from memory is often required of speakers when they make brief presentations such as toasts, congratulatory remarks, acceptance speeches, introductions, and the like. Speaking from memory is also required for prepared speeches in competitions such as the CCTV Cup and the 21st Century Cup. If you are giving a speech of this kind, be sure to memorize it so thoroughly that you will be able to concentrate on communicating with the audience, rather than on trying to remember the words.

SPEAKING IMPROMPTU

impromptu speech
A speech delivered with little or no immediate preparation.

An impromptu speech is delivered with little or no immediate preparation. Few people choose to speak impromptu, but sometimes it cannot be avoided. In fact, many of the speeches you give in life will be impromptu. You might be called on suddenly to "say a few words," or, in the course of a class discussion, business meeting, or committee report, you might want to respond to a previous speaker.

When such situations arise, don't panic. If you are in a meeting or discussion, pay close attention to what the other speakers say. Take notes of major points with which you agree or disagree. In the process, you will automatically begin to formulate what you will say when it is your turn to speak.

Whenever you are responding to a previous speaker, try to present your speech in four simple steps: First, state the point you are answering. Second, state the point you wish to make. Third, support your point with evidence and reasoning. Fourth, summarize your point. This four-step method will help you organize your thoughts quickly and clearly.

Video 11.1
View "Are We Becoming Too Susceptible to Advertising?" for an example of impromptu speaking.

Once you begin speaking, maintain strong eye contact with the audience. Help the audience keep track of your ideas with signposts such as "My first point is . . . ; second, we can see that . . . ; in conclusion, I would like to say. . . . " If you have had time to prepare notes, stick to what you have written. By stating your points clearly and concisely, you will come across as organized and confident.

As with other kinds of public speaking, the best way to become a better impromptu speaker is to practice. You can do this on your own. Simply choose a topic on which you are already well informed, and give a one- or two-minute impromptu talk on some

Extemporaneous speeches are prepared ahead of time, but the exact words are chosen at the moment of presentation. This allows for more direct delivery than does reading from a manuscript.

aspect of that topic. Any topic will do, no matter how serious or frivolous it may be. You don't even need an audience—you can speak to an empty room. Better yet, speak to a digital recorder and play it back to hear how you sound. The purpose is to gain experience in pulling your ideas together quickly and stating them succinctly.

extemporaneous speech
A carefully prepared and rehearsed speech that is presented from a brief set of notes.

SPEAKING EXTEMPORANEOUSLY

In popular usage, "extemporaneous" means the same as "impromptu." But technically the two are different. Unlike an impromptu speech, which is delivered off-the-cuff, an extemporaneous speech is carefully prepared and practiced in advance. In presenting the speech, the extemporaneous speaker uses only a set of brief notes or a speaking outline to jog the memory. The exact wording is chosen at the moment of delivery.

Video 11.2
View an excerpt from "Yoga: Uniting Mind, Body, and Spirit" for an example of conversational quality.

This is not as hard as it sounds. Once you have your outline (or notes) and know what topics you are going to cover and in what order, you can begin to practice the speech. Every time you run through it, the wording will be slightly different. As you practice the speech over and over, the best way to present each part will emerge and stick in your mind.

The extemporaneous method has several advantages. It gives more precise control over thought and language than impromptu speaking; it offers greater spontaneity and directness than speaking from memory or from a full manuscript; and it is adaptable to a wide range of situations. It also encourages the conversational quality audiences look for in speech delivery. "Conversational quality" means that no matter how many times a speech has been rehearsed, it still *sounds* spontaneous.

conversational quality
Presenting a speech so it sounds spontaneous no matter how many times it has been rehearsed.

Later in this chapter, we'll look at a step-by-step program for practicing your extemporaneous delivery.

The Speaker's Voice

A golden voice is an asset for any public speaker, but it is not a necessity. Some of the most famous speakers in history have had undistinguished voices. Abraham Lincoln had a harsh and penetrating voice; Winston Churchill suffered from a slight lisp and an awkward stammer. Like them, you can overcome natural disadvantages and use your voice to the best effect. Lincoln and Churchill learned to *control* their voices. You can do the same thing.

The aspects of voice you should work to control are volume, pitch, rate, pauses, variety, pronunciation, and articulation.

VOLUME

volume
The loudness or softness of a speaker's voice.

At one time, a powerful voice was essential for an orator. Today, electronic amplification allows even a soft-spoken person to be heard in any setting. Whether you speak with or without a microphone, be sure to adjust your voice to the acoustics of the room, the size of the audience, and the level of background noise. If you speak too loudly, your listeners will think you boorish. If you speak too softly, they will not understand you.

Remember that your own voice always sounds louder to you than to a listener. Soon after beginning your speech, glance at the people farthest away from you. If they look puzzled, are leaning forward in their seats, or are otherwise straining to hear, you need to talk louder.

PITCH

pitch
The highness or lowness of a speaker's voice.

Pitch is the highness or lowness of the speaker's voice. Changes in pitch are known as *inflections*. They give your voice luster, warmth, and vitality. Inflections reveal whether you are asking a question or making a statement, whether you are being sincere or sarcastic. Your inflections can also make you sound happy or sad, angry or pleased, dynamic or listless, tense or relaxed.

inflections
Changes in the pitch or tone of a speaker's voice.

Few people speak in an absolute monotone, with no variation whatever in pitch, but many fall into repetitious pitch patterns that are just as hypnotic. You can guard against this by recording your speeches as you practice them. If all your sentences end on the same inflection—either upward or downward—work on varying your pitch patterns to fit the meaning of your words.

RATE

rate
The speed at which a person speaks.

Rate refers to the speed at which a person speaks. Native speakers of English usually talk at a rate between 120 and 150 words per minute, but there is no uniform rate for effective speechmaking. The best rate depends on several things—the vocal attributes of the speaker, the mood she or he is trying to create, the composition of the audience, and the nature of the occasion.

Two obvious faults to avoid are speaking so slowly that your listeners become bored or so quickly that they lose track of your ideas. The key in both cases is to become aware of the problem and then to concentrate on solving it. Use a digital

The best rate of speech depends partly on the mood a speaker wants to create. To communicate the serenity of a mountain lake, you would probably speak at a slower-than-normal rate.

recorder to check how fast you speak. Pay special attention to rate when practicing your speech, and note where you need to slow down or speed up. Finally, be sure to include reminders about rate on your speaking outline so you won't forget to make the adjustments when you present your speech.

PAUSES

pause
A momentary break in the vocal delivery of a speech.

Learning how and when to pause is a major challenge for most beginning speakers. As you gain more poise and confidence, however, you will discover how useful the pause can be. It can signal the end of a thought unit, give an idea time to sink in, and lend dramatic impact to a statement. "The right word may be effective," said Mark Twain, "but no word was ever as effective as a rightly timed pause."

vocalized pause
A pause that occurs when a speaker fills the silence between words with vocalizations such as "um," "er," and "well."

Developing a keen sense of timing is partly a matter of common sense, partly a matter of experience. You will not always get your pauses just right at first, but keep trying. Listen to accomplished speakers to see how they use pauses to modulate their rate and rhythm. Work on pauses when you practice your speeches.

When you pause, make sure you do so at the end of thought units and not in the middle. Most important, do not fill the silence with "um," "er," or "well." These *vocalized pauses* are distracting to listeners and can damage a speaker's credibility.[1]

VOCAL VARIETY

vocal variety
Changes in a speaker's rate, pitch, and volume that give the voice interest and expressiveness.

Just as variety is the spice of life, so is it the spice of public speaking. A flat, listless, unchanging voice is just as deadly to speechmaking as a flat, listless, unchanging routine is to daily life. When giving a speech, you should vary the rate, pitch, and volume of your voice to communicate your ideas and feelings.

As you practice your speeches, record them to hear how they sound. Try them out on members of your family, a friend, or a roommate. Practice the vocal variety exercise

Internet Connection

Do you want to learn more about speech delivery? Perhaps gain additional experience after your speech class is over? You can do both by joining an organization such as Toastmasters International, which has more than 225,000 members and 11,500 clubs in 92 countries around the world. For information about Toastmasters, log on to its Web site at www.toastmasters.org.

You can access a number of excellent resources for nonnative speakers of English at the Purdue University ESL Web site for students and instructors (http://owl.english.purdue.edu/owl/resource/678/01/).

Video 11.3

View an excerpt from "Questions of Culture" for an excellent example of vocal variety.

at the end of this chapter. Above all, approach every speech as an opportunity to share ideas that are important to you. Your sense of conviction and your desire to communicate will give your voice the same spark it has in spontaneous conversation.

PRONUNCIATION

pronunciation
The accepted standard of sound and rhythm for words in a given language.

Pronunciation poses a challenge for anyone who presents speeches in a second language. Although native speakers of English are very tolerant of pronunciation errors by nonnative speakers in spontaneous conversation, they expect a higher degree of accuracy in formal speeches. As you work on your speeches, pay special attention to words that are difficult for you to pronounce and practice them until you can say them correctly. If you have any doubts about particular words, check an online dictionary that includes audio pronunciation.

ARTICULATION

articulation
The physical production of particular speech sounds.

Articulation and pronunciation are not identical. Sloppy articulation is the failure to form particular speech sounds crisply and distinctly. Most of the time, poor articulation is caused by laziness—by failing to manipulate the lips, tongue, jaw, and soft palate so as to produce speech sounds clearly and precisely.

One of the most common articulation errors by English speakers, native and nonnative alike, comes from the careless blending of two short words—such as saying "lemme" instead of "let me," "gonna" instead of "going to," and "didja" instead of "did you." Here are some other common errors in articulation you should work to avoid:

Word	Misarticulation
ought to	otta
don't know	dunno
have to	hafta
want to	wanna
will you	wilya

Video 11.4

View the beginning of "Globalization and Chinese Values of Harmony" for an example of excellent English articulation.

Good speakers such as Nobel Peace Prize Laureate Muhammad Yunus use a lively voice to bring their ideas to life. They also use gestures, eye contact, and facial expressions to create a bond with their audience.

The Speaker's Body

Posture, facial expression, gestures, eye contact—all affect the way listeners respond to a speaker. How we use these and other body motions to communicate is the subject of a fascinating area of study called kinesics. One of its founders, Ray Birdwhistell, estimated that more than 700,000 physical signals can be sent through bodily movement.

kinesics
The study of body motions as a systematic mode of communication.

Studies have shown that these signals have a significant impact on the meaning communicated by speakers. Research has also confirmed what the Greek historian Herodotus observed more than 2,400 years ago: "People trust their ears less than their eyes." When a speaker's body language is inconsistent with his or her words, listeners often believe the body language rather than the words.[2]

Here are the major aspects of physical action that will affect the outcome of your speeches.

PERSONAL APPEARANCE

A number of studies have confirmed that personal appearance plays an important role in speechmaking.[3] Listeners always see you before they hear you. Just as you adapt your language to the audience and the occasion, so should you dress and groom appropriately. Although the force of your speech can sometimes overcome a poor impression created by personal appearance, the odds are against it. Regardless of the speaking situation, you should try to evoke a favorable first impression.

EYE CONTACT

eye contact
Direct visual contact with the eyes of another person.

Like many elements of communication, eye contact is influenced by cultural background. When engaged in conversation, Arabs, Latin Americans, and Southern Europeans tend to look directly at the person with whom they are talking. People from some Asian countries and parts of Africa tend to engage in less eye contact.

When it comes to public speaking, there is wide agreement across cultures on the importance of some degree of eye contact. In most circumstances, one of the quickest ways to establish a communicative bond with your listeners is to look at them personally and pleasantly. Avoiding their gaze is one of the surest ways to lose them.

Video 11.5
View an excerpt from "Making a Difference Through the Special Olympics" for an example of strong eye contact.

When addressing a small audience, you can usually look briefly from one person to another. For a larger group, you will probably scan the audience rather than trying to engage the eyes of each person individually. No matter what the size of your audience, you want your eyes to convey confidence, sincerity, and conviction. They should say, "I am pleased to be able to talk with you. I believe deeply in what I am saying, and I want you to believe in it too."

GESTURES

gestures
Motions of a speaker's hands or arms during a speech.

Few aspects of delivery cause beginning speakers more anguish than deciding what to do with their hands. Even people who use their hands expressively in everyday conversation seem to regard them as awkward appendages when speaking before an audience.

Adroit gestures *can* add to the impact of a speech, but effective speakers do not need a vast repertoire of gestures. Some accomplished speakers gesture frequently; others, hardly at all. The primary rule is this: Whatever gestures you make should not distract from your message. They should *appear* natural and spontaneous, help clarify or reinforce your ideas, and be suited to the audience and occasion.

Gesturing tends to work itself out as you acquire experience and confidence. For now, make sure your hands do not upstage your ideas. Avoid flailing them about, wringing them together, or sticking them in your pockets. Once you have eliminated these distractions, forget about your hands. Think about communicating with your listeners, and your gestures will take care of themselves—just as they do in conversation.

MOVEMENT

Video 11.6
View an excerpt from "Tea Culture" for an example of poised delivery and movement.

Novice speakers are often unsure what to do with their body while giving a speech. Some pace back and forth across the podium or repeatedly shift their weight from one foot to another. Others turn into statues, standing rigid and expressionless from beginning to end. Such quirks usually stem from nervousness or inexperience. Once they are pointed out to you, concentrate on eliminating them in later speeches.

As important as how you act during the speech is what you do just *before* you begin and *after* you finish. As you rise to speak, try to appear calm, poised, and confident, despite the butterflies in your stomach. When you reach the lectern, don't lean on it, and don't rush into your speech. Give yourself time to get set. Arrange your notes just the way you want them. Stand quietly as you wait to make sure the audience is paying attention. Establish eye contact with your listeners. Then—and only then—should you start to talk.

When you reach the end of your speech, maintain eye contact for a few moments after you stop talking. This will give your closing line time to sink in. Unless you are staying at the lectern to answer questions, collect your notes and return to your seat. As you do so, maintain your cool, collected demeanor. Whatever you do, don't start to gather your notes before you finish talking; and don't cap off your speech with a huge sigh of relief or some remark like, "Whew! Am I glad that's over!"

When practicing your speeches, spend a little time rehearsing how you will behave at the beginning and at the end. It is one of the easiest—and one of the most effective—things you can do to improve your image with an audience.

As experienced speakers know, you need to practice a speech thoroughly before delivering it. If possible, try to rehearse under conditions as close as possible to those you will face during the speech itself.

Practicing Delivery

Popular wisdom promises that practice makes perfect. This is true, but only if we practice properly. You will do little to improve your speech delivery unless you practice the right things in the right ways. Here is a five-step method that has worked well for many speakers:

1. Go through your preparation outline *aloud* to check how it translates into spoken discourse. Is it too long? Too short? Are the main points clear when you speak them? Do the introduction and conclusion come across well? As you answer these questions, revise the speech as needed.

2. Prepare your speaking outline. In doing so, be sure to follow the guidelines in Chapter 9. Use the same visual framework as in the preparation outline. Make sure the speaking outline is easy to read at a glance. Give yourself cues on the outline for delivering the speech.

3. Practice the speech aloud several times using only the speaking outline. Be sure to "talk through" all examples and to recite in full all quotations and statistics. If your speech includes visual aids, use them as you practice. The first couple of times, you will probably forget something or make a mistake, but don't worry. Keep going and complete the speech as well as you can. Concentrate on gaining control of the *ideas*; don't try to learn the speech word for word. After a few tries, you should be able to get through the speech extemporaneously with surprising ease.

Checklist Delivery

YES	NO	
☐	☐	1. Do I understand the four methods of speech delivery?
☐	☐	2. Can I concentrate on communicating with my audience rather than on trying to remember what I want to say?
☐	☐	3. Have I recorded my speech when rehearsing to check volume, rate, pitch, and vocal variety?
☐	☐	4. Have I eliminated vocalized pauses from my speech?
☐	☐	5. Have I practiced the pronunciation and articulation of all challenging words?
☐	☐	6. Have I dressed properly for the audience and the occasion?
☐	☐	7. Have I rehearsed how I will act at the beginning and end of my speech to create a favorable impression?
☐	☐	8. Have I identified distracting mannerisms that I should avoid during the speech?
☐	☐	9. Have I gone over all aspects of the speech, including visual aids, in my practice sessions?
☐	☐	10. Have I practiced the timing of my speech so I can complete it in the allotted time?
☐	☐	11. Have I followed the five-step method of practicing delivery explained in this chapter?
☐	☐	12. Have I started practicing early enough that I will be fully prepared and confident on speech day?

4. Now begin to polish and refine your delivery. Practice the speech in front of a mirror to check for eye contact and distracting mannerisms. Record the speech to gauge volume, pitch, rate, pauses, and vocal variety. Most important, try it out on friends, roommates, family members—anyone who will listen and give you an honest appraisal. Since your speech is designed for people rather than for mirrors or recorders, you need to find out ahead of time how it goes over with people.

5. Finally, give your speech a dress rehearsal under conditions as close as possible to those you will face on speech day. Some students like to try the speech a couple of times in an empty classroom the day before the speech is due. Professional speakers usually familiarize themselves with the room in which they will be speaking. No matter where you hold your last practice session, you should leave it feeling confident and looking forward to addressing your audience.

If this or any practice method is to work, you must start early. Don't wait until the night before your speech to begin working on delivery. A single practice session—no matter how long—is rarely enough. Allow yourself plenty of time to gain command of the speech and its presentation.

SUMMARY

Speech delivery involves using the voice and body to convey the message expressed by a speaker's words. Rather than calling attention to itself, effective delivery conveys the speaker's ideas clearly, engagingly, and without distracting the audience.

There are four basic methods of delivering a speech: reading verbatim from a manuscript, reciting a memorized text, speaking impromptu, and speaking extemporaneously.

To use your voice effectively, you should work on controlling your volume, pitch, rate, pauses, vocal variety, pronunciation, and articulation. Volume is the relative loudness of your voice, and pitch is the relative highness or lowness. Rate refers to the speed at which you talk. Pauses, when carefully timed, can add impact to your speech, but you should avoid vocalized pauses ("er," "well," and the like). Vocal variety refers to changes in volume, pitch, rate, and pauses and is crucial to making your voice lively and engaging. For public speaking, you should be sure to pronounce words correctly and to articulate them distinctly.

Posture, personal appearance, facial expression, gestures, and eye contact also affect the way listeners respond to speakers. Dress and groom appropriately, use gestures and bodily movement to enhance your message, and make eye contact with your listeners.

You should practice all these aspects of delivery along with the words of your speech. Start your practice sessions early so you will have ample time to polish your presentation.

KEY TERMS

manuscript speech *(148)*
impromptu speech *(148)*
extemporaneous speech *(149)*
conversational quality *(149)*
volume *(150)*
pitch *(150)*
inflections *(150)*
rate *(150)*
pause *(151)*
vocalized pause *(151)*
vocal variety *(151)*
pronunciation *(152)*
articulation *(152)*
kinesics *(153)*
eye contact *(154)*
gestures *(154)*

Key-Term Exercise
Check your knowledge with the Key-Term Exercise for this chapter.

EXERCISES FOR THINKING AND SPEAKING

1. An excellent way to improve your vocal variety is to read aloud selections from poetry that require emphasis and feeling. Choose an English-language poem and practice reading it aloud. Use your voice to make the poem come alive. Vary your volume, rate, and pitch. Find the appropriate places for pauses. Underline the key words or phrases you think should be stressed. Use inflections for emphasis and meaning.

   If possible, practice reading the selection into a digital recorder. Listen to the playback. If you are not satisfied with what you hear, practice the selection some more and record it again. Finally, present the poem in class to receive feedback from your classmates and instructor.

2. Watch a 10-minute segment of a television drama with the sound turned off. What do the characters say with their dress, gestures, facial expressions, and the like? Do the same with a television comedy. How do the nonverbal messages in the two shows differ? Be prepared to report your observations in class.

3. Attend an English-language speech on campus. Prepare a brief report on the speaker's delivery. In your report, analyze the speaker's volume, pitch, rate, pauses, vocal variety, pronunciation, and articulation. Also evaluate the speaker's personal appearance, bodily action, gestures, and eye contact. Finally, note two techniques of delivery used by the speaker that you might want to try in your next speech.

4. Present a 1–2 minute report to your class analyzing the delivery of two of the speakers included on the CD-ROM for this chapter (Videos 11.1–11.6).

Public Speaking in Your Career

After receiving your master's degree, you accepted a job in the English department at a local university, where you have been teaching public speaking. Now you have been invited to attend a provincial conference on English public speaking instruction, at which you will present a paper on "The Three Most Important Elements of Speech Delivery." Prepare a 2-minute summary explaining the three elements of delivery that you believe are most important, and why.

12 Using Visual Aids

As the old saying tells us, one picture can be worth a thousand words. People find a speaker's message more interesting, grasp it more easily, and retain it longer when it is presented visually as well as verbally.[1] We have all heard that words can "go in one ear and out the other." Visual images tend to last. By using visual aids in your speeches, you can make it easier for listeners to understand exactly what you are trying to communicate.

When used properly, visual aids enhance almost every aspect of a speech. One study showed that an average speaker who uses visual aids will come across as better prepared, more credible, and more professional than a dynamic speaker who does not use visual aids. According to the same study, visual aids can increase the persuasiveness of a speech by more than 40 percent.[2] Visual aids can even help combat stage fright. They heighten audience interest, shift attention away from the speaker, and give the speaker greater confidence in the presentation as a whole.[3]

For all these reasons, you will find visual aids of great value in your speeches. In this chapter, we will look at the major kinds of visual aids and how to prepare and present them most effectively.

Kinds of Visual Aids

OBJECTS AND MODELS

Objects make excellent visual aids. If you are talking about Weifang kites, for example, you could bring one or two kites and explain them to your audience.

Some objects, however, cannot be used effectively in speeches. Some are too big. Others are too small to be seen clearly. Still others may not be available. If you were talking about a rare suit of armor in a local museum, you could, theoretically, transport it to your speech, but it is not likely that the museum would let you borrow it.

If the object you want to discuss is too large, too small, or unavailable, you may be able to work with a model. One option is a life-size model such as that used in the speech on CPR (rescue breathing) presented on Video 12.1. Another is a large-scale representation of a very small object, such as a model of a molecule or a strand of DNA.

model
An object, usually built to scale, that represents another object in detail.

Video 12.1
View an excerpt from "CPR."

PHOTOGRAPHS AND DRAWINGS

In the absence of an object or model, you may be able to use photographs or drawings. Neither, however, will work effectively unless they are large enough for the audience to see without straining. Normal-size photographs are too small to be seen without being passed around, which only diverts the audience from what you are saying. The same is true of photographs and drawings in books.

The most effective way to show drawings and photographs is with PowerPoint. Notice, for example, how the speaker in Video 12.2 uses PowerPoint to present a photograph of the famous Incan ruins at Machu Picchu, in Peru. No other method of showing the photograph would work as well.

Video 12.2
View an excerpt from "Machu Picchu: City of the Gods."

Internet Connection

Do you want to learn more about PowerPoint and other multimedia presentations? Check Presentation Tips (www.garrreynolds.com/Presentation/). Maintained by Garr Reynolds, author of *Presentation Zen*, this site contains a wealth of helpful tips, as well as updates on the latest technological developments.

GRAPHS

graph
A visual aid used to show statistical trends and patterns.

Audiences often have trouble grasping a complex series of numbers. You can ease their difficulty by using graphs to show statistical trends and patterns.

line graph
A graph that uses one or more lines to show changes in statistics over time or space.

The most common type of graph is the *line graph*. Figure 12.1 (below) shows such a graph, used in a speech about the American movie industry. If you look at Video 12.3, you can see how the speaker presented the graph.

Video 12.3
View the presentation of this graph in "American Movies: From the Studio System to the Video Age."

Movie Industry Revenues

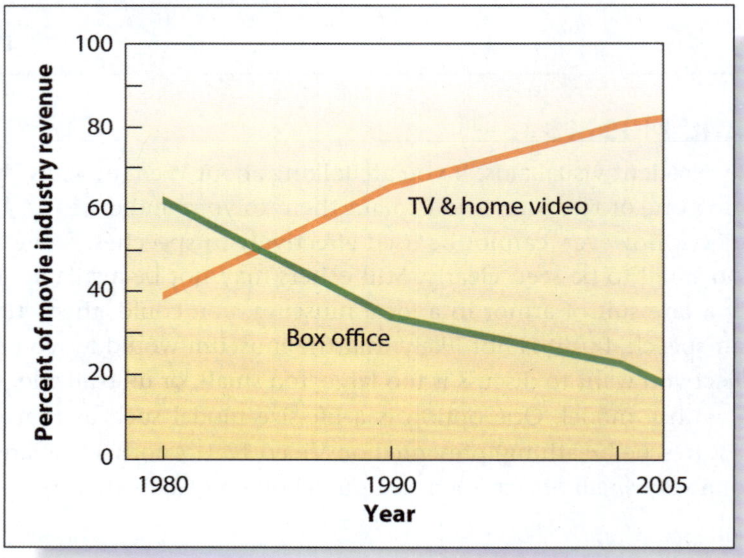

• **FIGURE 12.1**

A second type is the *pie graph*. It is best suited for illustrating simple distribution patterns. Figure 12.2 (page 163) shows how one speaker used a pie graph to visualize changes in marital status among U.S. working women during the past century.

Because a pie graph is used to dramatize relationships among the parts of a whole, you should keep the number of segments in the graph as small as possible. A pie graph should ideally have from two to five segments; under no circumstances should it have more than eight.

Women in the Work Force

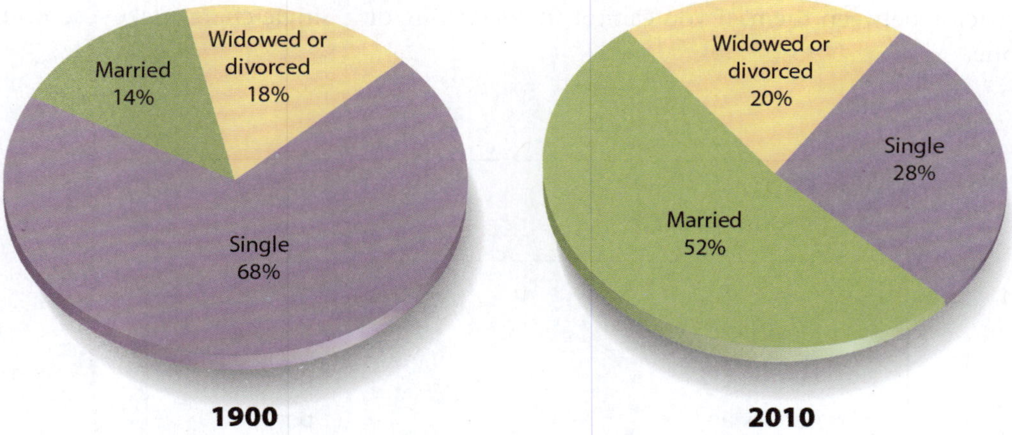

pie graph
A graph that highlights segments of a circle to show simple distribution patterns.

• **FIGURE 12.2**

A third type is the *bar graph*. It is a particularly good way to show comparisons among two or more items. Figure 12.3 (below) is an example of a bar graph from a speech titled "The Politics of Race in America." By using a bar graph, the speaker made his points more vividly than if he had just cited the numbers orally.[4]

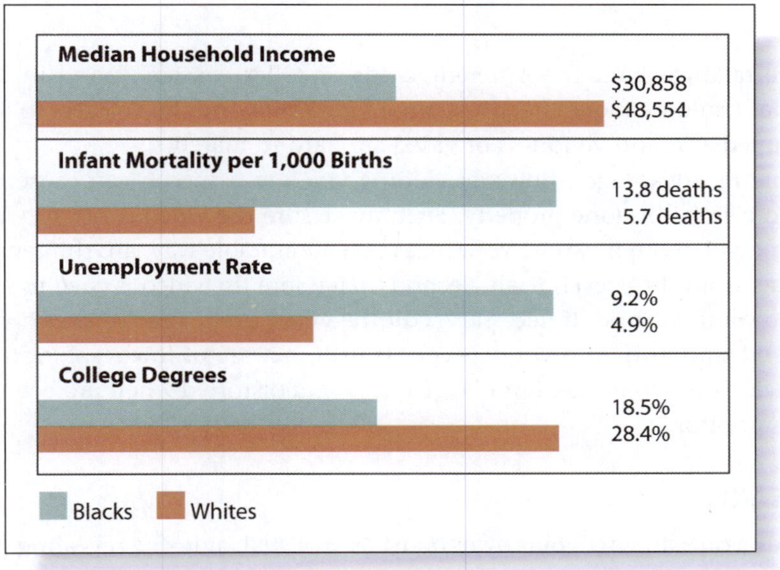

bar graph
A graph that uses vertical or horizontal bars to show comparisons among two or more items.

• **FIGURE 12.3**

CHARTS

Charts are especially useful for summarizing large blocks of information. Figure 12.4 (page 164) shows a chart listing the leading regions of the world for immigrants to the United States. These are too many categories for a pie graph. By listing them on a chart, the speaker made it easy for listeners to keep track of the information.

chart
A visual aid that summarizes a large block of information, usually in list form.

The biggest mistake speakers make when using a chart is to include too much information. Lists on a chart should rarely exceed seven or eight items, with generous spacing between them. If you cannot fit everything on a single chart, make a second one.

Video 12.4
View the presentation of this chart in "The United States: A Nation of Immigrants."

Region of Birth	Percent of U.S. Immigrants
Asia	36 percent
Mexico	14 percent
Europe	11 percent
Caribbean	11 percent
South America	10 percent
Africa	9 percent
Central America	5 percent
Other	4 percent

• **FIGURE 12.4**

VIDEO

If you are talking about the different kinds of roller coasters found in amusement parks, what could be more effective than a video showing the coasters in action? The detail, immediacy, and vividness of video are hard to match.

Despite its advantages, however, adding video to a speech can cause more harm than good if it is not done properly. First, make sure the video is not too long. While a 30-second video can illustrate your ideas in a memorable way, anything much longer will distract from the speech itself. Second, make sure the video is cued to start exactly where you want it. Third, if necessary, edit the video to the precise length you need so it will blend smoothly into your speech. Fourth, beware of low-resolution video that may look fine on a computer but will be blurry and distorted when projected on a large screen or monitor.

THE SPEAKER

Sometimes you can use your own body as a visual aid—by revealing the secrets behind magic tricks, by showing how to perform sign language for the deaf, and so forth. In addition to clarifying a speaker's ideas, doing some kind of demonstration helps keep the audience involved. It can also reduce a speaker's nervousness by providing an outlet for extra adrenaline.

Video 12.5
View an excerpt from "Yoga: Uniting Body, Mind, and Spirit."

Doing a demonstration well requires special practice to coordinate your actions with your words and to maintain eye contact with the audience. You can see an excellent example on Video 12.5, in which the speaker demonstrates how to perform yoga.

Sometimes a speaker can use his or her body as a visual aid, as in this speech demonstrating yoga postures. Such a speech requires careful practice to coordinate the speaker's actions and words while maintaining eye contact with the audience.

Special care is required if you are demonstrating a process that takes longer to complete than the time allowed for your speech. If you plan to show a long process, you might borrow the techniques of television chefs. They work through most of the steps in making a perfect Peking duck, but they have a second, finished duck ready to show you at the last minute.

POWERPOINT

When used well, PowerPoint is a great boon to communication. Unfortunately, it is not always used well. The biggest problem is that speakers often use PowerPoint to illustrate every point of their talk, so the speaker is virtually reading the speech to the audience as the words appear on screen. This is no more effective than reading dully from a manuscript, and it seldom produces genuine communication.

If you are going to use PowerPoint effectively, you need a clear idea of exactly why, how, and when you are going to use it in your speech. Rather than putting everything you say on screen for the audience to read, you need to choose which aspects of your speech to illustrate. This requires careful planning.

For an excellent example, view the speech on the Great Wall of China that is printed at the end of this chapter. As you will see, the speaker uses PowerPoint creatively and resourcefully without allowing it to overwhelm the entire speech. He also integrates his slides perfectly with his words, so as to produce a highly professional presentation.

Checklist Preparing Visual Aids

YES	NO	
☐	☐	1. Have I prepared my visual aids well in advance?
☐	☐	2. Are my visual aids clear and easy to comprehend?
☐	☐	3. Does each visual aid contain only the information needed to make my point?
☐	☐	4. Are my visual aids large enough to be seen clearly by the entire audience?
☐	☐	5. Do the colors on my visual aids work well together?
☐	☐	6. Is there a clear contrast between the lettering and background on my charts, graphs, and drawings?
☐	☐	7. Do I use line graphs, pie graphs, and bar graphs correctly to show statistical trends and patterns?
☐	☐	8. Do I limit charts to no more than eight items?
☐	☐	9. Do I use fonts that are easy to read?
☐	☐	10. Do I use a limited number of fonts?

If you have not used PowerPoint in a speech before, you may be surprised at how much preparation time it takes. In addition to all the other activities involved in speechmaking, you face the additional tasks of deciding where to use PowerPoint, of gathering images and/or sounds, of designing first-rate slides, and of mastering the equipment and PowerPoint commands needed to deliver the speech smoothly and expertly. Be sure to give yourself plenty of time to master all these tasks.

Tips for Preparing Visual Aids

Whether you are creating visual aids by hand or with PowerPoint, the following tips will help you design aids that are clear and visually appealing.

KEEP VISUAL AIDS SIMPLE

Visual aids should be simple, clear, and to the point. If you look back at the aids presented earlier in this chapter, you will see that all of them are clear and uncluttered. They contain enough information to communicate the speaker's point, but not so much as to confuse or distract the audience.

When using PowerPoint, limit your slides to no more than a half-dozen lines of type. If you are combining text with images, you may need to limit yourself to fewer lines to keep the text from getting too small. If you have a number of important points to cover, spread them out over multiple slides.[5]

MAKE SURE VISUAL AIDS ARE LARGE ENOUGH

A visual aid is useless if no one can see it. Keep in mind the size of the room in which you will be speaking and make sure your aid is big enough to be seen by everyone. Check its visibility by moving to a point as far away from it as your most distant listener will be sitting. If you are using PowerPoint, experts recommend using at least 44-point type for titles, 36-point type for subtitles, and 28-point type for other text.

What about using all capital letters? That might seem a great way to ensure that your print is large enough to be read easily. But research has shown that a long string of words in ALL CAPS is harder to read than is normal text. Reserve ALL CAPS for titles or for words that require special emphasis.

USE FONTS THAT ARE EASY TO READ

Not all fonts are suitable for visual aids. For the most part, you should avoid decorative fonts such as those on the left in Figure 12.5 (below). They are hard to read and can easily distract the attention of listeners. In contrast, the fonts on the right in Figure 12.5 are less exciting, but they are clear and easy to read.

font
A complete set of type of the same design.

Ineffective	More Effective
Airfoil Script	AHD Symbol
Bauble	Arial
Black Tie Engraved	Antique Olive
Corruga	Courier
Marker Board	Times New Roman
Twinkie	Univers
TWOSIE	Verdana

• **FIGURE 12.5**

USE COLOR EFFECTIVELY

As with other aspects of visual aids, colors need to be used thoughtfully. Some colors do not work well together. Red and green are a tough combination for anyone to read, and they look the same to people who are color-blind. Many shades of blue and green are too close to each other to be easily differentiated, as are orange and red, blue and purple.

It is also possible to have too many colors on a visual aid. In most cases, charts and graphs should be limited to a few colors that are used for strategic reasons—as in the chart used by one speaker to summarize the sound levels of everyday noises and to indicate their potential for causing hearing loss (Figure 12.6, below). Notice that he put sounds that are definitely harmful to hearing in red, sounds that may cause hearing loss in blue, and sounds that are safe in green.

IMPACT ON HEARING	DECIBEL LEVEL	TYPE OF NOISE
Harmful	140	Firecracker
to	130	Jackhammer
hearing	120	Jet engine
Risk	110	Rock concert
hearing	100	Chain saw
loss	90	Motorcycle
Loud	80	Alarm clock
but	70	Busy traffic
safe	60	Air conditioner

• **FIGURE 12.6**

Tips for Presenting Visual Aids

DISPLAY VISUAL AIDS WHERE LISTENERS CAN SEE THEM

Check the speech room ahead of time to decide exactly where you will display your visual aids. If you are showing an object or a model, be sure to place it where it can be seen easily by everyone in the room.

Once you have set the aid in the best location, don't undo all your preparation by standing where you block your audience's view of the aid. Stand to one side of the aid, and point with the arm nearest to it. If possible, use a pencil or some other pointer. This will allow you to stand farther away from the visual aid, thereby reducing the likelihood that you will obstruct the audience's view of it.

If you are using a projection screen, check ahead of time to make sure it is not located where you will cast a shadow on it while you are speaking. If necessary, move the lectern to the side of the screen.

EXPLAIN VISUAL AIDS

A visual aid is only as useful as the explanation that goes with it. The viewer needs to know what to look for and why. For example, Figure 12.7 (below) is an excellent visual aid, but do you know what it represents? You may if you suffer from migraine headaches, since it shows the different areas of pain experienced during a cluster migraine attack. But even then, the full meaning of the drawing may not be clear until it is explained to you.

FIGURE 12.7

View the presentation of this visual aid in "The Agony of Migraines."

Unfortunately, speakers often rush over visual aids without explaining them. Don't just say, "As you can see . . ." and then pass quickly over the aid. Tell listeners what the aid means. Describe its major features. Spell out the meaning of graphs and charts. Interpret statistics and percentages.

As you can see from Video 12.6, the speaker who used the diagram of the migraine headache discussed above did an excellent job explaining it. You should strive to do the same when presenting visual aids in your speeches.

AVOID PASSING VISUAL AIDS AMONG THE AUDIENCE

Once visual aids get in the hands of listeners, you are in trouble. At least three people will be paying more attention to the aid than to you—the person who has just had it, the person who has it now, and the person waiting to get it next. By the time the aid moves on, all three may have lost track of what you are saying.

Nor do you solve this problem by preparing a handout for every member of the audience. They are likely to spend a good part of the speech looking over the handout at their own pace, rather than listening to you. Although there are circumstances in which handouts can be valuable, they usually just create competition for the speaker.

Every once in a while, you will want listeners to have copies of some material to take home. When this occurs, keep the copies until you have finished talking, and distribute them at the end. Keeping control of your visual aids is essential to keeping control of your speech.

DISPLAY VISUAL AIDS ONLY WHILE DISCUSSING THEM

Just as circulating visual aids distracts attention, so does displaying them throughout a speech. If you are using an object or a model, keep it out of sight until you are ready to discuss it. When you finish your discussion, place the object or model back out of sight.

The same principle applies to PowerPoint slides. They should be visible only while you are discussing them. You can accomplish this by adding blank slides as needed, so the audience's attention will not be diverted by the previous slide. It is also a good idea to add a blank slide at the end of your presentation, so your last content slide will not continue to be exposed after you have finished discussing it.

TALK TO THE AUDIENCE, NOT TO YOUR VISUAL AIDS

When explaining a visual aid, it is easy to break eye contact with your audience. Of course, your listeners are looking primarily at the aid, and you may need to glance at it periodically as you talk. But if you keep your eyes fixed on the visual aid, you may lose your audience. By keeping eye contact with your listeners, you will also pick up feedback about how the visual aid and your explanation of it are coming across.

PRACTICE WITH YOUR VISUAL AIDS

No matter what kind of visual aid you choose, be sure to employ it when you practice your speech. Go through the speech multiple times, rehearsing how you will show your aids, the gestures you will make, and the timing of each move.

If you are using PowerPoint, don't just click the mouse casually or rush quickly over your words when you practice. Go through every part of the speech and make sure you know exactly when you want each slide to appear and disappear, and what you will say while each is on screen. Mark your speaking notes with cues that will remind you when to display each slide and when to remove it.

Video 12.7

View Stephen E. Lucas for more guidance on preparing and presenting visual aids.

Rehearse with the mouse and keyboard until you can use both without looking down for more than an instant when advancing your slides. Also concentrate on presenting the speech without looking back at the screen to see what is being projected on it. You can check what is on screen by glancing at the computer each time you advance a slide.

Given all the things you have to work on when practicing a speech with PowerPoint, you need to allow extra time for rehearsal. So get an early start and give yourself plenty of time to ensure that your delivery is as impressive as your slides.

CHECK THE ROOM AND EQUIPMENT

In ideal circumstances, you will be able to stop by the room a day or two beforehand to check the physical setting and to run through your visual aids with the same computer and projector you will use during your speech. If you can't get to the room

Presenting Visual Aids — Checklist

	YES	NO
1. Can I present my visual aids without writing or drawing on the chalkboard?	☐	☐
2. Have I checked the speech room to decide where I can display my visual aids most effectively?	☐	☐
3. Have I practiced presenting my visual aids so they will be clearly visible to everyone in the audience?	☐	☐
4. Have I practiced displaying my visual aids only while I am discussing them?	☐	☐
5. Have I practiced keeping eye contact with my audience while presenting my visual aids?	☐	☐
6. Have I practiced explaining my visual aids clearly and concisely in terms my audience will understand?	☐	☐
7. If I am using handouts, have I planned to distribute them after the speech rather than during it?	☐	☐
8. Have I double-checked all equipment to make sure it works properly?	☐	☐
9. Have I rehearsed my speech with the equipment I will use during the final presentation?	☐	☐
10. Do I have a backup plan in case there are problems with my visual aids on the day of my speech?	☐	☐

before the day of your speech, arrive an hour or so early to familiarize yourself with the equipment and to make sure it's working properly. Most experienced speakers arrange ahead of time to have a technician present when they arrive, so the technician can take care of any problems.

DEVELOP A BACKUP PLAN

Despite all your preparation and practice, it's possible that technology will fail you on the day of the speech. More than one speaker has arrived with PowerPoint in tow, only to discover that the computer is acting up, the projector will not work, or, especially in the case of international speakers, the room's power connections are not compatible with the speaker's computer.

What do you do if this happens? You can't just cancel the speech. This is why you always need a backup plan. At the very least, you should copy your slides to a USB flash drive so you can project them on another computer if something happens to yours. Another option is to print a hard copy of your slides to carry with you. The most important thing is to think through potential complications in advance and to have a backup plan ready just in case you need it.[6]

Sample Speech with Commentary

Video 12.8

View "The Great Wall of China."

The following informative speech was presented at the University of Wisconsin and illustrates the principles presented in this chapter for effective use of visual aids. As you can see from Video 12.8, the speaker employs PowerPoint creatively and professionally. Pay special attention to the quality of his slides, to how he integrates them with his words, and to the way he maintains eye contact with listeners while discussing his slides.

The Great Wall of China

COMMENTARY	SPEECH
The speaker begins by gaining attention and establishing his credibility.	In China there's a saying, "You won't be considered a great person until you've been to the Great Wall." I visited the wall last year while I was in China. I don't know if it made me a great person, but I do know that the wall is indeed great.
The speaker uses two slides in this paragraph. The first is a photograph of the Great Wall. The second shows how the wall extends across all of China.	As you can see from this photograph, the wall is great in beauty, with its long arms resting on rolling hills and its towers peering across the valleys. The wall stretches across more than half of China, from the sea in the east, past Beijing, to Gansu province in the west. At a total length of 4,000 miles, it is the longest human-made construction in the world. If the Great Wall were transported to the United States and stretched out in a straight line, it would run from New York City completely across the Atlantic Ocean—past Spain, England, and France, all the way to Berlin, Germany.
Here the speaker displays a blank slide so as not to distract his audience during the preview statement.	Today I would like to share with you some of the wonders of the Great Wall. I will focus on the three major stages of its construction, moving from the first phase during the Qin Dynasty, to the second phase during the Han Dynasty, and concluding with the third phase during the Ming Dynasty. Let's start more than 2,000 years ago, when the first parts of the wall were built.
As the speaker moves into his first main point, he shows a slide of Emperor Qin Shi Huang and the dates of the Qin Dynasty.	The beginning of the Great Wall as we know it dates back to 221 B.C., when Emperor Qin Shi Huang ordered his top general to lead 300,000 soldiers in rebuilding and connecting separate old walls that had been built by princes of warring states. In just 12 years, Qin had a 3,000-mile wall using primarily wood frames filled with stones and compacted earth.

Throughout the speech, visual aids are used only when needed to communicate the speaker's ideas. They are clear, simple, and highly effective.

While the wall proved effective in keeping out the tribes who threatened to invade China from the north, it created dissent within China. According to Arthur Waldron's *The Great Wall of China: From History to Myth,* "ditches on the roadside were filled with corpses of men who had been forced into construction of the Great Wall." Compelled into hard labor and burdened by heavy taxes to finance the project, the people grew unhappy, and a year after Qin's death, the peasants revolted. While the wall stood, the empire collapsed.

As in other parts of the speech, the slides in this paragraph are woven seamlessly with the speaker's words.

The second major period of construction for the Great Wall occurred during the Han Dynasty, which lasted from 206 B.C. to 220 A.D. Emperor Wu Di ordered expansion of the existing wall to protect land won when his armies defeated the northern tribes. Workers added 300 miles to the existing wall. They built wooden frames, which they filled with willow reeds and a mixture of fine gravel and water. As you can see from this picture of ruins of the Han wall, it was very different in construction and appearance from the Great Wall as it exists today.

The speaker starts his third main point with a slide that parallels the slides used in main points one and two. This reinforces the artistic unity of his speech.

The third major building period of the Great Wall occurred 1,100 years later during the Ming Dynasty. In 1368, during the first year of the Ming Dynasty, Emperor Zhu Yuanzhang ordered more expansion of the wall. Subsequent Ming emperors strengthened and extended the wall further until it reached its current length. Builders of the Ming wall made three important architectural advancements which resulted in the distinctive features of the wall as it exists today.

The speaker uses animation to make the appropriate text appear on his slide as he discusses each architectural feature of the Great Wall. This is an excellent example of how to use PowerPoint to maximum advantage.

You can see those features especially well in this photograph. First, rather than using earth and stone, they used kiln-fired bricks to create a stronger wall. Second, they erected more than 3,000 beacon towers to watch the mountain passes for potential invaders. These towers rise from the wall like mighty outposts and are one of the most striking aspects of the wall when you see them in person. Third, the Ming builders made the wall so large that it would be almost impossible to break through. In fact, the wall is so wide that soldiers could ride several horses abreast along the top of the wall.

To make sure the audience does not continue to focus on the architectural features of the wall, the speaker displays a blank slide that shifts attention back to him during the conclusion.

In conclusion, the Great Wall of China enjoys a rich history. Built over the course of more than 2,500 years during the Qin, Han, and Ming Dynasties, it is a magnificent feat of human engineering. While the wall no longer continues to defend China from invaders, it does continue to play a central role in Chinese culture and international identity. Now that you know a little more about the wall, I hope you have a fuller appreciation of why it's regarded as great, not just in China, but throughout the world.

SUMMARY

There are many kinds of visual aids. In some cases, you may be able to use the object about which you are speaking, or a model of it. You can also use photographs or drawings. Graphs are an excellent way to illustrate statistical trends, while charts are invaluable for summarizing large blocks of information.

Video can work well if it is limited in length, carefully edited, and skillfully worked into the speech. In some cases, you can act as your own visual aid by performing actions that demonstrate processes or ideas. PowerPoint allows you to integrate several kinds of visual aids into a speech. Rather than putting everything you say on screen for the audience to read, however, you need to plan carefully why, when, and how you are going to use PowerPoint.

No matter what kind of visual aid you employ, be sure to keep it simple, to use fonts that are easy to read, to utilize color strategically, and to avoid passing items among the audience. In addition, visual aids should be displayed only while you are discussing them and should be displayed where everyone can see them without straining. When presenting a visual aid, maintain eye contact with your listeners and explain the aid clearly and concisely.

You should always include visual aids when rehearsing your speech so you can present them smoothly and expertly. Check the speaking room ahead of time to make sure the equipment is working properly, and have a backup plan available in case you run into problems on the day of the speech.

KEY TERMS

Key-Term Exercise
Check your knowledge with the Key-Term Exercise for this chapter.

model *(161)*
graph *(162)*
line graph *(162)*
pie graph *(163)*
bar graph *(163)*
chart *(164)*
font *(167)*

EXERCISES FOR THINKING AND SPEAKING

1. Watch a how-to television program (a cooking show, for example) or the weather portion of a newscast. Notice how the speaker uses visual aids to help communicate the message. What kinds of visual aids are used? How do they enhance the clarity, interest, and retainability of the speaker's message? What would the speaker have to do to communicate the message effectively without visual aids?

2. Consider how you might use visual aids to explain each of the following. Be specific, and be prepared to discuss your ideas in class.

   a. Where to obtain information about study abroad.

   b. The amount of money spent each year on public education by China, Japan, Germany, Great Britain, and the United States.

   c. The wing patterns of various species of butterflies.

   d. How to change a car tire.

   e. The changes in global atmospheric temperature from 1980 to the present.

3. Plan to use visual aids in at least one of your classroom speeches. Be creative in devising your aids, and be sure to follow the guidelines discussed in the chapter for using them. After the speech, analyze how effectively you employed your visual aids, what you learned about the use of visual aids from your experience, and what changes you would make in using visual aids if you were to deliver the speech again.

Public Speaking in Your Career

As a spokesperson for the China National Tourism Association, you have been asked to deliver an oral briefing to the press. In the briefing, you plan to include statistics that (1) show the growth in the number of Chinese tourists traveling abroad during the past five years, and (2) compare the number of tourist arrivals each year in China, the United States, Spain, and France.

You decide to illustrate one set of statistics with a graph and one with a chart. For which set of statistics will a graph be more appropriate? For which will a chart be more appropriate? Of the three kinds of graphs discussed in this chapter (line, pie, bar), which will work best for your statistics, and why?

13 Speaking to Inform

Public speaking to inform occurs in a wide range of everyday situations: the business manager explaining next year's budget; the architect reviewing plans for a new building; the tour guide showing historical sites; the scientist presenting a paper at a conference; the teacher in a classroom. There are endless situations in which people need to inform others.

informative speech A speech designed to convey knowledge and understanding.

In one survey, college graduates were asked to rank the speech skills most important to their jobs. They rated informative speaking number one.[1] In another survey, 62 percent of respondents said they used informative speaking "almost constantly."[2] Competence in this form of communication will be valuable throughout your life.

When you speak to inform, your aim is to convey knowledge and understanding—not to advocate a cause. Your speech will be judged in light of three general criteria:

Is the information communicated accurately?

Is the information communicated clearly?

Is the information made meaningful and interesting to the audience?

In this chapter, we will look at four types of informative speeches and the basic principles of informative speaking. Along the way, we will apply various general principles discussed in previous chapters.

Types of Informative Speeches: Analysis and Organization

There are many ways to classify informative speeches. Here we focus on speeches about objects, speeches about processes, speeches about events, and speeches about concepts.

SPEECHES ABOUT OBJECTS

object Anything that is visible, tangible, and stable in form.

As the word is used here, "objects" include anything that is visible, tangible, and stable in form. Objects may have moving parts or be alive; they may include places, structures, animals, even people. Here are examples of subjects for speeches about objects:

Gobi Desert	computers
stock market	Sichuan masks
Xiang embroidery	panda

You will not have time to tell your classmates everything about any of these subjects. Instead, you will choose a specific purpose that focuses on one aspect of your subject. Working from the topics presented above, the following are examples of specific purpose statements for informative speeches about objects:

To inform my audience about geological features of the Gobi Desert.

To inform my audience about the latest developments in computer technology.

To inform my audience about the craftsmanship of Xiang embroidery.

Notice how precise these statements are. As we saw in Chapter 4, you should select a specific purpose that is not too broad to achieve in the allotted time. "To inform my audience about Zhao Mengfu" is far too general for a classroom speech. "To inform my audience about Zhao Mengfu's contributions to landscape painting" is more precise and is a purpose you could reasonably hope to achieve in a brief talk.

If your specific purpose is to explain the history or evolution of your subject, you will put your speech in *chronological* order. For example:

Specific Purpose: To inform my audience about the poetic career of Du Fu.

Central Idea: Judged by some experts to be the world's greatest poet, Du Fu expressed the people's spirit during a tumultuous period in Chinese history.

Main Points:
I. Du Fu was greatly influenced by his friendship with Li Bai during the 740s.
II. Du Fu blossomed as a poet during the 750s despite great turmoil in his personal life.
III. Du Fu reached a peak of creativity during his years in Chengdu from 759 to 765.
IV. Du Fu continued to write works of lasting importance until his death in 770.

If your specific purpose is to describe the main features of your subject, you may organize your speech in *spatial* order:

Specific Purpose: To inform my audience about the design of the Eiffel Tower.

Central Idea: The Eiffel Tower is divided into three sections, each with its own functions.

Main Points:
I. The lowest section of the tower contains the entrance, a gift shop, and a restaurant.
II. The middle section of the tower consists of stairs and elevators that lead to the top.
III. The top section of the tower includes an observation deck with a spectacular view of Paris.

As often as not, you will find that speeches about objects fall into *topical* order. For example:

Specific Purpose: To inform my audience about the four major elements of a Japanese garden.

Informative speeches about objects often call for visual aids. The speaker here is explaining a model car that runs on baking soda and vinegar. The car was entered in a contest sponsored by the American Institute of Chemical Engineers.

Central Idea: The four major elements of a Japanese garden are stones, sand, water, and plants.

Main Points:

I. The first element of a Japanese garden is stones, which symbolize mountains and islands.

II. The second element of a Japanese garden is sand, which symbolizes the sea or other vast areas.

III. The third element of a Japanese garden is water, which symbolizes cleansing and purity.

IV. The fourth element of a Japanese garden is plants, which symbolize life and the changing seasons.

No matter which organizational method you use—chronological, spatial, or topical—be sure to follow the guidelines discussed in Chapter 7: (1) limit the number of main points; (2) keep main points separate; (3) try to use the same pattern of wording for all main points; (4) balance the amount of time devoted to each main point.

SPEECHES ABOUT PROCESSES

A process is a systematic series of actions that leads to a specific result or product. Speeches about processes explain how something is made, how something is done, or how something works. Here are examples of specific purpose statements for speeches about processes:

To inform my audience how typhoons develop.

To inform my audience how to write an effective job resumé.

To inform my audience how to perform Tai Chi.

process
A systematic series of actions that leads to a specific result or product.

As these examples suggest, there are two kinds of informative speeches about processes. One kind explains a process so that listeners will *understand* it better. Your goal is to have your audience know the steps of the process and how they relate to one another. If your specific purpose is "To inform my audience how nuclear power plants work," you will explain the basic structure and mechanisms of a nuclear power plant. You will not instruct your listeners on how they can operate a nuclear power plant.

A second kind of speech explains a process so listeners will be better able to *perform* the process themselves. Your goal in this kind of speech is to have the audience learn a skill. Suppose your specific purpose is "To inform my audience how to take pictures like a professional photographer." You will present photographic techniques and show your listeners how they can use them.

Both kinds of speeches about processes may require visual aids. At the very least, you should prepare a chart outlining the steps or techniques of your process. In some cases you will need to demonstrate the steps or techniques by performing them in front of your audience. (If you are using visual aids of any kind, be sure to review Chapter 12.)

When informing about a process, you will usually arrange your speech in *chronological* order, explaining the process step by step from beginning to end. For example:

Specific Purpose: To inform my audience about the major rituals of a traditional Bengali wedding in India.

Central Idea: A traditional Bengali wedding consists of a series of rituals that take place before, during, and after the wedding ceremony.

Main Points:

I. Pre-wedding rituals include giving gifts to the bride and groom and dressing the bride in traditional fashion.

II. Rituals during the ceremony include an exchange of garlands between the bride and groom, the chanting of mantras, and the giving away of the bride by her uncle.

III. Post-wedding rituals include a celebration at the home of the bride's family, a reception at the home of the groom's family, and the formal exit of the bride and groom.

Sometimes, rather than moving through a process step by step, you will focus on the major principles or techniques involved in performing the process. Then you will organize your speech in *topical* order. Each main point will deal with a separate principle or technique. For example:

Specific Purpose: To inform my audience of the common methods used by stage magicians to perform their tricks.

Central Idea: Stage magicians use two common methods to perform their tricks—mechanical devices and sleight of hand.

Main Points: I. Many magic tricks rely on mechanical devices that may require little skill by the magician.

II. Other magic tricks depend on the magician's skill in fooling people by sleight-of-hand manipulation.

Concise organization is especially important in speeches about processes. You must make sure each step is clear and easy to follow. If your process has more than four or five steps, group the steps into units to limit the number of main points.

SPEECHES ABOUT EVENTS

The *Random House Dictionary* defines an event as "anything that happens or is regarded as happening." By this definition, the following are examples of suitable subjects for informative speeches about events:

event
Anything that happens or is regarded as happening.

insomnia	marriage
World Cup	Battle of Red Cliffs
tsunami	cyber crime

As usual, you will need to narrow your focus and pick a specific purpose you can accomplish in the allotted time. Here are examples of specific purpose statements for informative speeches about events:

To inform my audience about healthy cures for insomnia.

To inform my audience about events at the Battle of Red Cliffs.

To inform my audience about the major types of cyber crime.

There are many ways to discuss events. If your specific purpose is to recount the history of an event, you will organize your speech in *chronological* order, relating the incidents one after another in the order they occurred. For example:

Specific Purpose: To inform my audience about the history of the Paralympics.

Central Idea: Olympic-style games for athletes with physical disabilities have made great strides since the first competition more than 60 years ago.

Main Points: I. What would eventually become the Paralympics began in 1948 with a sports competition in Great Britain involving World War II veterans with spinal cord injuries.

II. In 1952, the event expanded when athletes from the Netherlands took part.

III. The first official Paralympic Games for international athletes took place in Rome in 1960.

IV. In 2001, an agreement was signed officially holding the Paralympic Games alongside the summer and winter Olympic Games.

Internet Connection

Visit TED: ideas Worth Spreading (www.ted.com/) to view informative talks by dozens of internationally acclaimed thinkers, writers, and artists. The talks cover a wide range of economic, philosophical, scientific, social, and cultural topics. Speakers include Microsoft founder Bill Gates, anthropologist Louise Leakey, novelist Amy Tan, biologist Robert Full, toy designer Caleb Chung, author Jennifer Lee, entrepreneur Shai Agassi, and former U.S. President Bill Clinton.

In an age of globalization, much informative speaking takes place in intercultural contexts. To learn about research on this topic, log on to www.immi.se/intercultural/, where you can read issues of the *Journal of Intercultural Communication* from its founding in 1999 to the present. Another useful source is the *International Journal of Communication*, an online publication that you can access at http://ijoc.org/ojs/index.php/ijoc.

You can approach an event from almost any angle or combination of angles—features, origins, implications, benefits, future developments, and so forth. In such cases, you will put your speech together in *topical* order, making sure that your main points subdivide the subject logically and consistently. For instance:

Specific Purpose: To inform my audience about the four major roles in Peking Opera.

Central Idea: The four major roles in Peking Opera are Sheng, Dan, Jing, and Chou.

Main Points:

I. Sheng is the primary male role.
II. Dan refers to any female role.
III. Jing is a painted-face male role.
IV. Chou is a male clown role.

SPEECHES ABOUT CONCEPTS

concept
A belief, theory, idea, notion, principle, or the like.

Concepts include beliefs, theories, ideas, principles, and the like. They are more abstract than objects, processes, or events. The following are examples of subjects for speeches about concepts:

Neo-Confucianism	theories of evolution
philosophies of education	motivational principles
military theory	constitutionalism

Taking a few of these general subjects, here are some specific purpose statements for speeches about concepts:

To inform my audience about basic points of the SMART principle.

To inform my audience about different philosophies of education in China and the United States.

To inform my audience about major theories explaining the extinction of dinosaurs.

Informative speeches take place in a wide range of situations. Here paleontologist Xu Xing speaks to an international audience in Beijing about the discovery of the world's largest birdlike dinosaur.

Speeches about concepts are usually organized in *topical* order and focus on the main features or aspects of your concept. For example:

Specific Purpose: To inform my audience about the Five Principles of Peaceful Coexistence.

Central Idea: The Five Principles of Peaceful Coexistence set forth norms for relations among nations.

Main Points:

I. The first principle is mutual respect for sovereignty and territorial integrity.
II. The second principle is mutual non-aggression.
III. The third principle is non-interference in each other's internal affairs.
IV. The fourth principle is equality and mutual benefit.
V. The fifth principle is peaceful coexistence.

Another approach is to explain competing schools of thought about the same subject. For example:

Specific Purpose: To inform my audience of arguments for and against Olympic Math.

Central Idea: Supporters and opponents of Olympic Math both have legitimate arguments.

Main Points:

I. Supporters of Olympic Math argue that it develops discipline, promotes math skills, and is necessary for admission to top middle schools.

II. Opponents of Olympic Math argue that it is suitable for only a few students, damages self-confidence in most, and destroys future interest in math for many.

Speeches about concepts are often more complex than other kinds of informative speeches. When dealing with concepts, pay special attention to avoiding technical language, to defining terms clearly, and to using examples and comparisons to illustrate the concepts.

The lines dividing speeches about objects, processes, events, and concepts are not absolute. Some subjects could fit into more than one category, depending on how you develop the speech. For example, a speech about the life of Yan Fu would treat its subject as an object, while a speech about Yan Fu's theory of translation would most likely treat its subject as a concept. The important step is to decide whether you will handle your subject as an object, a process, an event, or a concept. Once you do that, you can develop the speech accordingly.

Tips for Informative Speaking

All the previous chapters of this book relate to the principles of informative speaking. Selecting a topic and specific purpose, analyzing the audience, choosing supporting materials, organizing the speech, using language, delivering the speech—all must be done effectively if an informative speech is to be a success. Here we emphasize five additional points that will help make yours a success.

DON'T OVERESTIMATE WHAT THE AUDIENCE KNOWS

In a talk about meteorology, a speaker said, "The effects of the Bhola cyclone would have been reduced if better warning and response systems had been in place at the time." Then he was off to other matters, leaving his listeners to puzzle over what the Bhola cyclone was, when it happened, and what kind of destruction it wreaked.

The speaker assumed that the audience already knew these things. But his listeners were not experts on meteorology. Even those who had heard of the Bhola cyclone had only a fuzzy notion of it. Only the speaker knew that the cyclone, which killed 500,000 people when it struck East Pakistan (now Bangladesh) on November 12, 1970, is among the deadliest natural disasters in modern history.

As many speakers have discovered, it is easy to overestimate the audience's stock of information. In most informative speeches, your listeners will be only vaguely knowledgeable (at best) about the details of your topic. You cannot assume that they will know what you mean. Rather, you must lead them step by step, without any shortcuts. Be sure to define every special term, clarify every idea, illustrate every concept.

Informative speakers work on communicating their ideas in clear, nontechnical language, as illustrated here by paramedic Cheryl Bishop explaining the Heimlich maneuver to a group of middle-school students.

DON'T BE TOO TECHNICAL

What does it mean to say an informative speech is too technical? It may mean the subject matter is too specialized for the audience. Any subject can be popularized—but only up to a point. The important thing for a speaker to know is what can be explained to an audience of nonspecialists and what cannot.

Suppose your subject is electronic amplifiers. It's no trick to demonstrate how to operate an amplifier (how to turn it on and off, adjust the volume, set the tone and balance controls). It's also relatively easy to explain what an amplifier does (it boosts the sound received from a radio, MP3 player, or live performance). But to give a full scientific account of how an amplifier works—that is another matter. It cannot be done in any reasonable time unless the audience knows the principles of audio technology. The material is too technical to be understood by a general audience.

Even when the subject matter is not technical, the language used to explain it may be. Every activity has its jargon, whether it be ballet (arabesque, jeté, pas de deux), chemistry (colloid, glycogen, heavy water), or financial analysis (covered call, reverse bid, toehold acquisition). If you are talking to a group of specialists, you can use technical words and be understood. But you must do all you can to avoid technical words when informing an audience of nonspecialists.

personalize
To present one's ideas in human terms that relate in some fashion to the experience of the audience.

PERSONALIZE YOUR IDEAS

Listeners want to be entertained as they are being enlightened. Nothing takes the edge off an informative speech more than an unbroken string of facts and figures. And nothing enlivens an informative speech more than personal illustrations. Whenever possible, you should try to personalize your ideas and dramatize them in human terms.

Start right at the beginning. Instead of saying,

> I want to talk with you about chili peppers.

you could say:

> Imagine your mouth burning like wildfire, your eyes squirting out uncontrollable tears, and your face red and sweating profusely. Are you sick? No. You just took a bite of a screaming hot chili pepper. You're partaking in a worldwide tradition that has been spicing up lives and diets for thousands of years.

Video 13.1
View this excerpt from "The Hidden World of Chili Peppers."

But don't stop with the introduction. Whenever you can, work in examples that will put a human face on your topic while at the same time illustrating your ideas. Find ways to connect the speech with your listeners' interests and concerns.

Even words such as "you" and "your," "we" and "our," can make a big difference. Research shows that using these kinds of personal terms in an informative speech significantly increases the audience's understanding of a speaker's ideas.[3]

AVOID ABSTRACTIONS

description
A statement that depicts a person, event, idea, or the like with clarity and vividness.

Abstract ideas are less compelling to listeners than are concrete ideas. One way to avoid abstractions is through description. Here is how one speaker described his feelings the first time he went sky diving:

> As I jump out of the plane, I wonder, "What am I doing here?" The blast of air blows me backward like a leaf in the autumn wind. In 10 seconds, my body levels out and accelerates to a speed of 190 kilometers an hour. The air supports my body like an invisible flying carpet. Every nerve in my body is alive with sensation; yet I am overcome by a peaceful feeling that I am at one with the sky.

comparison
A statement of the similarities among two or more people, events, ideas, etc.

As we listen to the speaker, we feel his exhilaration as he floats effortlessly through the sky. The vivid description draws us in.

Another way to escape abstractions is with comparison and/or contrast. Both provide a way to put your subject in concrete, familiar terms. For example, suppose you want to convey what would happen if a comet or large asteroid struck the earth. You could say this:

contrast
A statement of the differences among two or more people, events, ideas, etc.

> If a comet or large asteroid struck the earth, the impact would be devastating.

True, but the statement is vague and abstract. Now suppose you add this:

> To give you an idea how devastating the impact would be, it would be like all the nuclear bombs in the world going off at one spot.

The comparison makes the abstract specific by relating it to something we know.

Regardless of the situation, informative speakers work to organize their ideas effectively and to explain them in clear, nontechnical language that is appropriate for their listeners' knowledge and interests.

BE CREATIVE

Whether you are seeking alternatives to technical language, avoiding abstractions, personalizing your ideas, or adapting to the audience's knowledge about the topic, you need to be creative in thinking about ways to achieve your objectives. A good informative speech is not an oral encyclopedia article. Like any other kind of speech, it requires a healthy dose of creativity.

If you look back at the examples discussed on the previous few pages, you will see that all of them involve creative thinking by the speaker. For one last example, we can turn to a speech about extended-wear contact lenses. The speech was given when such lenses first came on the market. Because the lenses were too small for his audience to see, the speaker used a glass plate, a paper plate, and a sheet of clear plastic wrap to illustrate how extended-wear lenses differ in flexibility from other kinds of contact lenses. As you can see from Video 13.2, it was a highly effective—and creative—solution.

Video 13.2

View an excerpt from "Extended-Wear Contact Lenses."

If, like this speaker, you think creatively when constructing your informative speeches, you are much more likely to be successful.

Sample Speech with Commentary

The following speech provides an excellent example of how to apply the tips for informative speaking discussed in this chapter. Pay attention to how crisply the speech is organized; to how the speaker uses clear, nontechnical language; and to how skillfully she demonstrates yoga postures as she explains them.

Video 13.3

View "Yoga: Uniting Mind, Body, and Spirit."

Yoga: Uniting Mind, Body, and Spirit

COMMENTARY	SPEECH
The speaker captures attention by adopting a yoga pose and asking a question about it.	What do you think of when I do this? If you said "Yoga," you are absolutely correct.
The speaker explains the origins of the word "yoga." Stella Weller's book is the first of several sources she will cite as the speech proceeds.	For 5,000 years, people have been practicing yoga to enhance their mental, physical, and emotional health. "Yoga" comes from the Sanskrit word meaning to "unite" or to "join." As Stella Weller says in her book *Yoga: Finding Balance and Serenity in Everyday Life*, yoga is the practice of uniting one's mind, body, and spirit.
This paragraph establishes the speaker's credibility and provides a clear preview of the main points to be discussed in the body.	I've been practicing yoga for over eight years, and I'm in the process of getting my certification to become a yoga instructor. Although there are many dimensions to yoga, today I'm going to focus on two—yoga breathing and yoga postures. Along the way, I'm going to share with you some of the health benefits that come along with these simple yoga practices. First, I'm going to go over yoga breathing.
Now the speaker moves into her first main point.	Breathing has been an essential part of yoga for centuries. There are four major stages in the breathing process. The first is inhalation; the second, pause; the third, exhalation; and the fourth, a pause.
The speaker demonstrates the yoga breathing process step by step. Notice how she uses "you" here and throughout the speech to personalize her ideas.	It goes something like this: When you inhale, you feel the breath coming from deep within your belly. And as you pause, you will feel the breath rising up. You focus to feel the breath around your heart. As you exhale, you feel the breath moving smoothly from your throat and out of your mouth. As you pause the final time, it needs to be prolonged and deliberate, because this is what completes the cycle of yoga breathing until the new inhalation begins.
The speaker anticipates what the audience is thinking and answers their question about why yoga concentrates so much on breathing. The quotation from Vimla Lalvani provides expert testimony.	Now you may be asking yourselves: Why does yoga concentrate on something so ordinary as breathing? The reason is this: When you breathe properly, the amount of oxygen that enters your brain and your bloodstream allows your body to relax, and it allows you to concentrate better than you normally would. As Vimla Lalvani, author of *The Power of Yoga*, writes: "Correct breathing rejuvenates the entire system by sending increased oxygen into the bloodstream to nourish and revitalize the internal organs. . . . The deeper you breathe, the calmer the mind becomes."

The speaker combines a transition with an internal preview as she moves to her second main point.

Now that we've learned about yoga breathing, I'm going to move on to yoga postures. I'm going to demonstrate three postures that I find extremely beneficial to me—the tree pose, the triangle bow pose, and the king of the dance pose.

As you can see from the video of this speech, the speaker demonstrates each yoga pose as she discusses it. Her sustained eye contact and extemporaneous delivery create a strong communicative bond with her audience.

First, let's start with the tree pose. I'm going to shift all of my weight onto my left foot. I'm then going to take my right foot and place it on the inside of my left thigh. I'm going to put my hands in front of me and press my palms together. And as I raise my arms over my head, I'm going to stare at a fixed point ahead of me. I usually hold this pose for about 30 seconds to a minute. This pose helps to strengthen your thighs, calves, ankles, and your back. It also helps to improve your balance.

The speaker's demonstration is perfectly timed with her words. This reflects her careful preparation and makes for an entertaining speech.

The second pose that I'm going to demonstrate is the triangle bow pose. You start with your feet a little wider than your shoulders. You then take your arms straight out across your body with your palms facing down. You touch your left hand to the floor while the opposite arm stretches towards the ceiling. You then turn your head and gaze up toward the ceiling. This pose helps with your blood circulation and it stretches your torso and your neck.

The speaker uses parallel structure as she explains each pose. First she shows how to perform the pose; then she notes the health benefits of the pose.

The third and final pose I'm going to do today is the king of the dance pose. You hold your right foot with your right hand and extend your left arm forward. As you raise your left arm, you raise your right leg as high as possible. You hold this pose for 30 seconds to a minute. Not only does this pose help greatly with balance, but it also stretches your hips, legs, and torso.

"So today" signals that the speaker is moving into her conclusion. She then restates her central idea.

So today we've learned about two important dimensions of yoga—yoga breathing and yoga postures. Developed across centuries and now practiced worldwide, yoga is helping millions of people unite their mind, body, and spirit.

The speaker uses a quotation to lead into her closing lines. As in the rest of the speech, her delivery reflects her enthusiasm about the topic and about the opportunity to share it with her audience.

Donna Farhi, author of five books on yoga, emphasizes that yoga affects the whole body and the whole person. "Each movement," she says, "demands that we hone some aspect of our consciousness and use ourselves in a whole new way." As yoga practitioners have known for centuries, a few simple movements can do a whole lot of good.

Thank you.

SUMMARY

Videos 13.4–13.7

View more sample informative speeches.

Informative speeches may be grouped into four categories: speeches about objects, processes, events, and concepts.

Objects include places, structures, animals, even people. Speeches about objects usually are organized in chronological, spatial, or topical order. A process is a series of actions that work together to produce a final result. Speeches about processes explain how something is made, how something is done, or how something works. The most common types of organization for speeches about processes are chronological and topical.

An event is anything that happens or is regarded as happening. Speeches about events are usually arranged in chronological or topical order. Concepts include beliefs, theories, ideas, and principles. Speeches about concepts are often more complex than other kinds of informative speeches, and they typically follow a topical pattern of organization.

No matter what the subject of your informative speech, there are several tips you can follow to make it successful. First, don't overestimate what your audience knows about the topic. Second, avoid being overly technical. Third, personalize your ideas and illustrate them in human terms. Fourth, use description, comparison, and contrast to make your ideas concrete rather than abstract. Fifth, be creative in finding ways to communicate your ideas as engagingly as possible.

KEY TERMS

Key-Term Exercise

Check your knowledge with the Key-Term Exercise for this chapter.

informative speech *(177)*
object *(177)*
process *(180)*
event *(181)*
concept *(182)*
personalize *(185)*
description *(186)*
comparison *(186)*
contrast *(186)*

EXERCISES FOR THINKING AND SPEAKING

1. Prepare a specific purpose statement for an informative speech about two of the topics listed below. Explain what method of organization you would most likely use in structuring a speech about each of your specific purpose statements.

hobbies	sports	technology
science	music	health

2. Popular nonfiction writing often provides helpful models of informative discourse on technical topics. Select an article of interest from the medicine, science, or business section

of an English-language magazine or newspaper. Prepare a brief report on the article answering each of the following questions:

a. How effectively does the author use explanation, description, comparison, contrast, and examples to make the subject clear and interesting to nontechnical readers?

b. Identify two techniques used in the article that you might want to try in your informative speeches.

3. Analyze "Questions of Culture," which is printed in the appendix of speeches for appreciation and analysis at the end of the book. Evaluate its use of the tips for informative speaking discussed in this chapter.

4. Select an informative speech topic that will contribute to your listeners' body of knowledge. Prepare a 4–5 minute informative speech introducing an object, explaining a concept, describing an event, or demonstrating a process. Develop your ideas by writing a preparation outline. Deliver the speech extemporaneously to your class audience using a speaking outline.

Public Speaking in Your Career

As the owner of a tropical fish store, you have been asked to speak to a group of consumers about how to establish a home aquarium. As you write down ideas for your speech, you find that you have the following main points:

I. You must choose the size of your tank.
II. You must determine the shape of your tank.
III. You must also decide how much you can afford to pay for a tank.
IV. Once you have the tank, you need a filter system.
V. You also need a heater.
VI. An air pump is also required.
VII. The tank also needs decorations.
VIII. Now you are ready to add the fish.
IX. Freshwater fish are the most common.
X. Saltwater fish are more expensive and require special care.

Having taken a speech class in college, you know these are too many main points for an audience to keep track of. As you look over your list again, however, you realize that it can easily be reorganized into three main points, each with several subpoints. What are those main points and subpoints?

14 Speaking to Persuade

Every day you are bombarded with persuasive messages: junk e-mails trying to sell a new ringtone, TV commercials promoting clothing and cosmetics, your boyfriend or girlfriend encouraging you to spend more time with them. Similarly, you spend part of your daily life persuading other people to do things for you or for themselves: asking your professor to extend the deadline for a paper, recommending a new movie to your roommate, urging a close friend to quit smoking.

persuasion The process of creating, reinforcing, or changing people's beliefs or actions.

Persuasion is the process of creating, reinforcing, or changing people's beliefs or actions.[1] The ability to speak (and write) persuasively will benefit you in every part of your life, from personal relations to career aspirations. Understanding the principles of persuasion is also vital to being an informed citizen and consumer. The more you know about persuasion, the more effectively you can use your powers of critical thinking to assess the barrage of persuasive messages you are exposed to every day.

When you speak to persuade, you act as an advocate. Your job is to get listeners to agree with you and, perhaps, to act on that belief. Your goal may be to defend an idea, refute an opponent, sell a program, or inspire people to action. Because persuasive speakers must communicate information clearly and concisely, you will need all the skills you used in speaking to inform. But you will also need new skills—skills that take you from giving information to affecting your listeners' attitudes, beliefs, or actions.

As with other kinds of public speaking, you are more likely to be effective at persuasion if you approach it systematically and with a clear understanding of the methods available to you. This chapter begins by looking at the psychology of persuasion and the target audience for persuasive speeches. It then turns to the three major kinds of persuasive speeches. Finally, it explores the methods of persuasion.

The Psychology of Persuasion

We often think of persuasion as something a speaker does to an audience. In fact, as a great deal of research shows, persuasion is something a speaker does *with* an audience. Listeners do not sit passively and soak in everything a speaker has to say. Instead, they engage in a mental give-and-take with the speaker.

While they listen, they assess the speaker's credibility, delivery, supporting materials, language, and reasoning. They may respond positively at one point, negatively at another. At times they may argue, inside their own minds, with the speaker. This mental give-and-take is especially vigorous when listeners are highly involved with the topic of the speech and believe it has a direct bearing on their lives.[2]

In a sense, the psychological interaction between a speaker and audience during a persuasive speech is similar to what happens vocally during a conversation—as in this example:

Xiangdong: China needs to take a more active role in combating global warming. There is only one Earth, and we all have to live on it.

Weihong: I agree that global warming is a serious problem, but China cannot be expected to do more than other countries. We are already leading the world in some areas of green technology. We cannot sacrifice economic progress at the altar of unproven environmental theories.

Xiangdong: Of course we must maintain prosperity, but ignoring the environment now will cost much more in the long run. China is already doing a lot, but we must do more in the future.

Weihong: How much more must we do? And how much are you willing to pay? People in prosperous areas can afford the luxury of strict pollution controls, but the same controls would bankrupt poorer areas.

Xiangdong: Environmental protection is not a luxury. We all breathe the same air. People in poorer areas deserve clean air as much as people in prosperous areas.

Much the same kind of interaction might occur during a persuasive speech, except that the listener would respond internally rather than out loud.

mental dialogue with the audience
The mental give-and-take between speaker and listener during a persuasive speech.

What does this mean to you as a speaker? It means you must think of your persuasive speech as a kind of a *mental dialogue* with your audience. You must anticipate possible objections the audience will raise to your point of view and then answer those objections in your speech. You cannot covert skeptical listeners unless you deal directly with the reasons for their skepticism.

As you prepare your persuasive speech, put yourself in the place of your audience and imagine how they will respond. Be as tough on your speech as your audience will be. Every place they will raise a question, answer it. Every place they will have a criticism, deal with it. Every place they will see a hole in your argument, fill it. Leave nothing to chance.[3]

The Target Audience

target audience
The portion of the whole audience that the speaker most wants to persuade.

Unfortunately, no matter how carefully you plot your speech, you will seldom be able to persuade all your listeners. Most often you will have a particular *part* of the whole audience that you want to reach with your speech. That part is called the target audience.

Concentrating on the target audience does not mean you should ignore or insult the rest of your listeners. You must always keep in mind the ideas and feelings of your entire audience. But no matter how noble your intentions or how hard you try, you can't persuade all the people all the time. It only makes sense to decide which portion of the audience you most want to reach.

When thinking about your target audience, it may be helpful to visualize listeners on a scale such as that shown in Figure 14.1. Listeners can range from strongly opposed to strongly in favor of a speaker's position. In most cases, the target audience will consist of people who are opposed to or neutral toward the speaker's position. The further one moves toward the right of the scale, the less need there is for persuasion.

TARGET AUDIENCE

Strongly Opposed	Moderately Opposed	Slightly Opposed	Neutral	Slightly in Favor	Moderately in Favor	Strongly in Favor

• **FIGURE 14.1**

If your target audience is strongly opposed, you cannot expect to convert them with a single speech. Instead, you can consider your speech a success if it leads even a few listeners to reexamine their views and to reduce the level of their opposition. If, on the other hand, your target audience is neutral or only slightly opposed, you have a realistic chance of moving them closer to your position.

Later in this chapter, we'll examine methods you can use to hit the target in your persuasive speeches. First, however, we need to explore the three major kinds of persuasive speeches and how to organize them most effectively. We'll look first at speeches on questions of fact, then at speeches on questions of value, and finally at speeches on questions of policy.

Persuasive Speeches on Questions of Fact

When was the Temple of Heaven built? What was the first Chinese volleyball team to win a world championship? How far is it from Shanghai to Paris? These questions of fact can be answered absolutely. The answers are either right or wrong.

Many questions of fact, however, cannot be answered absolutely. There is a true answer, but we don't have enough information to know what it is. Will the economy be better or worse in two years? Who will win the next World Cup? Did William Shakespeare really write the plays attributed to him? No one knows the final answers to these questions, but that doesn't stop people from speculating about them or from trying to convince other people that they have the best possible answers.

question of fact
A question about the truth or falsity of an assertion.

ANALYZING QUESTIONS OF FACT

In some ways, a persuasive speech on a question of fact is similar to an informative speech. But the two kinds of speeches take place in different situations and for different purposes.

The situation for an informative speech is *nonpartisan*. The speaker acts as a lecturer or a teacher. The aim is to give information as impartially as possible, not to argue for a particular point of view. On the other hand, the situation for a persuasive speech on a question of fact is *partisan*. The speaker acts as an advocate. His or her aim is not to be impartial but to present one view of the facts as persuasively as possible. The speaker may mention competing views of the facts, but only to refute them.

Consider, for example, the assassination of U.S. President John F. Kennedy. After almost 50 years, there is still much debate about what really happened in Dallas on

November 22, 1963. Did Lee Harvey Oswald act alone, or was he part of a conspiracy? How many shots were fired at President Kennedy and from what locations? If there was a conspiracy, who was involved in it?

The informative speaker would merely recite the known facts on both sides of these questions without drawing a conclusion about which side is correct. The persuasive speaker, however, would draw a conclusion and would try to convert listeners to his or her point of view.

ORGANIZING SPEECHES ON QUESTIONS OF FACT

Persuasive speeches on questions of fact are usually organized *topically.* Suppose, for example, that you want to persuade an audience about the health dangers of cigarette smoking. Each main point in your speech will present a *reason* why someone should agree with you:

Specific Purpose: To persuade my audience that cigarette smoking causes serious health dangers.

Central Idea: There is overwhelming evidence that cigarette smoking causes serious dangers to human health.

Main Points:

I. Studies in China show that cigarette smoking is a major cause of cancer, tuberculosis, and heart disease.

II. Scientists estimate that half of today's smokers in China will eventually be killed by tobacco.

To take another example, suppose you are trying to convince your classmates that William Shakespeare did not write the plays attributed to him. Your specific purpose, central idea, and main points might be:

Specific Purpose: To persuade my audience that William Shakespeare did not write the plays attributed to him.

Central Idea: There is considerable evidence that the plays attributed to William Shakespeare were actually written by someone else.

Main Points:

I. Biographical and textual evidence suggest that Shakespeare did not write the plays attributed to him.

II. Historical evidence indicates that Shakespeare's plays were probably written by either Francis Bacon or Edward de Vere, 17th Earl of Oxford.

Notice in these examples that the speaker's purpose is limited to persuading the audience to accept a particular view of the facts. Sometimes, however, the dispute that gives rise to a persuasive speech will go beyond a question of fact and will turn on a question of value.

Many persuasive speeches revolve around questions of value. Here Irish musician Bob Geldof speaks about the moral commitment of Western nations to help African nations deal with famine and disease.

Persuasive Speeches on Questions of Value

Who is the best Chinese actor? Is cloning morally justifiable? What are the ethical responsibilities of journalists? Such questions not only involve matters of fact, but they also demand *value judgments*—judgments based on a person's beliefs about what is right or wrong, good or bad, moral or immoral, proper or improper, fair or unfair.

Take the issue of cloning. It can be discussed at a purely factual level by asking such questions as "What are the scientific methods of cloning?" Or "What are the laws about cloning in different countries?" These are factual questions. The answers you reach are independent of your belief about the morality of cloning.

question of value
A question about the worth, rightness, morality, and so forth of an idea or action.

But suppose you ask, "Is it morally justifiable to clone human beings?" Or "Is it ethically acceptable to clone human cells in an effort to cure diseases such as diabetes and cancer?" Now you are dealing with questions of value. How you answer will depend not only on your factual knowledge about cloning, but also on your moral values.

ANALYZING QUESTIONS OF VALUE

Contrary to what many people think, questions of value are not simply matters of personal opinion or whim. If you say, "I enjoy bicycle riding," you do not have to give a reason why you enjoy it. You are making a statement about your personal taste. Even if bicycle riding were the most unpleasant activity ever invented, it could still be one of your favorites.

On the other hand, if you say, "Bicycle riding is the ideal form of land transportation," you are making a statement about a question of value. Whether bicycling is the ideal form of land transportation does not depend on your own likes and dislikes. To defend the statement, you cannot say, "Bicycle riding is the ideal form of land transportation because I like it."

Instead you must *justify* your claim. The first step is to define what you mean by an ideal form of land transportation. Do you mean a mode of transportation that gets people where they want to go as fast as possible? That is relatively inexpensive? Nonpolluting? Beneficial for the user? In other words, you must establish your *standards* for an ideal form of land transportation. Then you can show how bicycle riding measures up against those standards.

Whenever you give a speech on a question of value, be sure to give special thought to the standards for your value judgment.

ORGANIZING SPEECHES ON QUESTIONS OF VALUE

Persuasive speeches on questions of value are almost always organized *topically*. The most common approach is to devote your first main point to establishing the standards for your value judgment and your second main point to applying those standards to the subject of your speech.

Think back for a moment to the speech about bicycle riding as the ideal form of land transportation. If you organized this speech in topical order, your first main point would identify the standards for an ideal form of land transportation. Your second main point would show how biking measures up against those standards. Here is how your specific purpose, central idea, and main points might look:

Specific Purpose: To persuade my audience that bicycle riding is the ideal form of land transportation.

Central Idea: Bicycle riding is the ideal form of land transportation because it is faster than walking or running, is nonpolluting, and promotes the health of the rider.

Main Points:

I. An ideal form of land transportation should meet three major standards.
   A. It should be faster than running or walking.
   B. It should be nonpolluting.
   C. It should be beneficial for the person who uses it.

II. Bicycle riding meets all these standards for an ideal form of land transportation.
   A. It is faster than walking or running.
   B. It is not a source of air, land, water, or noise pollution.
   C. It is beneficial for the health of the rider.

Speeches on questions of value may have strong implications for our behavior, but they do not argue directly for or against particular courses of action. Once you go beyond arguing right or wrong to arguing that something should or should not be done, you move from a question of value to a question of policy.

Questions of policy arise daily in almost everything we do. At home we debate where to go during Spring Festival, whether to buy a new television, which movie to see on the weekend. At work we discuss whether to change jobs, what strategy to use in selling a product, how to improve communication between management and employees. As citizens we ponder measures to improve health care, how to preserve historical sites, what to do about cross-Strait relations.

question of policy
A question about whether a specific course of action should or should not be taken.

All these are questions of policy because they deal with specific courses of action. Questions of policy inevitably involve questions of fact. (How can we decide how to improve health care unless we know the facts of the current situation?) They may also involve questions of value. (The policy you favor on cloning will be affected by whether you think cloning is moral or immoral.) But questions of policy *always* go beyond questions of fact or value to decide whether something should or should not be done.

When put formally, questions of policy usually include the word "should," as in these examples:

What measures should be taken against college students who are caught cheating?

Should celebrities who endorse shoddy products be punished?

Should excavation of the Terracotta Army at Xi'an be resumed?

TYPES OF SPEECHES ON QUESTIONS OF POLICY

When you speak on a question of policy, your goal may be either to gain passive agreement or to motivate immediate action from your listeners. Deciding which goal you want to achieve will affect almost every aspect of your speech.

Speeches to Gain Passive Agreement

If your goal is passive agreement, you will try to get your audience to agree with you that a certain policy is desirable, but you will not necessarily encourage the audience to do anything to enact the policy. For example, suppose you want to persuade people that smoking should be banned in public parks and buildings. If you seek passive agreement, you will try to get your audience to concur, but you will not urge the audience to take any action right now to help change smoking regulations.

speech to gain passive agreement
A persuasive speech in which the speaker's goal is to convince the audience that a given policy is desirable, without encouraging the audience to take action in support of the policy.

Here are some specific purpose statements for policy speeches that seek passive agreement:

To persuade my audience that there should be stricter safety standards for amusement-park rides.

To persuade my audience that our city should begin a mandatory recycling program.

To persuade my audience that public speaking should be a required course for English majors.

In each case, the speaker's aim is to convince listeners that the speaker's policy is necessary and practical. The speaker is not trying to get listeners to take action in support of the policy.

Speeches to Gain Immediate Action

speech to gain immediate action
A persuasive speech in which the speaker's goal is to convince the audience to take action in support of a given policy.

When your goal is immediate action, you want to do more than get your listeners to nod their heads in agreement. You want to motivate them to act. Here are some examples of specific purpose statements for policy speeches that seek immediate action:

> To persuade my audience to donate blood on a regular basis.
>
> To persuade my audience to start a regular exercise program.
>
> To persuade my audience to volunteer to help the elderly.

Some experts say you should seek action from your audience whenever possible. Although it is much easier to evoke passive agreement than to elicit action, the listener is not making much of a commitment by thinking, "Sure, I agree with you." Within a day or two, that same listener may forget about your speech—and about his or her agreement with it.

Action, however, reinforces belief. Research shows that once a listener acts on behalf of a speaker's position, even if the action is minor, he or she is more likely to remain committed to that position and to take future action in support of it.[4]

When you call for action in a persuasive speech, you should make your recommendations as specific as possible. Don't just urge listeners to "do something." Tell them exactly what to do and how to do it. The more specific your instructions are, the more likely your listeners are to act on them.[5]

ORGANIZING SPEECHES ON QUESTIONS OF POLICY

Effective organization is crucial when you seek to persuade listeners on a question of policy. Although any of the basic patterns of organization explained in Chapter 7 can be used, four special patterns are especially valuable for policy speeches. They are problem-solution order, problem-cause-solution order, comparative advantages order, and the motivated sequence.

Problem-Solution Order

If you advocate a change in policy, your main points often will fall naturally into problem-solution order. In the first main point, you demonstrate the need for a new policy by showing the extent and seriousness of the problem. In the second main point, you explain your plan for solving the problem. For example:

Video 14.1
View an excerpt from "Bursting the Antibacterial Bubble."

Specific Purpose: To persuade my audience that the use of antibacterial chemicals in household products should be reduced.

Central Idea: The use of antibacterial chemicals in household products is a serious problem that requires action by government and consumers alike.

Regardless of how you organize your persuasive speech, you will need strong supporting materials. The better your research is, the more convincing your arguments are likely to be.

Main Points: I. Rather than making us healthier, antibacterial chemicals in household products are creating long-term health problems.

II. Solving these problems requires a combination of government regulation and consumer action.

You can use the problem-solution format just as easily to organize a speech opposing a change in policy. In such a speech, your job is to defend the current system and to attack your opponents' proposed policy. Thus in the first main point, you might argue that there is not a need for change. In the second main point, you might show that even if there were a serious problem, the suggested new policy would not solve it and would create serious problems of its own. For example:

problem-solution order
A method of organizing persuasive speeches in which the first main point deals with the existence of a problem and the second main point presents a solution to the problem.

Specific Purpose: To persuade my audience that the city council should not pass legislation merging the police and fire departments.

Central Idea: Merging the police and fire departments is neither necessary nor practical.

Main Points: I. Merging the police and fire departments is not necessary.

A. The police department has a reputation as one of the best in China.

B. The fire department is also highly respected.

II. Besides being unnecessary, merging the police and fire departments is impractical.

A. Rather than saving money, merging the departments will increase costs.

B. Merging the departments will also make both less efficient.

Problem-Cause-Solution Order

problem-cause-solution order
A method of organizing persuasive speeches in which the first main point identifies a problem, the second main point analyzes the causes of the problem, and the third main point presents a solution to the problem.

For a variation on problem-solution order, you might arrange your speech in problem-cause-solution order. This produces a speech with three main points—the first identifying a problem, the second analyzing the causes of the problem, and the third presenting a solution to the problem. For example:

Specific Purpose: To persuade my audience that steps should be taken to deal with the problem of childhood obesity.

Central Idea: Childhood obesity is a serious problem that can be controlled by changes in diet and exercise.

Main Points:

I. Childhood obesity is a serious problem in China.
   A. National surveys show that childhood obesity is growing rapidly.
   B. The increase in obesity is producing health problems among children.

II. There are two major causes of the increase in childhood obesity.
   A. One cause is the popularity of American fast food.
   B. A second cause is physical inactivity.

III. Solving the problem requires dealing with both causes.
   A. Families must make sure children eat healthy foods.
   B. Families must also make sure children get enough exercise.

One benefit of this method of organization is that it requires the speaker to identify the causes of the problem. This in turn makes it easier to check whether the proposed solution will actually remedy the causes.

Comparative Advantages Order

comparative advantages order
A method of organizing persuasive speeches in which each main point explains why a speaker's solution to a problem is preferable to other proposed solutions.

When your audience already agrees that a problem exists, you can devote your speech to comparing the advantages and disadvantages of competing solutions. In such a situation, you might put your speech in comparative advantages order, devoting each main point to explaining why your solution is preferable to other proposed solutions.

Suppose you want to convince your audience that automakers should put greater emphasis on developing hydrogen fuel-cell cars than gas-electric hybrid cars. Using comparative advantages order, you would compare hydrogen cars with hybrid cars and show why the former are a better choice. Your specific purpose, central idea, and main points might look like this:

Specific Purpose: To persuade my audience that automakers should put greater emphasis on developing hydrogen fuel-cell cars than hybrid cars.

Central Idea: Unlike hybrid cars, hydrogen cars run entirely without gasoline and do not emit air-polluting exhaust.

Main Points:

I. Unlike hybrid cars, hydrogen cars run entirely without gasoline.

II. Unlike hybrid cars, hydrogen cars do not emit any air-polluting exhaust.

Although it was written more than 2,000 years ago, Aristotle's *Rhetoric* remains the classic work on the methods of persuasion. You can access the full text at http://classics.mit.edu/Aristotle/rhetoric.html. Book I defines rhetoric and explores the major genres of oratory. Book II deals with evidence, proof, reasoning, and emotional appeal. Book III focuses on language and speech organization. For commentary on the *Rhetoric*, check the Stanford Encyclopedia of Philosophy at http://plato.stanford.edu/entries/aristotle-rhetoric/.

Internet Connection

Motivated Sequence

The motivated sequence is tailor-made for policy speeches that seek immediate action. It has five steps that follow the psychology of persuasion:

motivated sequence
A method of organizing persuasive speeches that seek immediate action. The five steps of the motivated sequence are attention, need, satisfaction, visualization, and action.

1. *Attention.* First you gain the attention of your audience by using one or more of the methods described in Chapter 8.
2. *Need.* Next you make the audience feel a need for change. You show there is a serious problem with the existing situation.
3. *Satisfaction.* Having aroused a sense of need, you satisfy it by providing a solution to the problem. You present your plan and show how it will work.
4. *Visualization.* Having given your plan, you intensify desire for it by visualizing its benefits. Use vivid imagery so listeners can see how much better conditions will be once your plan is adopted.
5. *Action.* Once the audience is convinced that your policy is beneficial, you are ready to call for action. Say exactly what you want listeners to do—and how to do it. Then conclude with a final stirring appeal that reinforces their commitment to act.

Many speakers prefer the motivated sequence because it is more detailed than problem-solution order. It follows the process of human thinking and leads the listener step by step to the desired action. One indication of its effectiveness is that it is widely used by people who make their living by persuasion—especially advertisers. The next time you watch television, pay close attention to the commercials. You will find that many of them follow the motivated sequence.

The following outline shows how one U.S. speaker incorporated the motivated sequence into a speech urging her audience to donate blood:

Specific Purpose: To persuade my audience to become regular blood donors.

Central Idea: By becoming regular blood donors, you can help save lives and replenish the U.S. blood supply.

Video 14.2
View an excerpt from "The Ultimate Gift."

Introduction

Attention: I. Are you at least 17 years old? Do you weigh more than 110 pounds? Do you consider yourself fairly healthy?

The motivated sequence is especially useful for persuasive speakers who seek immediate action from their listeners, as is the case with actor and activist Danny Glover in this address to garment workers.

II. If you answered yes to these questions, you should be donating blood every two months.

III. Today I will show you why donors are in such desperate need and encourage you to become a donor.

Body

Need: I. The lack of participation by eligible blood donors poses a threat to the lives of many Americans.

A. Someone in the U.S. undergoes a blood transfusion every three seconds.

B. This amounts to 3,000 gallons of blood every hour of every day.

C. Current donation levels are too low to meet this need.

Satisfaction: II. You can help by becoming a regular blood donor.

A. You can donate at your local Red Cross.

B. The process is simple, easy, and painless.

Visualization: III. Every unit of blood you donate can help save three lives.

A. The blood is divided into red blood cells, white blood cells, and platelets, each of which can help a different person.

B. If you donate 6 times a year, you can help 18 people.

C. If you donate for 10 years, you can help save 180 lives.

Conclusion

Action: I. So I encourage each of you to become a regular blood donor.

II. Give the ultimate gift—the gift of life.

What makes a speaker persuasive? Why do listeners accept one speaker's views and reject those of another? How can a speaker motivate listeners to act in support of a cause, a campaign, or a candidate? People have been trying to answer these questions for thousands of years—from the ancient Greek philosopher Aristotle to modern-day communication researchers. Although many answers have been given, we can say that listeners will be persuaded by a speaker for one or more of four reasons:

Because they perceive the speaker as having high credibility.

Because they are won over by the speaker's evidence.

Because they are convinced by the speaker's reasoning.

Because their emotions are touched by the speaker's ideas or language.

Let us look at each in turn.

BUILDING CREDIBILITY

Here are two sets of imaginary statements. Which one of each pair would you be more likely to believe?

"Within ten years, changes in technology will make today's personal computers seem hopelessly old-fashioned." (Bill Gates)

"Personal computers are not likely to be much different in ten years than they are today." (Zhang Yimou)

"Despite changes in audience values, there will always be a market for well-made kung fu films." (Zhang Yimou)

"There is no longer a significant market for kung fu films." (Bill Gates)

Most likely you chose the first option in each pair of statements. If so, you were probably influenced by your perception of the speaker. You are more likely to respect the judgment of Bill Gates, founder of Microsoft, when he talks about the future of personal computers, and to respect the judgment of heralded director Zhang Yimou when he talks about the future of kung fu films. Some scholars call this factor *credibility*. Others refer to it as *ethos*, the name given by Aristotle.

ethos
The name used by Aristotle for what modern students of communication refer to as credibility.

Factors of Credibility

Many things affect a speaker's credibility, including sociability, dynamism, physical attractiveness, and perceived similarity between speaker and audience. Above all, though, credibility is affected by two factors:

- *Competence*—how an audience regards a speaker's intelligence, expertise, and knowledge of the subject.
- *Character*—how an audience regards a speaker's sincerity, trustworthiness, and concern for the well-being of the audience.

credibility
The audience's perception of whether a speaker is qualified to speak on a given topic.

The more favorably listeners view a speaker's competence and character, the more likely they are to accept what the speaker says.

It is important to remember that credibility is an attitude. It exists not in the speaker, but in the mind of the audience. A speaker may have high credibility for one audience and low credibility for another. A speaker may also have high credibility on one topic and low credibility on another.

Enhancing Your Credibility

How can you build credibility in your speeches? At one level, the answer is frustratingly general. Since everything you say and do in a speech will affect your credibility, you should say and do *everything* in a way that will make you appear capable and trustworthy. In other words, give a brilliant speech and you will achieve high credibility!

The advice is sound, but not all that helpful. There are, however, some specific ways you can boost your credibility while speaking. They include explaining your competence, establishing common ground with the audience, and speaking with genuine conviction.

Explain Your Competence

As we saw in Chapter 8, one way to enhance your credibility is to mention your expertise on the speech topic. Did you investigate the topic thoroughly? Then say so. Do you have experience that gives you special knowledge or insight? Again, say so.

Here is how two speakers revealed their qualifications. The first stressed his study and research:

> I never knew much about UFOs until I did a research project on them last year. Since then, I have read a lot more about the subject, including reports by scientists from the National Society of Extraterrestrial Studies. As a result, I have decided that the evidence strongly suggests that Earth has been—and continues to be—v sited by spaceships from other planets.

The second speaker emphasized her background and personal experience:

> We all have some desire to study abroad. But I never realized just how valuable it would be until I spent last year in the United States. Not only did I become much better in my use of English, but I made so many new friends and learned so much about American culture. Today I want to persuade all of you to do everything you can to participate in some kind of study-abroad program.

Both speakers increased their persuasiveness by establishing their credibility.

Establish Common Ground with Your Audience

Another way to bolster your credibility is to establish common ground with your audience. You do not persuade listeners by assaulting their values and rejecting their opinions. As the old Western saying goes, "You catch more flies with honey than with vinegar." The same is true of persuasion. Show respect for your listeners. You can make your speech more appealing by identifying your ideas with those of your audience—by showing how your point of view is consistent with what they believe.[6]

Here is an example from a speech favoring a tuition increase at the speaker's school—an unpopular point of view with his audience. He began by saying:

A speaker's credibility has a powerful impact on how her or his speech is received. One way to boost your credibility is to deliver your speeches expressively and with strong eye contact.

As we all know, there are many differences among the people in this class. But regardless of age, major, background, or goals, we all share one thing in common—we are all concerned with the quality of education at this school. And that quality is clearly in danger. Because of budget reductions, faculty salaries have fallen below those at comparable schools, library hours have been cut back, and more and more students are being crowded out of classes they need to take.

Whether we like it or not, we have a problem—a problem that affects each of us. This morning I would like to discuss this problem and whether it can be solved by an increase in tuition.

Video 14.3
View this excerpt from "Let's Protect the Quality of Our Education."

By stressing common perceptions of the problem, the speaker hoped to get off on the right foot with his audience. Once that was done, he moved gradually to his more controversial ideas.

Deliver Your Speeches Fluently, Expressively, and with Conviction

There is a great deal of research to show that a speaker's credibility is strongly affected by his or her delivery. Moderately fast speakers, for example, are usually seen as more intelligent and confident than slower speakers. So too are speakers who use vocal variety to communicate their ideas in a lively, animated way. On the other hand, speakers who consistently lose their place or pepper their talk with vocalized pauses are seen as less competent than speakers who are poised and dynamic.[7] All of this argues for practicing your persuasive speech fully ahead of time so you can deliver it fluently and expressively.

Speaking techniques aside, the most important way to strengthen your credibility is to deliver your speeches with genuine conviction. American President Harry Truman once said that in speaking, "sincerity, honesty, and a straightforward manner are more important than special talent or polish." If you want others to believe and care about your ideas, you must believe and care about them yourself. Your spirit, enthusiasm, and conviction will carry over to your listeners.

Checklist Evidence

YES	NO	
☐	☐	1. Are all my major claims supported by evidence?
☐	☐	2. Do I use sufficient evidence to convince my audience of my claims?
☐	☐	3. Is my evidence stated in specific rather than general terms?
☐	☐	4. Do I use evidence that is new to my audience?
☐	☐	5. Is my evidence from credible, unbiased sources?
☐	☐	6. Do I identify the sources of my evidence?
☐	☐	7. Is my evidence clearly linked to each point that it is meant to prove?
☐	☐	8. Do I provide evidence to answer possible objections the audience may have to my position?

USING EVIDENCE

evidence
Supporting materials used to prove or disprove something.

Evidence consists of supporting materials—examples, statistics, testimony—used to prove or disprove something. As we saw in Chapter 6, careful listeners are skeptical. They are suspicious of unsupported generalizations. They want speakers to justify their claims. If you hope to be persuasive, you must support your views with evidence.

Evidence is especially crucial when your target audience opposes your point of view. Listeners in such a situation will mentally argue with you—asking questions, raising objections, and creating counterarguments to "answer" what you say. The success of your speech will depend partly on how well you anticipate these internal responses and give evidence to refute them.

Any of the supporting materials discussed in Chapter 6—examples, statistics, testimony—can work as evidence in a persuasive speech. As we saw in that chapter, there are guidelines for using each kind of supporting material regardless of the kind of speech you are giving. Here we look at three special tips for using evidence in a persuasive speech.

Use Specific Evidence

No matter what kind of evidence you employ, it will be more persuasive if you state it in specific rather than general terms.[8] When speaking about diabetes, for example, a speaker should not say, "Lots of people in China suffer from diabetes." This will leave the audience wondering how many "lots" amounts to. The statement will have more impact if the speaker says, "According to statistics in *Shanghai Daily*, more than 80 million Chinese have some form of diabetes." This will also enhance the speaker's credibility by showing that he or she has a firm grasp of the facts.

Persuasive speeches need strong evidence to convince skeptical listeners. Finding the best evidence often takes hard digging, but it is well worth the effort.

Use Novel Evidence

Evidence is more likely to be persuasive if it is new to the audience.[9] You will gain little by citing facts and figures that are already well known to your listeners. If they have not persuaded your listeners already, they will not do so now. You must go beyond what the audience already knows and present new evidence that will get them to say, "Hmmm, I didn't know *that*. Maybe I should rethink the issue." Finding such evidence usually requires resourceful research, but the rewards are worth the effort.

Use Evidence from Credible Sources

Listeners find evidence from competent, credible sources more persuasive than evidence from less qualified sources.[10] Above all, listeners are suspicious of evidence from sources that appear to be biased or self-interested. In assessing the current state of airline safety, for example, they are more likely to be persuaded by testimony from impartial aviation experts than from an airline's public relations department. If you wish to be persuasive, rely on evidence from objective, nonpartisan sources.

logos
The name used by Aristotle for the logical appeal of a speaker. The two major elements of *logos* are evidence and reasoning.

Evidence is one element of what Aristotle referred to as *logos*—the logical appeal of a speaker. The other major element of *logos* is reasoning, which works in combination with evidence to help make a speaker's claims persuasive.

reasoning
The process of drawing a conclusion on the basis of evidence.

REASONING

Reasoning is the process of drawing a conclusion on the basis of evidence. Sometimes we reason well—as when we conclude that ice particles forming on the trees may mean that the roads will be slippery. Other times we reason less effectively—as when we conclude that a jumpy right eyelid will bring bad luck. Most superstitions are actually no more than instances of faulty reasoning.

As a public speaker, you have two major concerns with respect to reasoning. First, you must make sure your own reasoning is sound. Second, you must try to get listeners to agree with your reasoning. Let us look, then, at four basic methods of reasoning and how to use them in your speeches.

Reasoning from Specific Instances

reasoning from specific instances
Reasoning that moves from particular facts to a general conclusion.

When you reason from specific instances, you progress from a number of particular facts to a general conclusion.[11] For example:

Fact 1: My physical education course last term was easy.

Fact 2: My roommate's physical education course was easy.

Fact 3: My brother's physical education course was easy.

Conclusion: Physical education courses are easy.

As this example suggests, we use reasoning from specific instances daily. The speaker who concludes that unethical business practices are common in the United States because several major corporations have been guilty of fraud in recent years is reasoning from specific instances. So is the speaker who argues that cheating is increasing on college campuses because there have been a number of well-publicized cases of cheating at schools across China.

Such conclusions are never foolproof. No matter how many specific instances you give (and you can give only a few in a speech), it is always possible that an exception exists. Throughout the ages people observed countless white swans without seeing any of a different color. It seemed an undeniable fact that all swans were white. Then, in the 19th century, black swans were discovered in Australia!

When you reason from specific instances, you should follow three basic guidelines:

hasty generalization
An error in reasoning from specific instances, in which a speaker jumps to a general conclusion on the basis of insufficient evidence.

First, avoid generalizing too hastily. Beware of the tendency to jump to conclusions on the basis of insufficient evidence. Make sure your sample of specific instances is large enough to justify your conclusion.

Second, make sure the instances you present are fair, unbiased, and representative. (Are three physical education courses *enough* to conclude that physical education courses in general are easy? Are the three courses *typical* of most physical education courses?)

Third, reinforce your argument with statistics or testimony. Since you can never give enough specific instances to make your conclusion irrefutable, you should supplement them with testimony or statistics demonstrating that the instances are representative.

Reasoning from Principle

Reasoning from principle is the opposite of reasoning from specific instances. It moves from the general to the specific.[12] When you reason from principle, you progress from

Reasoning is an important part of persuasive speaking. In a Western legal trial, for example, neither the prosecution nor the defense is likely to sway the jury unless their reasoning is clear and convincing.

a general principle to a specific conclusion. We are familiar with this kind of reasoning from statements such as the following:

1. All people are mortal.
2. Socrates is a person.
3. Therefore, Socrates is mortal.

You begin with a general statement ("All people are mortal"), move to a minor premise ("Socrates is a person"), and end with a specific conclusion ("Socrates is mortal").

reasoning from principle
Reasoning that moves from a general principle to a specific conclusion.

Speakers often use reasoning from principle when trying to persuade an audience. One of the clearest examples from American history is Susan B. Anthony's famous speech "Is It a Crime for U.S. Citizens to Vote?" Delivered on numerous occasions in 1872 and 1873, at a time when women were legally barred from voting, Anthony's speech reasoned along the following lines:

1. The United States Constitution guarantees all U.S. citizens the right to vote.
2. Women are U.S. citizens.
3. Therefore, the United States Constitution guarantees women the right to vote.

This argument progresses from a general principle ("The United States Constitution guarantees all U.S. citizens the right to vote") through a minor premise ("Women are U.S. citizens") to a conclusion ("Therefore, the United States Constitution guarantees women the right to vote").

When you use reasoning from principle in a speech, pay special attention to your general principle. Will listeners accept it without evidence? If not, give evidence to support it before moving to your minor premise. You may also need to support your minor premise with evidence. When both the general principle and the minor premise are soundly based, your audience will be more likely to accept your conclusion.

Causal Reasoning

causal reasoning
Reasoning that seeks to establish the relationship between causes and effects.

There is a patch of ice on the sidewalk. You slip, fall, and break your arm. You reason as follows: "*Because* that patch of ice was there, I fell and broke my arm." This is an example of causal reasoning, in which someone tries to establish the relationship between causes and effects.

As any scientist (or detective) will tell you, causal reasoning can be tricky. The relationship between causes and effects is not always clear. There are two common errors to avoid when using causal reasoning.

false cause
An error in causal reasoning in which a speaker mistakenly assumes that because one event follows another, the first event is the cause of the second.

The first is the fallacy of false cause. This fallacy is often known by its Latin name, *post hoc, ergo propter hoc*, which means "after this, therefore because of this." In other words, the fact that one event happens after another does not mean that the first is the cause of the second. The closeness in time of the two events may be entirely coincidental. If you hear a black crow cry and five minutes later you fall and break your arm, you needn't blame your accident on the poor crow.

A second error to avoid when using causal reasoning is assuming that events have only one cause. In fact, most events have several causes. What causes the economy to boom or bust? Interest rates? Oil prices? Tax policy? Labor costs? World affairs? *All* these factors—and others—affect the economy. When you use causal reasoning, be wary of the temptation to attribute complex events to single causes.

Analogical Reasoning

analogical reasoning
Reasoning in which a speaker compares two similar cases and infers that what is true for the first case is also true for the second.

What do these statements have in common?

> If you're good at Ping-Pong, you will probably be good at tennis.
>
> In Great Britain the general election campaign for Prime Minister lasts less than three weeks. Surely the same can be done with the U.S. presidential election.

Both statements use reasoning from analogy. By comparing two similar cases, they infer that what is true for one must be true for the other.

The most important question in assessing analogical reasoning is whether the two cases being compared are essentially alike. If they are essentially alike, the analogy is valid. If they are not essentially alike, the analogy is invalid.

Look back at the analogies at the start of this section. Is playing Ping-Pong the same as playing tennis? Not exactly. But they are close enough that being skillful at one greatly increases the odds of being skillful at the other. The analogy is valid.

invalid analogy
An analogy in which the two cases being compared are not essentially alike.

What about the second analogy? That depends on how much alike the British and American political systems are. Are the countries similar in size? Is it possible for candidates in both countries to canvass the entire land in less than three weeks? Does the party system operate the same in both countries? In other words, are the factors that allow Great Britain to elect a Prime Minister in less than three weeks also present in the United States? Because the answer is no, the analogy is invalid.

In addition to using evidence to support their ideas, effective speakers such as Bill Richardson take care to avoid fallacies in reasoning that may undermine their credibility and persuasiveness.

Reasoning from analogy is used most often in persuasive speeches on questions of policy. When arguing for a new policy, you should find out whether it has been tried elsewhere. You may be able to claim that your policy will work because it has worked in similar circumstances.

By the same token, if you argue against a change in policy, you should check whether the proposed policy—or something like it—has been implemented elsewhere. If it was unsuccessful there, you may be able to reason that it will also be unsuccessful in the new circumstances.

Because argument from analogy can be used on both sides of an issue, you are more likely to persuade your audience if the analogy shows a truly parallel situation.

Fallacies

A fallacy is an error in reasoning. As a speaker, you need to avoid fallacies in your speeches. As a listener, you need to be alert to fallacies in the speeches you hear.

fallacy
An error in reasoning.

Logicians have identified more than 125 different fallacies. Earlier in this chapter, we discussed three of the most important: hasty generalization, false cause, and invalid analogy. Here we look at four other fallacies you should guard against.

Red Herring

The name of this fallacy comes from an old trick used by farmers in England to keep fox hunters and their hounds from galloping through the crops. By dragging a smoked

red herring
A fallacy that introduces an irrelevant issue to divert attention from the subject under discussion.

herring with a strong odor along the edge of their fields, the farmers could throw the dogs off track by destroying the scent of the fox.

A speaker who uses a red herring introduces an irrelevant issue in order to divert attention from the subject under discussion. For instance:

> How dare my opponents accuse me of corruption when we are working to improve the quality of life for all people in our province?

What does the speaker's concern about the quality of life in the province have to do with whether he is guilty of corruption? Nothing! It is a red herring used to divert attention away from the real issue.

Ad Hominem

ad hominem
A fallacy that attacks the person rather than dealing with the real issue in dispute.

Latin for "against the man," *ad hominem* refers to the fallacy of attacking the person rather than dealing with the real issue in dispute. For instance:

> The mayor has a number of interesting economic proposals, but let's not forget that she has just had her second divorce.

By impugning the mayor's personal life rather than dealing with the substance of her economic proposals, the speaker is engaging in an *ad hominem* attack.

Sometimes, of course, a person's character or integrity can be a legitimate issue, as in the case of a police chief who violates the law or a corporate president who swindles stockholders. In such cases, a speaker might well raise questions about the person without being guilty of the *ad hominem* fallacy.

Bandwagon

bandwagon
A fallacy that assumes that because something is popular, it is therefore good, correct, or desirable.

How often have you heard someone say, "It's a great idea—everyone agrees with it"? This is a classic example of the bandwagon fallacy, which assumes that because something is popular, it is therefore good, correct, or desirable.

Much advertising is based on the bandwagon fallacy. The fact that more people in China drink Coca-Cola than Pepsi Cola does not prove that Coca-Cola is made of healthier ingredients. Coca-Cola's popularity could be due to aggressive marketing. The question of which drink has healthier ingredients is a medical issue that has nothing to do with popularity.

The bandwagon fallacy is also evident in political speeches. Consider the following statement:

> The U.S. President must be correct in his approach to international policy; after all, polls show that 60 percent of the American people support him.

This statement is fallacious because popular opinion cannot be taken as proof that an idea is right or wrong. Remember, "everyone" used to believe that the world is flat, that space flight is impossible, and that women should not attend college with men!

Slippery Slope

The slippery slope fallacy takes its name from the image of a boulder rolling uncontrollably down a steep hill. Once the boulder gets started, it can't be stopped until it reaches the bottom.

slippery slope
A fallacy that assumes that taking a first step will lead to subsequent steps that cannot be prevented.

A speaker who commits the slippery slope fallacy assumes that taking a first step will lead inevitably to a second step and so on down the slope to disaster—as in the following example:

> It never fails: Once a child starts playing video games, his work ethic weakens, his grades collapse, and he loses all chance of getting into a top university.

If a speaker claims that taking a first step will lead inevitably to a series of disastrous later steps, he or she needs to provide evidence or reasoning to support the claim. To assume that all the later steps will occur without proving that they will is to commit the slippery slope fallacy.[13]

APPEALING TO EMOTIONS

Emotional appeals—what Aristotle referred to as *pathos*—are intended to make listeners feel sad, angry, guilty, afraid, happy, proud, sympathetic, reverent, or the like. These are often appropriate reactions when the question is one of value or policy. As George Campbell wrote in his *Philosophy of Rhetoric,* "When persuasion is the end, passion also must be engaged."[14]

pathos
The name used by Aristotle for what modern students of communication refer to as emotional appeal.

Below is a list of some emotions evoked most often by public speakers. Following each emotion are a few examples of subjects that might stir that emotion:

- *Fear*—of serious illness, of natural disasters, of economic hardship.
- *Compassion*—for people with disabilities, for neglected animals, for starving children, for victims of fraud.
- *Pride*—in one's country, in one's hometown, in one's family, in one's school, in one's personal accomplishments.
- *Anger*—at terrorists and their supporters, at unethical business leaders, at corrupt officials, at vandals and thieves.
- *Reverence*—for an admired person, for traditions and institutions, for one's cultural heritage.

You can appeal to these and other emotions by using emotional language, by developing vivid examples, and by speaking with sincerity and conviction. No matter what kind of emotional appeal you use, however, you want to make sure it is appropriate and ethical.

For example, emotional appeals are usually inappropriate in a persuasive speech on a question of fact. Here you should deal only in specific information and logic. Suppose

Emotional appeals often make a persuasive speech more compelling. Such appeals should always be used ethically and should not be substituted for facts and logic.

someone charges an official in your local area with fraud and embezzlement. If you respond by saying, "I'm sure the charge is false because I have always admired the official," or "I'm sure the charge is true because I have always disliked the official," then you are guilty of applying emotional criteria to a purely factual question.

On the other hand, if you want to move people to act on a question of policy, emotional appeals are not only legitimate but perhaps necessary. You will need to appeal to your listeners' hearts as well as to their heads.

Even when trying to move listeners to action, however, you should never substitute emotional appeals for evidence and reasoning. You should *always* build your persuasive speech on a firm foundation of facts and logic. This is important for practical reasons as well as ethical reasons. Unless you prove your case, careful listeners will not be stirred by your emotional appeals. You need to build a good case based on reason *and* kindle the emotions of your audience.[15]

Sample Speech with Commentary

Video 14.4
View "Making a Difference Through the Special Olympics."

The following persuasive speech deals with a question of policy and is organized according to the motivated sequence. As you read, notice how the speaker utilizes the methods of persuasion discussed in this chapter. The speech also provides an excellent example of how delivery can enhance a speaker's credibility as well as the impact of his or her emotional appeals.

Making a Difference Through the Special Olympics

COMMENTARY	SPEECH
The first step in the motivated sequence is gaining attention, which the speaker does with an extended example. In this case, the example has strong emotional appeal.	In Seattle, nine young athletes gathered at the starting line for the 100-yard dash. At the gun, they all started off, not exactly in a dash, but with a desire to run the race to the finish and win. All except one little boy who stumbled on the asphalt, tumbled over a couple of times, and began to cry. The other runners heard the boy cry. They stopped; they looked back. Then they all went back to the boy's side—every single one of them. One girl with Down's syndrome kissed him and said, "This will make it better." Then all nine linked arms and walked to the finish line—together.
The speaker moves from her opening example to reveal the topic of her speech.	These athletes were not competing on national television. They were not sponsored or idolized. But they were given the opportunity to flourish under the glow of their own spotlight, to feel the brush of the ribbon cross their chests as they ran through their own finish line in their own Olympics—the Special Olympics.
After stating the goals of Special Olympics, the speaker relates the topic to her audience at a personal level.	Founded in 1968, Special Olympics invited the world to let go of limiting views, unyielding prejudices, and ignorant misconceptions about people with cognitive disabilities and to embrace the idea that they can be respected, valued, contributing members of society. Just think, one of the kids who ran through that finish line could have fallen into your arms. Or, maybe one day, could be your own child.
The speaker establishes her credibility and provides a preview statement that leads into the body of the speech.	After working as a volunteer for the Special Olympics and doing additional research for this speech, I'd like to encourage you to become involved as a volunteer for the Special Olympics. We'll start by looking at the need for volunteers.
The speaker begins the need step of the motivated sequence by providing information about the number of participants in Special Olympics.	According to the Special Olympics Web site, more than 1.3 million people compete in Special Olympics around the world. Participants must be at least eight years old and be identified as having a cognitive or intellectual disability. There are currently 200 Special Olympics programs running in over 150 countries.
The speaker discusses the need for volunteers by focusing on Wisconsin, where the speech was delivered.	As the Special Olympics continues to grow, so does the need for volunteers. Here in Wisconsin, there are 10,000 athletes and 3,500 volunteer coaches. But because of all the individual attention required by Special Olympics athletes, there's always a need for more volunteer coaches, or for loads of other volunteers as well.

This paragraph begins with a transition into the satisfaction section of the speech. The speaker explains that one does not need to be a great athlete or have prior coaching experience to volunteer as a Special Olympics coach.

Now you know the need for Special Olympics volunteers. So the question is: What can you do to help? The answer is: Become a volunteer. The most obvious way to become a volunteer is to become a coach. Now, you don't have to be a great athlete. You don't have to have any prior coaching experience. Special Olympics offers a general course on the principles of coaching, in addition to a mentoring program in which the new coaches receive guidance from the experienced coaches.

The speaker provides options for her listeners by noting that one's contributions to Special Olympics can vary depending on personal circumstances.

If you don't want to be a coach, there are other ways to help out as well. You can work behind the scenes by assisting with fund-raising or organizing events or any of the other countless details involved in running a huge organization such as Special Olympics. It's also very important that you know that your contribution to Special Olympics can last from a day to a year to a lifetime, depending on the level of commitment that you're ready to make.

The speaker moves into the visualization section, in which she demonstrates the benefits of her plan. This is one of the most important aspects of any persuasive speech on a question of policy.

No matter how you decide to help, I guarantee you that working with the Special Olympics will be immensely rewarding. As a coach, your instruction and support will help your athletes develop physical skills, while your interaction and friendship will help them develop socially. Ronna Vanderslice, author of the article "Special Olympics: Beneficial to All," reports that individuals who get involved in sports and recreation through Special Olympics develop larger networks of friends, are more likely to socialize with others, and receive more social support.

Drawing on her own experience as a volunteer boosts the speaker's credibility. As you can see from the video of the speech, the speaker's sincerity adds immensely to the impact of her ideas.

But it's not just the athletes who benefit from Special Olympics. In my case, working with Special Olympics is one of the most gratifying things I have ever done in my life. Not only do I have the satisfaction that comes from helping others improve the quality of their lives, but I've met so many amazing people and met so many great friends that, really, I would not trade the experience for anything.

A transition signals that the speaker is moving into the action section of her speech. Notice how she relates to the audience by using "you" and "your."

Now you know the need for Special Olympics volunteers, some ways that you can help out, and the benefits to the volunteers and athletes alike, so now I'd like to ask you to take the step of getting involved with the Special Olympics. If you want more information, you can check out the Web site for the Special Olympics or visit the local headquarters located on Monona Drive here in Madison. I also have brochures with contact information that I'll be handing out after the speech.

The speaker again stresses that listeners can adjust volunteering to fit their personal schedules.	I know you may not have a lot of time available right now, but you can volunteer for the time that fits your schedule. The most important thing is to get involved in some capacity, for whatever amount of time you can manage.
By returning to her opening story, the speaker unifies the entire speech and reinforces its emotional appeal. The closing quotation provides an excellent ending.	Remember the nine children I mentioned at the beginning of this speech. Think of their happiness and their support for one another. Think of how much they gained from running in that race. And think of how you can help others experience the same benefits as they strive to fulfill the motto of the Special Olympics: "Let me win. But if I can't win, let me be brave in the attempt."

SUMMARY

Persuasion is the process of creating, reinforcing, or changing people's beliefs or actions. When you speak to persuade, you should think of your speech as a mental dialogue with your audience. Identify your target audience, anticipate objections they may have to your point of view, and answer those objections in your speech.

Persuasive speeches on question of fact come into existence when there is debate about the facts of a given situation. Speeches on questions of value seek to persuade listeners about what is right or wrong, good or bad, ethical or unethical, but they do not argue for or against particular courses of action.

Speeches on questions of policy deal with whether something should or should not be done. They can seek either passive agreement or immediate action. Methods of organizing speeches on questions of policy include problem-solution order, problem-cause-solution order, comparative advantages order, and a special pattern known as the motivated sequence.

Videos 14.5–14.6
View more sample persuasive speeches.

There are four primary methods of persuasion. The first is establishing credibility, which is affected above all by the audience's view of the speaker's character and competence. The second is supporting ideas with evidence. Research shows that evidence will be most persuasive if it is specific, novel, and derived from credible sources.

The third method of persuasion involves reasoning—from specific instances, from general principle, from cause, or from analogy. Whatever kind of reasoning a speaker uses, he or she should be on guard against fallacies such as hasty generalization, false cause, invalid analogy, red herring, *ad hominem*, bandwagon, and slippery slope.

The fourth method of persuasion is appealing to emotions. Such appeals are most appropriate in speeches on questions of policy that seek immediate action from listeners.

KEY TERMS

Key-Term Exercise
Check your knowledge with the Key-Term Exercise for this chapter.

persuasion *(193)*
mental dialogue with the audience *(194)*
target audience *(194)*
question of fact *(195)*
question of value *(197)*
question of policy *(199)*
speech to gain passive agreement *(199)*
speech to gain immediate action *(200)*
problem-solution order *(201)*
problem-cause-solution order *(202)*
comparative advantages order *(202)*
motivated sequence *(203)*
ethos *(205)*
credibility *(205)*
evidence *(208)*
logos *(209)*
reasoning *(209)*
reasoning from specific instances *(210)*
hasty generalization *(210)*
reasoning from principle *(211)*
causal reasoning *(212)*
false cause *(212)*
analogical reasoning *(212)*
invalid analogy *(212)*
fallacy *(213)*
red herring *(214)*
ad hominem *(214)*
bandwagon *(214)*
slippery slope *(215)*
pathos *(215)*

EXERCISES FOR THINKING AND SPEAKING

1. Below are four specific purposes for persuasive speeches. In each case, explain whether the speech associated with it concerns a question of fact, a question of value, or a question of policy. Then rewrite the specific purpose statement to make it appropriate for a speech about one of the other two kinds of questions. For instance, if the original purpose statement is about a question of policy, write a new specific purpose statement that deals with the same topic as either a question of fact or a question of value.

   a. To persuade my audience to engage in extracurricular activities.

   b. To persuade my audience that media violence is a major cause of violent behavior in society.

   c. To persuade my audience that alternate-day driving in private cars should be mandatory in all cities of five million people or more.

   d. To persuade my audience that it is unethical for businesses to use genetic testing when evaluating potential employees.

2. Choose a topic for a persuasive speech on a question of policy. Create two specific purpose statements about that topic—one for a speech to gain passive agreement, another for a speech to motivate immediate action. Once you have the specific purpose statements, explain how the speech seeking immediate action would differ in organization and persuasive appeals from the speech seeking passive agreement.

3. Identify the fallacy in each of the following statements.
   a. Raising a child is like having a pet—you need to feed it, play with it, and everything will be fine.
   b. Every time the cheerleaders have worn blue ribbons, the basketball team has won. If the team wants to keep winning, the cheerleaders should continue wearing blue ribbons.
   c. No one in my family has ever suffered from diabetes. Therefore, I don't think it is such a serious problem in China.
   d. The murder suspect claims he is innocent, but why should anyone listen to him? He is a high-school dropout.
   e. Surely, Olympic Math is good for children. After all, it is popular throughout China.
4. Work with a group of four to five classmates. Compose a 1–2 minute speech designed to sell a household item (rubber band, stapler, hairbrush, tea pot, etc.) to the class. There are two special requirements. First, your group must come up with a completely new use for your item. For example, if your item is a can opener, you must devise some use for it other than opening cans or bottles. Second, the speech must be organized according to the motivated sequence. Have a member of your group present the speech to the class.
5. Analyze Barbara Bush's "Choices and Change," which is printed in the appendix of speeches for appreciation and analysis at the end of the book. Evaluate its use of the methods of persuasion discussed in this chapter.
6. Prepare a 5–6 minute persuasive speech on a question of policy. Your speech should deal with a current issue that you feel is highly relevant and worthy of the audience's attention. After selecting a topic and formulating a specific purpose, choose a method of organization that will work best for achieving your purpose. Develop your ideas by writing a preparation outline. Deliver the speech extemporaneously to your class audience using a speaking outline.

Public Speaking in Your Career

As a volunteer worker at the local branch of the All-China Women's Federation, you are scheduled to speak to a group of 150 women who have just been laid off and are looking for reemployment opportunities in a highly competitive job market. The purpose of your speech is to persuade listeners to sign up for free workshops that offer life-skills training programs such as catering, tailoring, hairstyling, nursing, housekeeping, and the like.

Because training is free, the biggest challenge for your audience is the demanding time commitment. To get a graduating certificate from the program, they have to attend training sessions eight hours a day, five days a week, for three consecutive months.

Before writing your speech, you need to develop a plan for using all four methods of persuasion discussed in this chapter. Identify specific strategies you might use for enhancing your credibility, persuading your audience with evidence and reasoning, and employing emotional appeals.

15 Speaking on Special Occasions

- Speeches of Introduction
- Speeches of Presentation
- Speeches of Acceptance
- Toasts
- Commemorative Speeches

Special occasions are the punctuation marks of day-to-day life, the high points that stand out above ordinary routine. Weddings, funerals, graduations, award ceremonies, retirement dinners, anniversaries—all are special occasions to the people who participate in them. They are also occasions for speechmaking. These speeches are part of the ceremonial aura that marks the event.

Speeches for special occasions are different from the speeches we have considered so far in this book. They may convey information or persuade, but that is not their primary purpose. Rather, they aim to fit the particular needs of a special occasion. In this chapter, we look at some of the most important kinds of special occasions and the speeches appropriate for each.

Speeches of Introduction

A speech of introduction is an address that introduces the main speaker to the audience. If you are presenting such an address, you need to accomplish three purposes:

speech of introduction
A speech that introduces the main speaker to the audience.

Build enthusiasm for the upcoming speaker.

Build enthusiasm for the speaker's topic.

Establish a welcoming climate that will boost the speaker's credibility.

Following are some tips for speeches of introduction.

Be Brief

Everyone who has ever sat through a long-winded speech of introduction knows how dreary it can be. The purpose of the speech is to focus attention on the main speaker, not on the person making the introduction. A speech of introduction will usually be no more than two to three minutes long and may be shorter if the speaker is already well known to the audience.

Make Sure Your Remarks Are Completely Accurate

Many an introducer has embarrassed himself or herself, as well as the main speaker, by garbling basic facts. Always check with the speaker ahead of time to make sure your introduction is accurate in every respect.

Above all, get the speaker's name right. This may seem obvious, but it bears repeating. Remember that nothing is more important than a person's name. If the speaker's name is at all difficult—especially if it involves a foreign pronunciation—practice saying it enough times in advance that you can deliver it without error or hesitation.

Adapt Your Remarks to the Occasion

In preparing your introduction, you may be constrained by the nature of the occasion. Formal occasions require formal speeches of introduction. If you were presenting a guest speaker at an informal business meeting, you might be much more casual than at a formal banquet.

Adapt Your Remarks to the Main Speaker

No matter how well it is received by the audience, a speech of introduction that leaves the main speaker feeling uncomfortable has failed in part of its purpose. How can you make a main speaker uncomfortable? One way is to overpraise the person—especially for his or her speaking skills. Never say, "Our speaker will keep you on the edge of your seat from beginning to end!" You create a set of expectations that are almost impossible to fulfill.

Another way to create discomfort is by revealing embarrassing details of the speaker's personal life or by making remarks that are in poor taste. An introducer may think this line is funny: "Why, I've known Tina Liu since she was 10 years old and so overweight that everybody called her a fat goose!" To the speaker, however, the statement will probably not be a bit funny and may be painful.

Adapt Your Remarks to the Audience

Just as you adapt other speeches to particular audiences, so you need to adapt a speech of introduction to the audience you are facing. Your aim is to make *this* audience want to hear *this* speaker on *this* subject.

If you were introducing the same speaker to two different groups, some of the information in the speeches of introduction might be the same, but it would be slanted differently. Suppose, for example, that J. K. Rowling, author of the Harry Potter series, is going to address two groups—an audience of elementary school children and an audience of educators at the annual meeting of the International Reading Association. The introduction to the schoolchildren might go something like this:

> Children, we have a very important guest today. You know her by the character she has created—Harry Potter. What you don't know is all the hard work that goes into writing the books that we all love to read. Today she is going to tell us how she came up with the idea of Harry Potter and his friends and how she goes about writing her books. Let's give a big round of applause to J. K. Rowling.

But the introduction to the International Reading Association would be along these lines:

> Ladies and gentlemen, it is my privilege to introduce to you today the world's best-selling author. We are all well acquainted with her Harry Potter series that has captured the imagination of children—and more than a few adults—around the globe.
>
> Many of us know the remarkable story of her writing life: The inspiration for Harry Potter came on a train ride from Manchester to London in 1990. Over the next few years, she compiled notes as the story took shape in her mind. The bulk of the writing took place when she was a single mother on public assistance in Edinburgh. She was teaching French to teenagers in the mid-1990s when she heard that the first Harry Potter book had been accepted for publication. The rest is literary history.
>
> This afternoon, she will be telling us more about what inspired her fascinating story of wizardry, where she gets her ideas, and what kinds of books she wants to write next. Please give a warm welcome to J. K. Rowling.

Speeches for special occasions are part of the ceremonial aura that helps make certain events special, as in this commencement address by U.S. Congresswoman Linda Sanchez.

Try to Create a Sense of Anticipation and Drama

You may have noticed one detail shared by the two speeches introducing J. K. Rowling: In both cases the speaker's name was saved for last. This is a convention in speeches of introduction. While there may occasionally be a good reason to break the convention, usually you will avoid mentioning the speaker's name until the final moment—even when the audience knows exactly whom you are discussing. By doing this, you build a sense of drama, and the speaker's name comes as the climax of your introduction.

Above all, if you expect to be creative and dramatic, be sure to practice your speech of introduction thoroughly. You should be able to deliver it extemporaneously, with sincerity and enthusiasm.

Speeches of Presentation

Speeches of presentation are given when someone receives a gift, an award, or some other form of public recognition. Usually such speeches are brief. They may be no more than a mere announcement ("And the winner is . . .") or be up to four or five minutes in length.

speech of presentation
A speech that presents someone a gift, an award, or some other form of public recognition.

The main purpose of a speech of presentation is to tell the audience why the recipient is receiving the award. Point out his or her contributions, achievements, and so forth. Do not deal with everything the person has ever done. Focus on achievements related to the award, and discuss these achievements in a way that will make them meaningful to the audience.

Depending on the audience and the occasion, you may also need to discuss two other matters in a speech of presentation. First, if the audience is not familiar with the award, you should explain it briefly. Second, if the award was won in a public competition and the audience knows who the losers are, you might take a moment to praise the losers as well.

Below is a sample speech of presentation. It was delivered by U.S. President Bill Clinton in presenting the Congressional Gold Medal to former South African President Nelson Mandela. Because the Congressional Gold Medal is a special honor, there are no public competitors for the award. Thus Clinton did not need to say anything about the "losers." His speech focused on Mandela's battle against apartheid and his efforts to promote reconciliation among the people of South Africa.

Presenting the Congressional Gold Medal

Bill Clinton

To my friend, President Mandela, Americans as one today, across all the lines that divide us, pay tribute to your struggle, to your achievement, and to the inspiration you have given us to do better. Today we offer a man who has received the Nobel Prize the highest honor within the gift of this country. . . .

Those of us who share his vision and lift him up in honor today owe it to him to build a permanent partnership between Americans and Africans—for the education of our children, for the solution of our problems, for the resolution of our differences, for the elevation of what is best about us all. . . .

In forgiving those who imprisoned him, he reminded us of the most fundamental lesson of all—that in the end apartheid was a defeat of the heart, the mind, the spirit. It was not just a structure outside and jail houses within which people were kept; it was a division of the mind and soul against itself. We owe it to Nelson Mandela not simply to give him this award, but to live by the lesson he taught us and to tear down every last vestige of apartheid in our own hearts—everything that divides us, one from another.

For those of us who have been privileged to know this remarkable man, no medal, no award, no fortune, nothing we could give him could possibly compare to the gift he has given to us and to the world. The only gift that is true recompense is to continue his mission and to live by the power of his profound and wonderful example.

Now, as prescribed by the law, it is my privilege to present the Congressional Gold Medal to President Nelson Mandela.

Speeches of Acceptance

acceptance speech
A speech that gives thanks for a gift, an award, or some other form of public recognition.

The purpose of an acceptance speech is to give thanks for a gift or an award. When giving such a speech, you thank the people who are bestowing the award and recognize the people who helped you gain it.

The acceptance speech on the next page is the companion piece to the speech of presentation by Bill Clinton. It was delivered by Nelson Mandela in accepting the Congressional Gold Medal, and it exemplifies the major traits of a good acceptance speech—brevity, humility, and graciousness.[1]

Accepting the Congressional Gold Medal

Nelson Mandela

Thank you. President Clinton, Mr. Speaker, distinguished members of the Senate and the House, ladies and gentlemen . . .

It has been my great privilege to serve a people whose bondage to an inhuman system evoked the solidarity of all those who love freedom and justice, a people whose triumph over the divisions of racist doctrine has given new life to humanity's hope for a world without hatred and discrimination. I am conscious that in bestowing the Congressional Gold Medal upon me you are evoking these bonds between our nations and paying tribute to the whole South African nation for its achievements in realizing our shared ideals.

It is in that spirit that I humbly accept the award, aware at the same time of the great honor you do me by using me as the vehicle of a unique distinction conferred by this hallowed institution of American democracy. As one who has dedicated his life to the pursuit of unity, I am moved by the consensus in your nation's regard for the achievements of my people. And I feel a great pride in the fact that with a few citizens of other countries who have received this high honor, the name of an African is now added. . . .

The award with which you honor me today is an expression of the common humanity that binds us, one person to another, nation to nation, and people of the North to people of the South. I receive it with pride as a symbol of partnership for peace, prosperity, and equity as we enter the new millennium. I thank you.

Toasts

The toast is one of the oldest speeches in the world. The custom of saying a few words of greeting, celebration, or thanks in conjunction with a meal or reception can be found in most civilizations throughout history.

toast
A speech of greeting, celebration, or thanks, usually in conjunction with a meal or reception.

Some toasts are very brief—a few sentences of welcome or of wishes for good health, a joyful marriage, or a prosperous career. Often such toasts are capped off with raised glasses and a brief phrase such as "Gan Bei," "Cheers," or "Here's to good friends." If you anticipate giving this kind of toast in a cross-cultural situation, be sure to check in advance any special phrases or pronunciations associated with the toast.

In some situations, toasts are longer and more complex. This is especially true of foreign diplomacy and international business, in which there may be a formal dinner or banquet where the major figures deliver reciprocal toasts. As with shorter toasts, these speeches need to exhibit warmth and sincerity, but they may also need to articulate some important principles with regard to the upcoming meetings or negotiations. Such principles, however, must be stated briefly, graciously, and circumspectly. They must be consistent with the convivial nature of the occasion, and they must not produce loss of face for any of the participants.

Regardless of the kind of toast you are giving, you should rise from your chair and speak to the entire room. At the conclusion, raise your glass to shoulder level, make eye contact with the honored person, and consume your drink. Regardless of circumstances, a toast should rarely exceed three to five minutes.

Below is one of the most famous English-language toasts of modern times. It was presented by U.S. President Richard Nixon on February 21, 1972, at a banquet hosted by Premier Zhou Enlai on the first day of Nixon's historic visit to China. The banquet was held at the Great Hall of the People, and the words of both leaders were broadcast around the world. After Premier Zhou's remarks, which were delivered in Chinese, Nixon responded as follows:

Toast in Response to Premier Zhou Enlai

Richard M. Nixon

Mr. Prime Minister and all of your distinguished guests this evening:

On behalf of all of your American guests, I wish to thank you for the incomparable hospitality for which the Chinese people are justly famous throughout the world. I particularly want to pay tribute, not only to those who prepared the magnificent dinner, but also to those who have provided the splendid music. Never have I heard American music played better in a foreign land.

Mr. Prime Minister, I wish to thank you for your very gracious and eloquent remarks. At this very moment, through the wonder of telecommunications, more people are seeing and hearing what we say than on any other such occasion in the whole history of the world. Yet, what we say here will not be long remembered. What we do here can change the world.

As you said in your toast, the Chinese people are a great people, the American people are a great people. If our two peoples are enemies, the future of this world we share together is dark indeed. But if we can find common ground to work together, the chance for world peace is immeasurably increased.

In the spirit of frankness which I hope will characterize our talks this week, let us recognize at the outset these points: We have at times in the past been enemies. We have great differences today. What brings us together is that we have common interests which transcend those differences. As we discuss our differences, neither of us will compromise our principles. But while we cannot close the gulf between us, we can try to bridge it so that we may be able to talk across it.

So let us, in these next five days, start a long march together, not in lockstep, but on different roads leading to the same goal, the goal of building a world structure of peace and justice in which all may stand together with equal dignity and in which each nation, large or small, has a right to determine its own form of government, free of outside interference or domination. . . .

There is no reason for us to be enemies. Neither of us seeks the territory of the other; neither of us seeks domination over the other; neither of us seeks to stretch out our hands and rule the world.

Chairman Mao has written, "So many deeds cry out to be done, and always urgently. The world rolls on. Time passes. Ten thousand years are too long. Seize the day, seize the hour."

This is the hour, this is the day for our two peoples to rise to the heights of greatness which can build a new and a better world.

In that spirit, I ask all of you present to join me in raising your glasses to Chairman Mao, to Prime Minister Zhou, and to the friendship of the Chinese and American people which can lead to friendship and peace for all people in the world.

Whether given on the world stage or in one's local community, speeches for special occasions should seek to invest the occasion with dignity, meaning, and honest emotion.

Commemorative Speeches

commemorative speech
A speech that pays tribute to a person, a group of people, an institution, or an idea.

Commemorative speeches are speeches of praise or celebration. Eulogies, National Day speeches, and dedications are examples of commemorative speeches. Your aim in such speeches is to pay tribute to a person, a group of people, an institution, or an idea.

As in an informative speech, you probably will have to give the audience information about your subject. After all, the audience must know *why* your subject is praiseworthy. As in other speeches, you may draw on examples, testimony, even statistics to illustrate the achievements of your subject.

Your fundamental purpose in a commemorative speech, however, is not to inform your listeners but to *inspire* them—to arouse and heighten their appreciation of or admiration for the person, institution, or idea you are praising. If you are paying tribute to a person, for example, you should not simply recount the details of the person's life. Rather, you should penetrate to the *essence* of your subject and generate in your audience a deep sense of respect.

When speaking to commemorate, you want to express feelings, to stir sentiments—joy and hope when a new building is dedicated, anticipation and good wishes at a commencement celebration, lament and consolation at a funeral, admiration and respect at a testimonial dinner. A commemorative speech is like an impressionist painting—"a picture with warm colors and texture capturing a mood or a moment."[2]

But while the painter works with brush and colors, the commemorative speaker works with language. Of all the kinds of speeches, none depends more on the creative and subtle use of language. Some of the most memorable speeches in history, including Abraham Lincoln's Gettysburg Address, have been commemorative. We continue to find such speeches meaningful and inspiring in part because of their eloquent use of language.

When speaking to commemorate, your success will depend on your ability to put into language the thoughts and emotions appropriate to the occasion. It is easy—too easy—to fall back on clichés and trite sentiments. Your challenge will be to use language imaginatively to invest the occasion with dignity, meaning, and honest emotion.

In doing so, you may want to utilize the special resources of language discussed in Chapter 10. Metaphor, simile, parallelism, repetition, antithesis, alliteration—all are appropriate for commemorative speeches. Some highly acclaimed commemorative speeches—including Martin Luther King's "I Have a Dream" and John Kennedy's inaugural address—are distinguished by their creative use of such devices.

Confronted with the evocative speeches of a Kennedy or a King, you may decide that the speech of commemoration is far beyond your abilities. But many people who are not famous have delivered excellent commemorative speeches.

Video 15.1

View "My Crazy Aunt Sue."

Look, for example, at "My Crazy Aunt Sue," which is printed below. The speaker is a student in the United States, and her purpose is to pay tribute to her aunt, who for years has battled rheumatoid arthritis. Although the speaker provides basic information about aunt Sue, the speech is not a biography. Rather than recounting the details of aunt Sue's life, it focuses on her courage, her sense of humor, and her refusal to complain about her fate. Vivid language, parallel structure, and repetition reinforce the ideas and give the speech an elegant tone.

My Crazy Aunt Sue

The strongest person I know cannot peel a potato. The strongest person I know has trouble putting on her makeup. The strongest person I know needs a special key holder to turn the key in her car's ignition.

For the past fifteen years, my 47-year-old aunt Sue has been living with rheumatoid arthritis, a painfully debilitating disease in which the joints of the body become intensely inflamed due to the immune system's activity. Yet despite the daily torments of this disease, my aunt Sue is stronger than any woman or man I have ever met.

Not a moment passes that my aunt Sue is not confronted with this demon of a disease and reminded of her disability through the pills she must take and the pain she must endure. It hurts to stand, it hurts to walk, it hurts to sit. After an infinite number of failed medications, aunt Sue is now undergoing her most aggressive treatment, which includes weekly oral chemotherapy. After half a dozen surgeries, her frail body is in need of still more.

And yet despite all of this, I can't recall ever hearing her complain about her fate. After all the indignities and inconveniences her illness has thrown at her, my aunt Sue still finds the energy to devote much of her time not to herself, but to those less fortunate than her. This past Thanksgiving, for example, she helped organize a dinner for more than 500 poor and homeless people. My aunt Sue, who has her medications put in non-childproof containers so she can open them, helped coordinate a dinner for those in need.

The picture I have painted of my aunt Sue thus far is of a kind woman, a determined woman, a warm-hearted woman whose own suffering seems inconsequential when compared to that of others. This is all completely true, but there is something else about my aunt Sue that makes me admire her so. Actually, it's what makes me love her as much as I do.

At five feet two inches, and 105 pounds, with the spunk of a teenager, she introduces herself as "Crazy Sue"—and sometimes I'd have to agree with her. Somehow she is able to approach this demonic disease with a sense of humor. And not just any sense of humor. My Aunt Sue is one of the funniest people I know.

Years ago, when the disease began to hit her really hard, one of the attorneys at her law firm asked why she was limping. She told him she fell off a trapeze performing her weekend hobby—and he believed her! Following an ankle sprain and further complications, her ankle became deformed and the arch of her foot completely collapsed. Whereas most people would wallow in their misery, aunt Sue calls it her "cartoon foot."

My aunt Sue has made a positive impression on countless people throughout her life, but I hope she knows how much of an impression she has made on me—and how much I admire her.

I complain about trudging through the snow to class, but I'm walking pain free. I complain about driving my friends around town, but I'm steering the wheel pain free. I complain about the final exams I'll have to write, but I have the mobility in my wrist to write pain free. I have learned from my aunt Sue that I need to do a better job about being happy for the things that I have, rather than worrying about the not-so-perfect things in my life.

Aunt Sue may call herself crazy, but I call her phenomenal—a joy to be around and a reminder that having a physical disability in no way diminishes a person's spirit or inner beauty.

SUMMARY

This chapter has dealt with several kinds of speeches for special occasions. Your job in a speech of introduction is to establish a welcoming climate for the main speaker. Keep your remarks brief, and make sure they are entirely accurate.

Video 15.2

View one more sample commemorative speech.

Speeches of presentation are given when someone receives a gift or an award. The main objective of such a speech is to acknowledge the recipient's achievements. In contrast, the purpose of an acceptance speech is to give thanks for a gift or an award. It should be brief, humble, and gracious.

Toasts can run from one or two sentences to several minutes. Regardless of length, they should be warm and sincere. When giving a toast in a cross-cultural situation, be sure to check in advance any special phrases or pronunciations associated with the toast.

A commemorative speech is an address of praise or celebration. It should inspire the audience, and its success depends largely on how well the speaker puts into language the thoughts and feelings appropriate to the occasion.

KEY TERMS

Key-Term Exercise

Check your knowledge with the Key-Term Exercise for this chapter.

speech of introduction *(223)*
speech of presentation *(225)*
acceptance speech *(226)*
toast *(227)*
commemorative speech *(229)*

EXERCISES FOR THINKING AND SPEAKING

1. Observe several speeches of presentation and acceptance—at a campus awards ceremony or a television program such as the Academy Awards, Grammy Awards, or Golden Rooster and Hundred Flowers Awards. Which speeches do you find most effective? Least effective? Why?
2. Analyze the toast by Richard Nixon printed on page 228. How well does it fulfill the requirements for a toast presented in this chapter? Be prepared to share your thoughts in class.
3. Imagine yourself being able to invite any well-known figure, living or dead, to address your speech class on a topic of your choice. Following the guidelines for speeches of introduction presented in this chapter, prepare a 1–2 minute speech introducing your chosen person to the class. Deliver the speech in class.
4. Analyze "My Crazy Aunt Sue" (pages 230–231) in light of the criteria for commemorative speaking presented in this chapter.
5. Prepare a 3-minute commemorative speech paying tribute to a person, a group, an institution, or an idea. In addition to following the guidelines for commemorative speaking discussed in this chapter, include various of the devices for vivid language discussed in Chapter 10. Develop your ideas by writing a complete manuscript. Deliver the speech to your class from manuscript or from memory.

Public Speaking in Your Career

You have been working as a math teacher at a local high school for two years. You have just learned that you have won the Teacher of the Year Award by popular vote among your students. The award will be presented at a year-end party organized by the school's teachers union. At the party, you will deliver a brief formal speech accepting your award. Prepare a draft of your speech.

16 Speaking Competiti

Every year, thousands of college students throughout China participate in English public speaking competitions, especially the CCTV Cup and the 21st Century Cup. Starting at the local level and culminating in gala national championships, these competitions are exciting events for speakers and spectators alike. Only one person can win the grand prize in any given competition, but all participants benefit from the experience.

In this chapter, we will discuss the major kinds of competition speeches. As we shall see, there are no magic secrets that will allow you to become an instant winner. As in other aspects of life, success in public speaking requires the steady, systematic cultivation of one's natural talents. If you learn the principles discussed in previous chapters and apply them astutely, you will have a solid foundation for success. But you also need to adapt those principles to the special challenges posed by speech competitions.

Competitions as Communication

Many people think of competitions as artificial speaking situations. In some ways, of course, they are. The speeches at a competition are not part of a negotiation, a conference, or a public commemoration. They are created specifically for the competition, and they are presented in accord with strict rules of eligibility, conduct, and judging. No business deals, no educational programs, no environmental policies, no promotions ride on the outcome. The ultimate measure of success or failure is the decision of the judges, not the approval of the larger audience.

Because of this, it is easy to lose sight of the fact that competition speeches are acts of communication. The most successful speakers, whether in a competition or any other situation, are those who communicate most effectively with their listeners. This is why the winners of speech competitions are not always the students with the very best technical skills in oral English.

Of course, the winners need a very high level of English proficiency. They should exhibit a strong vocabulary, excellent pronunciation, and correct articulation. But they are not judged solely on their vocabulary, pronunciation, or articulation. Rather, they are judged on their ability to use English as a working language in formulating and communicating their ideas.

The question is: Communicate to whom? There are two primary audiences in a speech competition. One is the general group of people assembled to hear the speeches. In a local competition, the number of listeners might be fairly small. In the grand finals of the CCTV Cup or the 21st Century Cup, the live audience may be more than a thousand people, with television and Internet viewers numbering in the millions.

Your second audience is composed of the judges. They have designated criteria for assessing the speakers, but like the larger audience, they also make an overall assessment based on the speakers' ability to think clearly and to communicate effectively. As this chapter proceeds, we will look at various examples of successful competition speeches. In each case, you will see that the speaker, in addition to having a strong technical command of English, is an excellent communicator.

Prepared Speech

The prepared speech is the first event in most speech competitions. It may not be worth the highest number of points, but it is the foundation for everything that follows. A strong prepared speech is vital to getting started on the right foot. It creates a favorable first impression with the judges and builds the speaker's confidence for the rest of the competition. You cannot win a competition on the basis of your prepared speech alone, but it is almost impossible to recover from a poor prepared speech.

PREPARATION AND PRESENTATION

All the principles discussed in previous chapters apply to the prepared speech. Although most prepared speeches have an assigned topic, you must decide how to develop the topic most effectively within the time limit. You must focus on a limited number of main points and back them up with high-quality supporting materials. Clear organization is imperative. Your introduction should gain attention and get the audience involved in the speech. Your main points should flow naturally from one to the next. Your conclusion should create a memorable final impression. As in any speech, your language should be accurate, clear, vivid, and appropriate.

Because the prepared speech is delivered without notes, you must know it so well that you can concentrate on communicating with the audience, rather than on trying to remember the words. Your vocal and physical delivery should enhance the impact of your words. This requires dynamic vocal variety, with complete control of volume, pitch, rate, and pauses. Pronunciation and articulation should be flawless. You do not need a large number of gestures, but all your gestures should appear natural and spontaneous. Your facial expressions and eye contact should reinforce your ideas and create a communicative bond with the audience.

CREATIVITY

Beyond these basic principles, the most important element of a successful prepared speech is creativity. It transcends all the aspects of public speaking we have discussed so far, and it usually makes the difference between an ordinary speech and a superb one. Public speaking is not a matter of following a formula. It is not like cooking, in which one follows a recipe exactly and gets a great meal. The top speakers bring their ideas to life with creativity.

This is true of masterpieces such as Abraham Lincoln's Gettysburg Address, Martin Luther King's "I Have a Dream," John F. Kennedy's Inaugural Address, and the Earl of Spencer's eulogy to Princess Diana. But it is also true of competition speeches. The speeches that fare best in the 21st Century Cup and CCTV Cup are those that use the elements of public speaking not only correctly, but also imaginatively, resourcefully, and creatively.

In fact, the need for creativity is almost greater in speech competitions than in other situations. On any given day of a major competition, the judges will listen to 25 or 30 prepared speeches. After a while, it becomes increasingly difficult to distinguish

National speech competitions such as the CCTV Cup and the 21st Century Cup are dramatic events for speakers and spectators alike. The skills developed in these competitions benefit contestants throughout the rest of their lives.

one speech from another. The speakers are all talented, and they are all addressing the same topic. One path to a winning performance is to be creative in making your speech stand out positively in the judges' minds.

There are two kinds of speech creativity. The first is micro-creativity, which refers to creativity in a particular passage or section of a speech. It is usually manifested in a powerful insight, a compelling example, a memorable turn of phrase, or a poignant emotional appeal. One way to think of micro-creativity is as a brilliant spark that stands out from the rest of the speech and captures the audience's imagination at a crucial moment.

micro-creativity Creativity in a particular passage or section of a speech.

The second type of creativity is macro-creativity, which runs through an entire speech, from beginning to end. It usually involves several major elements of the speech—content, language, organization, delivery, or some combination thereof. Whereas micro-creativity is like a spark that stands out from the rest of the speech, macro-creativity is like a fire that blazes ever more brightly as the speech proceeds.

macro-creativity Creativity that runs through an entire speech.

SAMPLE SPEECH WITH COMMENTARY

The following prepared speech illustrates both levels of creativity. It was delivered by Qi Yue, a student at Beijing Language and Culture University, during the 2001 21st Century Cup. The theme was "Beijing 2008: The Meaning of the Bid." From a technical standpoint, Qi Yue's speech is virtually flawless, with worthy content, exemplary organization, admirable language, and superb delivery. But it is also creative, especially in its use of the colors yellow, red, and green to symbolize the Olympic Games, to link the Games with national pride and tradition, and to provide a unifying principle for the speech. In a competition that included many fine presentations, Qi Yue's creativity elevated her in the judges' minds and helped her win the grand prize.

Video 16.1
View "New Beijing: The Three-Colored Olympics."

New Beijing: The Three-Colored Olympics

COMMENTARY	SPEECH
	Good afternoon, ladies and gentlemen:
The speaker's opening sets the tone for the rest of the speech. Each sentence builds on the previous one, leading to the speaker's central idea, which she identifies at the end of the paragraph.	Bidding for the Olympic Games is, in a way, an image-creating undertaking. The first and foremost thing is to let people fall in love with the city at first sight, attracting them by its unique image. What image does Beijing intend to create for itself once it has the opportunity to host the 2008 Olympics? It is known to all that the Beijing Municipal Government has already set the theme for the future Games: "New Beijing, Great Olympics." For me, the 2008 Olympics will be a great green Olympics illuminated with two more special colors, yellow and red.
A signpost ("First") lets the audience know that the speaker is moving into the body of her speech. Her use of a different color for each main point as the speech proceeds makes her ideas distinct and memorable.	First, yellow is a meaningful color. The Yellow River is China's mother river and the cradle of Chinese civilization. We are of the yellow race and descendants of the Yellow Emperor. This color has a special origin and great significance for the Chinese people. Beijing is the capital of New China, and previously the capital for nine dynasties in Chinese history. So yellow will naturally add splendor to the 2008 Games.
Another signpost ("Secondly") makes the speaker's second main point stand out in the audience's mind. She develops the point with vivid, stirring imagery and clear, uncluttered language.	Secondly, the 2008 Olympics will be a red pageant. Red is another traditionally cherished color for the whole country. We adore red. On big occasions, we like to decorate our homes in red. It is the color of double happiness, representing joyous moments, auspiciousness, enthusiasm, and prosperity. Red is one of the most suitable colors to describe the future of Beijing. Beijing, together with the whole country, is becoming more and more prosperous in the process of modernization. Should the 2008 Olympics be held in Beijing, the whole city will be a sea of red—the red torch, red flags, red flowers, and the radiant faces of millions of joyful people.
A final signpost ("Above all") indicates that the speaker is starting her last main point. Her notion of a green Olympics provides artistic unity by paralleling her use of yellow and red in the previous main points.	Above all, the 2008 Olympics will be a green Olympics. Adding a green ingredient is essential in creating an appealing image, as we can't deny the fact that Beijing, at the moment, is not as green a city as we would like it to be. Striving for an environmentally appealing city has become a central task for all the citizens of Beijing. Big efforts have been made in pollution control, replanting, and beautification of the city.
The speaker uses statistics to illustrate the efforts to ensure a green Olympics in Beijing. She rounds off her statistics and identifies her sources.	According to a project entitled "The Green Olympic Action Plan," between 1998 and 2007, Beijing will have invested 100 billion RMB in preserving and protecting the environment. Some 12.5 million trees and over 1 million acres of grass will be planted along the fourth ring road. By then, the city's green area will make up 40 percent of its total. The city will also dredge its reservoirs used as a water supply to Beijing residents,

	controlling industrial pollution and moving out the 200 factories presently located within the city proper.
Here, as throughout the speech, the speaker's ideas are strengthened by her delivery and her high English skills.	Certainly, all of this is no easy task. But I am sure that all of us have confidence that we will realize these green goals. For now, we have the full support and participation of the environmentally conscious citizens. Each citizen is showing great concern for every one of the steps the city government takes. As the saying goes, "United we stand," and a great Beijing will be achieved.
The conclusion incorporates both the Olympic theme mentioned in the introduction and the three colors discussed in the body.	When our aspiration becomes a reality, it will be a unique Olympics. "New Beijing, Great Olympics" will be weaved of these three superb colors: yellow, red, and green. Let us welcome it and look forward to it!
Most competition speeches end by thanking the audience.	Thank you.

Impromptu Speech

In most speech competitions, the impromptu speech follows the prepared speech. In the CCTV Cup finals, each contestant receives the impromptu topic on stage and has 15 seconds to prepare his or her remarks. In the 21st Century Cup, competitors receive the impromptu topic backstage, 20 minutes before presentation of the prepared speech. Once they are onstage, they deliver the prepared speech, followed immediately by the impromptu speech. Here are a few impromptu speech questions from recent competitions:

Is globalization widening the gap between the rich and the poor?

Which is happier, to love or to be loved?

Should students be provided with more rigorous training in character development?

Are foreign films a positive or negative influence on the development of China's film industry?

As you can see, topics run the gamut from personal to political, campus issues to current affairs. Because all contestants have plenty of time to work on their prepared speech, they usually receive good marks for it. Many falter, though, when it comes to the impromptu speech. If you want to finish near the top, it is essential that you receive high scores for this event.

Speaking impromptu is difficult even for students who are using their native tongue. It is more demanding for students who are speaking in a foreign language. However, it provides excellent training for life after college, when you will face many situations in which you will need to present your ideas clearly and persuasively on the spur of the moment.

PREPARATION AND PRESENTATION

In Chapter 11, we discussed general principles for impromptu speaking. As we noted there, the most important elements in an effective impromptu speech are precise thought and clear organization. In a competition, impromptu speeches usually run one to two minutes in length. You must use that time to maximum advantage. Settle on two or three major points that you want to cover, and discuss each point clearly and concisely. Support your points as necessary with examples, statistics, or testimony. Because some impromptu topics ask for your personal opinion, feel free to draw upon your own experiences in the speech.

Above all, avoid the temptation to ramble or to repeat yourself. Once you have made a point, move on to the next one. Use signposts to identify each new point and to help the audience keep track of your ideas. When you reach the end of your speech, wrap things up quickly and thank the audience for their attention.

When delivering your impromptu speech, try to look calm and assured regardless of how nervous you might be. If you misspeak or lose your train of thought during the speech, don't panic. If you make a small mistake, chances are no one will notice; just continue as if nothing happened. If you make a bigger mistake, don't be afraid to say something like "I'm sorry, I meant to say . . ." and then move on.

As in your prepared speech, maintain eye contact with the audience and avoid vocalized pauses. The less you stumble around searching for words, the more polished and confident you will appear. If you talk at a clear, deliberate pace and maintain your composure throughout the speech, you will have a much better chance of making a favorable impression on the judges.

Although there is no way to know the topic of your impromptu speech before the day of the competition, this does not mean you have to wait until the last minute to prepare. As you get ready for the competition, ask your tutor to give you sample topics, and then practice giving impromptu speeches in response. As you practice, work on all the suggestions presented in the preceding paragraphs. In the early practice sessions, make an audio recording of your speeches to check your organization, clarity, fluency, and pronunciation. In later practice sessions, use a video recording to make sure you look confident, maintain strong eye contact, and avoid distracting gestures or mannerisms.

DEVELOPING A FUND OF KNOWLEDGE

Being an effective impromptu speaker is more than a matter of technique and delivery. Above all, you must have something to say. This requires an inquiring mind and a fund of knowledge about topics ranging from current events, economics, science, philosophy, and education to literature, popular culture, history, and the environment.

Given the complexity of the modern world, of course, no one can know everything about all subjects. The aim is to know as much as you can in comparison with your peers. You should be a regular consumer of the mass media, including English-language newspapers, magazines, and television newscasts. *China Daily*, CCTV-9, and China Radio International can help sharpen your English skills and keep you informed about what is happening in China and the world. Also valuable are Western media

Like other events at speech competitions, impromptu speaking requires creativity, high communication skills, and a strong fund of knowledge. Speakers should focus on two or three key points and discuss them clearly and concisely.

outlets such as the *New York Times*, *USA Today*, CNN, and the BBC. Get in the habit of taking notes on stories dealing with major issues of the day. Also pay attention to words and expressions that are frequently mentioned in these stories so you will know how to say them properly in English.

At the same time, read books and other sources to develop a broad stock of general knowledge. You should know, for example, that William Shakespeare was the author of *Hamlet*, that most of the countries in South America used to be Spanish colonies, and that the Cold War refers to the rivalry that developed after World War II between the United States and the Soviet Union and their respective allies.

Your reading, however, should not be limited to Western issues and sources. To be an informed speaker, you need a deep understanding of China's history and cultural heritage. The *Analects* of Confucius; Sunzi's *The Art of War*; the Tang poets; the inventions of the Song Dynasty; the arts of calligraphy, embroidery, and landscape painting; the architecture of Longxing Temple, the White Pagoda, and the Temple of Heaven—these are only a few of the subjects that might arise in conjunction with impromptu speaking. The more you know about them, the better you will be able to respond.

Before we move on, it is important to stress that the need for a strong fund of knowledge is not limited to impromptu speaking. Prepared speeches, question-and-answer sessions, and debates also require substantial, well-developed content. If you aim to be successful in any kind of speech, you need to acquire knowledge on a wide array of topics. As the great Roman speaker Cicero stated centuries ago, "It is the duty of the true orator to seek out, hear, read, discuss, handle, and ponder everything that befalls in the life of man."

SAMPLE SPEECHES WITH COMMENTARY

We can illustrate the principles of impromptu speaking by looking at two examples. The first was presented by Zhang Ruiting, of Southwest Jiaotong University, in the finals of the 2008 CCTV Cup. Her topic was "Would rebuilding the Old Summer Palace be a celebration of past glory or a betrayal of history?" Because she had only one minute to respond, her remarks had to be sharp, clear, and precise. But she is also creative, especially in her use of antithesis, repetition, and parallelism. Her delivery is equally impressive. Poised and confident, she speaks with conviction, has excellent eye contact, and possesses superb articulation and pronunciation.

Videos 16.2–16.3

View "We Should Not Rebuild the Old Summer Palace" and "The First Chinese Astronaut to the Moon."

The second speech is by Sun Ning, from Beijing Foreign Studies University, grand-prize winner at the 2002 21st Century Cup. He had two minutes to respond to the topic, "If you were the first Chinese astronaut to go to the moon, and you could leave three objects, what would they be?" The organization of his speech is impeccable. He states each point with utter clarity, and he develops each cogently and thoughtfully. His delivery is direct and engaging. The impression is that of a confident speaker fully in control of his thoughts. Like Zhang Ruiting's speech, Sun Ning's is distinguished by its strong content, and it would be of superior quality even if presented by a native speaker of English.

We Should Not Rebuild the Old Summer Palace

COMMENTARY	SPEECH
The speaker states her position on the topic clearly and decisively.	Ladies and gentlemen: I think we shouldn't restore the Old Summer Palace because it indeed would be a betrayal of history. It is our cultural heritage, and it should be kept as it is.
The speaker's first main point builds to a compelling antithesis between the Old Summer Palace as an ornament and as a monument. This is an excellent example of micro-creativity.	The tragedy that happened in 1860 is something we should all remember and something we should all keep in mind. It is a reminder to us of what happened in the past, and an important page in Chinese history. Maybe restoring it will make it look as glorious as before, but that is not the true meaning of this building. It is not there as an ornament, but as a monument, a monument of the past.
The speaker's second main point also builds to a strong climax. Her use of repetition and parallelism adds rhythm, force, and artistic flair.	Also, if we restore it into another site, it would take away the historical reality that it has become. If we move it away, it would lose its original meaning. It was built in Beijing, it was destroyed in Beijing, and it should remain in Beijing.
	Thank you very much!

The First Chinese Astronaut to the Moon

COMMENTARY	SPEECH
Stating the central idea is usually all that time allows at the start of an impromptu speech.	Well, if I were the first Chinese astronaut to go to the moon, I would like to bring with me the following three items:
The speaker develops his first main point. Here, as throughout the speech, he uses personal pronouns such as "I," "you," "we," and "our" to create a bond with the audience.	First of all, I would like to bring a toy, or rather a miniature, of panda. Panda is our Chinese national treasure, and it's known to all that it is unique to our Chinese habitat, to our Chinese environment, to our Chinese climate. If you look at panda, under a cute appearance and a seemingly awkward movement, you can see that it's very composed in manner. It is at peace with other species and at peace with the environment. That is something we need to learn from the pandas.
The speaker's signpost indicates that he is moving to his second main point. His explanation of traditional Chinese painting is informed and illuminating.	Second, I would like to bring a man-made object, and it will be a traditional Chinese painting. I learned Chinese traditional painting in my childhood for years, and I hope it's done by me. When I learned that, I know that it is even more important to notice what is left unpainted on the picture. And also on the typical Chinese painting you also see a poem—and usually written in beautiful Chinese calligraphy—and also there is a seal there. And usually a Chinese painting will portray the beautiful Chinese landscape.
The speaker's third main point focuses on his dual identity as a Chinese citizen and a global citizen. His use of language is skillful and sophisticated.	And third, I would like to bring a map of the world. Well, some of you might be surprised. Why not a map of China? First and last, I know that I'm a Chinese man, but I'm also aware that in this age of increasing interconnectedness, I'm also a citizen of the world. I couldn't confine my horizons only within the Chinese borders; I need to look beyond that. I also should know that there are vast areas of seas and lands beyond our borders, and it is important that we reach out and understand them.
	And that's all. Thank you.

Question-and-Answer Session

At major speech competitions, speakers are usually queried by a panel of question masters, commentators, or challengers after either the prepared speech or the impromptu speech. Here are some examples of questions from recent competitions:

Unlike Western speech competitions, those in China usually include a question-and-answer session. Here Stephen E. Lucas, author of *The Art of Public Speaking*, queries a contestant at the 21st Century Cup.

To move from "Made in China" to "Created in China," what steps do you suggest Chinese enterprises take to move up the value chain and create sustainable product lines of their own?

If you join an Internet dating service, how would you describe yourself? What kind of picture would you paint?

In your speech, you mentioned the miserable job-seeking experience of some college graduates. In your view, what qualities should college graduates have so as to avoid such miserable experience?

What do you think a society will look like if divorce is disallowed?

PREPARATION AND PRESENTATION

As with the impromptu speech, you must practice for the Q&A session before you get to the competition. Look over your prepared speech and anticipate possible questions about it. When you practice the speech in front of other people, invite them to ask you questions. Make a list of the questions you come up with, as well as those asked by the people who listen to your speech. Then work out answers to the questions. Outline your answers to make sure you have thought them through fully and can answer them concisely within the one-minute time limit.

Once you have a set of potential questions and answers, practice delivering your answers orally. It is crucial that you do this on a regular basis. The more you practice answering questions, the more comfortable you will be on the day of the competition. As you practice, work on making your answers brief and to the point. Also work on delivering the answers with poise and confidence. As with other aspects of preparing for the competition, you should make a video recording as you practice for the Q&A session so you can identify weak spots and work on correcting them.

No matter how much you work ahead of time, of course, there is no way to predict exactly what questions you will receive during the contest. Be certain to listen carefully to the questions you are asked on the day of the competition. When faced with an unclear query, ask the question master or the challenger to restate the question. If you still don't understand, ask the questioner to give an example of what he or she means.

If you are given a question for which you have prepared in advance, consider yourself fortunate and make the most of your opportunity. Beware of the temptation, however, to recite an answer you have worked out ahead of time but that does not truly address the question posed to you. This is a sure way to lose points. Judges understand how difficult the Q&A session can be. They do not expect perfect answers, but they do expect answers that respond directly to the questions that are asked.

SAMPLE SPEECH WITH COMMENTARY

The following remarks illustrate the elements of a strong Q&A. The speaker is Ma Tingting, from Guangdong University of Foreign Studies. After her prepared speech at the 2004 CCTV Cup, in which she told the story of Sally, a university student who had committed suicide, she was asked the following question: "Is there something we can do about this problem, or must we accept the tragic situation of Sally—and all the other Sallies like her—as one of the inevitable costs of the quest for personal excellence or national achievement?" Tingting's answer is substantive, detailed, and directly responsive to the question. She presents it with poise, strong eye contact, and natural gestures.

Video 16.4
View "Preventing Suicide Among College Students."

Preventing Suicide Among College Students

COMMENTARY	SPEECH
It is customary to begin the Q&A by expressing thanks for the question.	Thank you for the question.
The speaker focuses primarily on steps universities can take to prevent student suicides. She presents each step clearly and straightforwardly.	Actually, there are some things we can do. For the universities, they can give lectures instructing students how to cope with the pressures in life. At the same time, they can hire psychotherapists to provide consulting services for these students in need. And lastly, they can employ a system called tutorship to let the students have more contact with their teachers. They're experienced in life, so through this contact students can learn something from their teachers and cope with the pressures in life.
The speaker ends by mentioning the role of family and friends in suicide prevention.	At the same time, family and friends are also a way to help solve this problem. They can offer a helping hand for the students in need, and listen to them.

Debate

As in the West, debate tournaments in China are usually team events that are held separately from public speaking competitions. However, the national finals of the CCTV Cup English Speaking Contest includes debates between individual contestants and a panel of three challengers. The debate takes place immediately after each student's impromptu speech. Students must defend the position taken in the impromptu speech against the challengers' queries and counterarguments. Criteria for judging include substance of response, use of supporting materials, command of grammar and vocabulary, and quickness and persuasiveness of arguments.

STRATEGIES AND TECHNIQUES

Debates at the CCTV Cup require all the skills used in Q&A and impromptu speaking, but they present additional challenges. Foremost is sustaining your argument across the three-minute debate. This is not a matter of simply repeating your main points over and over. Rather, you must be able to counter the debate panel's questions and challenges by expanding upon and extending the position taken in your impromptu speech.

Ideally, you will be able to do so by drawing upon appropriate examples, statistics, and/or testimony. As we saw in Chapter 6, these kinds of supporting materials are important in any kind of speech, but they are especially vital in debate. They can be used both to strengthen your position and to weaken that of the challengers. For example, if you contend that smoking should be banned in all public buildings, you will make a stronger impression if you can cite statistics showing the health dangers from smoking, or testimony from experts supporting a ban on smoking in public facilities.

As the debate proceeds, keep track of how the challengers respond to your evidence. If they do not contest it, be sure to point that out. You might say something like the following:

> You raise a legitimate question about the convenience of nonsmoking laws. But before answering that question, I want to point out that everyone on the debate panel appears to accept the testimony I presented earlier from medical experts who believe that banning smoking in public places would help reduce the number of smoking-related deaths and illnesses throughout China. Even though such a ban might be inconvenient for some people, how can we place convenience above preserving health and saving lives?

Reasoning is another crucial weapon in debate. As we saw in Chapter 14, the four methods of reasoning used most often in public speaking are reasoning from specific instances, reasoning from principle, causal reasoning, and analogical reasoning. You should be familiar with all four and know how to use them soundly and persuasively. Consider, for example, the topic we looked at earlier in this section: Should smoking be banned in public buildings? All four methods of reasoning could come into play with regard to this topic, as follows:

Debates are one of the most exciting events at the CCTV Cup. Successful competitors are poised, confident, and quick-witted. They are also adept at using evidence and reasoning to defend their position against questions and challenges.

- Reasoning from specific instances: Are there sufficient cases of people who have been harmed by second-hand smoke to conclude that banning smoking from public buildings will improve public health?
- Reasoning from principle: How does one balance the right of people to work and socialize in a healthy environment against the right of people to smoke in places where they work and socialize?
- Causal reasoning: Is there a demonstrated causal connection between smoking in public buildings and health problems among nonsmokers?
- Analogical reasoning: What lessons for China can be drawn from the experience of Western countries in which smoking has been banned in public buildings?

Any of these questions could arise in the ebb and flow of debate. Recognizing the kind of reasoning involved in each case will allow you to make a stronger argument for your position and, perhaps, to spot weaknesses in the arguments of the debate panel.

The same is true with regard to the fallacies discussed in Chapter 14. If you can point out instances in which the challengers commit a particular fallacy, you will receive credit from the judges. Consider the following response to a challenger's statement that many people in China oppose a ban on smoking in public buildings:

> Just because a large number of people support or oppose a given policy cannot be taken as evidence that the policy is right or wrong. This is an error in reasoning known as the bandwagon fallacy. The question is not what is popular, but what is right. Earlier in this debate, I gave you evidence from medical authorities documenting that banning smoking in public buildings will improve public health. That is the right thing to do, regardless of its popularity.

In addition, you could go on to address the challenger's popularity point by making an analogy:

> We know from the experience of Western countries that public opinion initially opposed bans on smoking in public buildings. But once those laws were enacted and people saw their benefits, the overwhelming majority came to support the laws. Just as attitudes in China have changed about many things in recent years, so eventually will they change on the subject of smoking in public buildings.

This kind of one-two punch puts you in a position of logical superiority and makes it even harder for the opposition to respond.

PREPARATION AND PRACTICE

Coming up with effective responses in the midst of a debate is not easy. It takes a great deal of knowledge, poise, self-assurance, and practice. As we discussed in the section on impromptu speaking, acquiring knowledge is a matter of sustained and systematic inquiry. You need to read broadly, think deeply, and seek ideas from a wide range of sources. No aspect of preparing for debate is more important than developing a strong, flexible fund of knowledge that will help you respond to the wide range of subjects that can arise in debate.

Of course, you also need to develop your debate skills so you can apply your knowledge effectively. Even though the debate topic is the same as that for your impromptu speech, you should probably not begin by practicing both at the same time. Work first on impromptu speaking. Once you have acquired confidence in that event, add debating to your practice sessions. After giving a sample impromptu speech, ask your tutor or classmates to engage in debate with you following the same format as the CCTV Cup. Do not look for easy questions. Instead, ask for tough, probing queries that will sharpen your wits and prepare you for the rigors of competition. Record your practice sessions on video so you can see what works most effectively and what most needs improvement.

As you practice, pay special attention to your rate of speech and the pitch of your voice. When speaking in English, some Chinese students have a tendency to talk faster and faster as a debate heats up. In the process, the pitch of their voice often becomes higher and higher, especially among female speakers. These vocal characteristics can make the speaker appear nervous and disorganized. Although there is no perfect rate for any kind of speech, effective debaters usually maintain a controlled pace, which helps them appear poised and confident despite the stress of the situation.

In addition, take time to view debates from previous CCTV Cups. If a given speaker is not effective, try to determine why. If he or she is effective, try to pick out techniques you can use yourself. Pay attention to the speaker's method of argument as well as to delivery. How does the speaker frame his or her responses to the debate panel? What methods does she or he employ when dealing with difficult questions? Notice how effective debaters maneuver out of difficult spots and expose weaknesses in the challengers' points without being disrespectful. As you watch, think of strategies you can use in your own debates, and then make a conscious effort to rehearse those strategies in your practice sessions.

SAMPLE SPEECH WITH COMMENTARY

The following selection from the 2007 CCTV Cup illustrates the dynamic give-and-take of effective debate.[1] The speaker is Wang Liansi, from Hunan University. In her impromptu speech, she had argued that people educated in foreign universities are not entitled to a higher salary when they return to China for work. Two of her challengers in the debate, Beijing Foreign Studies University professor Teng Jimeng and CCTV anchor Rui Chenggang, received their degrees abroad. Rather than being intimidated, Wang Liansi held her ground superbly, spoke calmly and confidently, and supported her position with pertinent examples and quick-witted reasoning. Her performance won her an audience choice award and earned her the top score for any speaker during the first three days of the competition.

Video 16.5

View "Are People Educated Overseas Entitled to a Higher Salary?"

Are People Educated Overseas Entitled to a Higher Salary?

COMMENTARY	SPEECH
The opening challenge presents three points against Wang Liansi's position that foreign-educated students do not deserve higher salaries than those educated in China.	**Teng Jimeng:** I think you are sadly wrong in terms of saying that they do not deserve the high salary. On the contrary, we argue for a high salary for these returnees, first things first, for the international exposure, and secondly, the kind of state-of-the-art expertise and knowledge they bring back to China, or maybe any other countries. Thirdly, they are also very well known for using interpersonal skills in communicating.
Wang Liansi responds to the challenger's points clearly and systematically. She begins by defending the communication skills of college students educated in China.	**Wang Liansi:** Well, you do have a point. However, you mentioned that they have communication skills, but are you trying to say that these employees, these college students who are studying in China, do not have the communication skills? No. I am a college student. I study in Hunan University, but I don't see that I'm in lack of any communication skills.
By enumerating her points, Wang Liansi comes across as a focused and organized thinker. She states her points clearly and concisely.	And secondly, you mentioned that they are exposed to foreign cultures, so they have a state-of-the-art expertise. But you have to know that China's higher education is also flourishing. Peking University, Tsinghua University, as well as universities in Hong Kong, can also compete with foreign universities as well.
Wang Liansi echoes an analogy from her impromptu speech, in which she said that students educated overseas were like foreign fruits: "No matter how far away they come from, how fragrant they smell, how exotic they look, what counts most is whether they're delicious enough."	And the third point I remember you said was they are more professional. But, you know, many people refer to the returnees from overseas as bananas. They have yellow skins, but inside they are white. But personally, I don't like to eat bananas, and I doubt that those employers in the companies will like bananas. We need apples; we need other common fruits as well.

	Teng Jimeng: What's wrong with being a banana, as long as we can kind of reach a deal?
Again using analogical reasoning, Wang Liansi responds deftly to the challenger's question by defending the principle of equal treatment versus special privilege.	**Wang Liansi:** Being a banana is fine, but are you willing to pay like ten yuan for a banana, when you can enjoy the same nutrition by paying five yuan for an apple? Of course not. I mean each kind of fruit should be treated equally, and it doesn't mean that if you are a banana, you have to be paid a higher price or you are in any way superior to those common fruits.
	Rui Chenggang: If you are a Harvard business school MBA and you are working in Beijing, you are entitled to a salary amounting to 100,000 U.S. dollars. You have a problem with that?
Wang Liansi does not get flustered, even though she is cut off part way through her response.	**Wang Liansi:** I don't have a problem with that, as long as he has the ability. We are talking about whether these returnees . . .
	Rui Chenggang: But his salary will be much higher than the same MBA from Peking University and Tsinghua University. . . .
	Teng Jimeng: Right. Think about Yang Lan, for example. She actually is now the head of a corporation, a kind of multinational corporation. And she is a graduate from Columbia University.
Wang Liansi scores strongly by countering the challenger's example of Yang Lan with the case of Liu Xin, CCTV anchor and hostess of the 2007 competition.	**Wang Liansi:** Yang Lan is very successful, but our hostess Liu Xin is also very successful. Do you remember that she has won the first prize in the international English speaking competition? That was about a decade, or ten years ago. At that time, she had never been abroad, but she competed with those people who have international backgrounds and she won. What's your opinion about it?
	Rui Chenggang: Many good students educated overseas have a very heavy student loan. That's why they have to have a higher salary—to pay back the student loan. They are paying a very high price for going to top schools in the world.
Wang Liansi supports her position by drawing on her personal experience. As elsewhere in the debate, she rises to every challenge from the debate panel.	**Wang Liansi:** According to my observation in Sydney, I saw a lot of Chinese students there, but I haven't seen them with any particular advantages of being an international student. They didn't work very hard. They were very rich students, so they went to Sydney, but they didn't study well. But students around me, my classmates, they've been working really hard, and I believe that in future, when they are applying for the same company, the latter, the person who has real ability, can have a higher salary.

SUMMARY

Speech competitions are exciting events for participants and spectators alike. They require competitors to think on their feet, to analyze topics quickly and clearly, and to use English effectively in formulating and communicating ideas.

The prepared speech requires all the skills of public speaking discussed earlier in this book, but it also needs the spark of creativity. That creativity can be manifested in particular passages or sections of the speech, or it can run throughout the entire speech, from beginning to end. The aim is to be resourceful in making your speech stand out positively in the judges' minds.

Success in the impromptu speech is based above all on firm knowledge, clear thinking, and sharp organization. It should be delivered at a deliberate pace with poise, composure, and strong eye contact. If you practice impromptu speaking on a regular basis, you will find it much less stressful when the day of competition arrives.

Question-and-answer sessions also require systematic practice and preparation. Anticipate possible questions about your prepared speech and sketch out answers in advance. At the competition, listen carefully to the question master and answer the specific question you are asked.

Speech competitions may also include debates between individual contestants and a panel of challengers. The strategic use of evidence and reasoning is vital in these debates, as is a poised and confident delivery. Successful debaters also need a strong and flexible fund of knowledge that they can draw upon when responding to the many questions and challenges that arise during a debate.

Videos 16.6–16.8
View more sample speeches in competitions.

KEY TERMS

micro-creativity *(237)*   macro-creativity *(237)*

Key-Term Exercise
Check your knowledge with the Key-Term Exercise for this chapter.

EXERCISES FOR THINKING AND SPEAKING

1. View the videos of each of the sample speeches with commentary printed in this chapter. Which speech, in your judgment, has the strongest delivery, and why? Be prepared to share your comments in class.

2. Below are topics from recent national speech competitions:

   Living with Globalization

   The Greatest Invention in My Eyes

   College Education in Today's Competitive World

   My Definition of Success

   Select one of these topics and write an original 2-minute prepared speech that is clearly organized and creatively developed. Deliver your speech in class. Be ready for a Q&A session following the speech.

3. Get together with three or four peers and compose a list of five impromptu topics. Each of you should give a 1-minute practice speech on one of these topics. Critique each other's performances, noting both the strong points and the points that need improvement. Deliver your speeches again in light of the comments you received.

4. Using the same groups as in Exercise 3, practice debating, as follows: After each member of the group gives his or her impromptu speech, the other members of the group should act as a debate panel and pose questions to the speaker. Each debate should last 4–5 minutes, including the time used for questions.

Public Speaking in Your Career

As a recent university graduate with strong English public speaking skills, you are excited when you learn that CCTV-9 is holding open tryouts for a new public affairs show designed for young people. Part of the tryout will involve a debate with current CCTV anchors and commentators on a topic of the job candidate's choice. Select your topic and prepare a 1-minute speech on it. After you have written the speech, identify three questions that you anticipate might be asked in response to it. Prepare concise, convincing answers to the questions.

Speeches for Appreciation and Analysis

Appendix

I Have a Dream

Martin Luther King, Jr.

Martin Luther King's "I Have a Dream" is widely regarded as a masterpiece. It was delivered August 28, 1963, to some 200,000 people who had come to Washington, D.C., to participate in a peaceful demonstration to further the cause of equal rights for African Americans. King spoke from the steps of the Lincoln Memorial, in the "symbolic shadow" of Abraham Lincoln, and the crowd filled the vast area between the Memorial and the Washington Monument. In addition, millions of Americans watched the speech on television or listened to it on the radio.

Like most ceremonial addresses, "I Have a Dream" is relatively short. Although it took King only 16 minutes to deliver the speech, he prepared it more carefully than any other speech in his career to that time. His purpose was to set forth as succinctly and as eloquently as possible the guiding principles of the civil rights movement, and to reinforce the commitment of his listeners to those principles.

One of the most interesting features of the speech is King's use of language to make the abstract principles of liberty and equality clear and compelling. Throughout, King relies on familiar, concrete words that create sharp, vivid images. He uses many more metaphors than do most speakers, but they are appropriate to the occasion and help to dramatize his ideas. Finally, he makes extensive use of repetition and parallelism to reinforce his message and to enhance the momentum of the speech.

If you have heard a recording of "I Have a Dream," you know its impact was heightened by King's delivery. In his rich baritone voice, marked by the fervor of the crusader and modulated by the cadences of the Southern Baptist preacher, King gained the total involvement of his audience. As William Robert Miller says, "The crowd more than listened, it participated, and before King had reached his last phrase, a torrent of applause was already welling up."

1 I am happy to join with you today in what will go down in history as the greatest demonstration for freedom in the history of our nation.

2 Five score years ago, a great American, in whose symbolic shadow we stand today, signed the Emancipation Proclamation. This momentous decree came as a great beacon light of hope to millions of Negro slaves, who had been seared in the flames of withering injustice. It came as a joyous daybreak to end the long night of their captivity.

3 But one hundred years later, the Negro still is not free. One hundred years later, the life of the Negro is still sadly crippled by the manacles of segregation and the chains of discrimination. One hundred years later, the Negro lives on a lonely island of poverty in the midst of a vast ocean of material prosperity. One hundred years later, the Negro is still languished in the corners of American society and finds himself an exile in his own land. And so we've come here today to dramatize a shameful condition.

4 In a sense we've come to our nation's Capitol to cash a check. When the architects of our republic wrote the magnificent words of the Constitution and the Declaration of Independence, they were signing a promissory note to which every American was to fall heir. This note was a promise that all men—yes, black men as well as white

men—would be guaranteed the unalienable rights of life, liberty, and the pursuit of happiness.

5 It is obvious today that America has defaulted on this promissory note insofar as her citizens of color are concerned. Instead of honoring this sacred obligation, America has given the Negro people a bad check—a check which has come back marked "insufficient funds."

6 But we refuse to believe that the bank of justice is bankrupt. We refuse to believe that there are insufficient funds in the great vaults of opportunity of this nation. And so we've come to cash this check—a check that will give us upon demand the riches of freedom and the security of justice.

7 We have also come to this hallowed spot to remind America of the fierce urgency of now. This is no time to engage in the luxury of cooling off or to take the tranquilizing drug of gradualism. Now is the time to make real the promises of democracy. Now is the time to rise from the dark and desolate valley of segregation to the sunlit path of racial justice. Now is the time to lift our nation from the quicksands of racial injustice to the solid rock of brotherhood. Now is the time to make justice a reality for all of God's children.

8 It would be fatal for the nation to overlook the urgency of the moment. This sweltering summer of the Negro's legitimate discontent will not pass until there is an invigorating autumn of freedom and equality. Nineteen sixty-three is not an end, but a beginning. Those who hope that the Negro needed to blow off steam and will now be content will have a rude awakening if the nation returns to business as usual. There will be neither rest nor tranquility in America until the Negro is granted his citizenship rights. The whirlwinds of revolt will continue to shake the foundations of our nation until the bright day of justice emerges.

9 But there is something that I must say to my people, who stand on the warm threshold which leads into the palace of justice. In the process of gaining our rightful place, we must not be guilty of wrongful deeds. Let us not seek to satisfy our thirst for freedom by drinking from the cup of bitterness and hatred.

10 We must forever conduct our struggle on the high plane of dignity and discipline. We must not allow our creative protest to degenerate into physical violence. Again and again we must rise to the majestic heights of meeting physical force with soul force.

11 The marvelous new militancy which has engulfed the Negro community must not lead us to a distrust of all white people. For many of our white brothers, as evidenced by their presence here today, have come to realize that their destiny is tied up with our destiny. They have come to realize that their freedom is inextricably bound to our freedom. We cannot walk alone.

12 As we walk, we must make the pledge that we shall always march ahead. We cannot turn back. There are those who are asking the devotees of civil rights, "When will you be satisfied?" We can never be satisfied as long as the Negro is the victim of the unspeakable horrors of police brutality. We can never be satisfied as long as our bodies, heavy with the fatigue of travel, cannot gain lodging in the motels of the highways and the hotels of the cities. We cannot be satisfied as long as the Negro's basic mobility is from a smaller ghetto to a larger one. We can never be satisfied as

long as our children are stripped of their selfhood and robbed of their dignity by signs stating "For Whites Only." We cannot be satisfied as long as a Negro in Mississippi cannot vote and a Negro in New York believes he has nothing for which to vote. No, no, we are not satisfied, and we will not be satisfied until justice rolls down like waters, and righteousness like a mighty stream.

13 I am not unmindful that some of you have come here out of great trials and tribulations. Some of you have come fresh from narrow jail cells. Some of you have come from areas where your quest for freedom left you battered by the storms of persecution and staggered by the winds of police brutality. You have been the veterans of creative suffering. Continue to work with the faith that unearned suffering is redemptive.

14 Go back to Mississippi, go back to Alabama, go back to South Carolina, go back to Georgia, go back to Louisiana, go back to the slums and ghettos of our Northern cities, knowing that somehow this situation can and will be changed. Let us not wallow in the valley of despair.

15 I say to you today, my friends, so even though we face the difficulties of today and tomorrow, I still have a dream. It is a dream deeply rooted in the American dream.

16 I have a dream that one day this nation will rise up and live out the true meaning of its creed, "We hold these truths to be self-evident, that all men are created equal."

17 I have a dream that one day on the red hills of Georgia the sons of former slaves and the sons of former slaveowners will be able to sit down together at the table of brotherhood.

18 I have a dream that one day even the state of Mississippi, a state sweltering with the heat of injustice, sweltering with the heat of oppression, will be transformed into an oasis of freedom and justice.

19 I have a dream that my four little children will one day live in a nation where they will not be judged by the color of their skin but by the content of their character. I have a dream today.

20 I have a dream that one day, down in Alabama, with its vicious racists, with its governor having his lips dripping with the words of interposition and nullification, one day right there in Alabama little black boys and black girls will be able to join hands with little white boys and white girls as sisters and brothers. I have a dream today.

21 I have a dream that one day every valley shall be exalted, every hill and mountain shall be made low, the rough places will be made plane and the crooked places will be made straight, and the glory of the Lord shall be revealed, and all flesh shall see it together.

22 This is our hope. This is the faith that I go back to the South with. With this faith we will be able to hew out of the mountain of despair a stone of hope. With this faith we will be able to transform the jangling discords of our nation into a beautiful symphony of brotherhood. With this faith we will be able to work together, to pray together, to struggle together, to go to jail together, to stand up for freedom together, knowing that we will be free one day.

23 This will be the day—this will be the day when all of God's children will be able to sing with new meaning, "My country 'tis of thee, sweet land of liberty, of thee I sing. Land where my fathers died, land of the pilgrim's pride, from every mountainside, let freedom ring." And if America is to be a great nation, this must become true.

24 So let freedom ring from the prodigious hilltops of New Hampshire. Let freedom ring from the mighty mountains of New York. Let freedom ring from the heightening Alleghenies of Pennsylvania!

25 Let freedom ring from the snowcapped Rockies of Colorado! Let freedom ring from the curvaceous slopes of California!

26 But not only that. Let freedom ring from Stone Mountain of Georgia!

27 Let freedom ring from Lookout Mountain of Tennessee!

28 Let freedom ring from every hill and molehill of Mississippi. From every mountainside, let freedom ring.

29 And when this happens, when we allow freedom ring—when we let it ring from every village and every hamlet, from every state and every city—we will be able to speed up that day when all of God's children, black men and white men, Jews and Gentiles, Protestants and Catholics, will be able to join hands and sing in the words of the old Negro spiritual, "Free at last! Free at last! Thank God almighty, we are free at last!"

Cultural Programs and the 2008 Olympic Games

Yang Lan

A television star, journalist, and businesswoman, Yang Lan is also one of China's foremost cultural ambassadors. Her intelligence, refinement, and English public speaking skills have drawn praise from audiences around the globe. A longtime supporter of the Olympic movement in China, she was a natural choice to be a member of the delegation that presented Beijing's bid to host the 2008 Games.

Video A.1

View "Cultural Programs and the 2008 Olympic Games."

Delivered in Moscow on July 13, 2001, her speech to the International Olympic Committee preceded the closing address by delegation chair He Zhenliang. Focusing on cultural aspects of the bid, she explained that holding the Games in Beijing would celebrate the universal aspirations of humanity and would enhance harmony between China and the diverse cultures of the world. "You are going to have a great time in Beijing," she promised. "Beijing will prove to be a land of wonders to . . . athletes, spectators, and the worldwide television audience alike. Come and join us."

The speech was elegant, personable, and uplifting. Yang Lan's command of English was pitch-perfect, and her conversational tone was highly pleasing. Her remarks had been revised and rehearsed countless times, but they came across as fresh and invigorating. Other speakers explained why China should receive the bid; Yang Lan made listeners *want* to come to Beijing.

To ensure accuracy, the text of this speech has been transcribed from a video recording.

1 Mr. President, ladies and gentlemen, good afternoon. Before I introduce our cultural programs, let me tell you one thing first about 2008: You are going to have a great time in Beijing.

2 Many people are fascinated by China's sports legends in history. For example, back to Song Dynasty, which was the 11th century, people in our country started to play a game called *cuju*, which is regarded as the origin of ancient football. The game

was so popular that women were also participating. So now you will probably understand why our women's football team does so well today.

3 There are a lot more wonderful and exciting events waiting for you in the new Beijing, a modern metropolis with 3,000 years of cultural treasures woven into the urban tapestry. Along with the iconic imagery of the Forbidden City, the Temple of Heaven, and the Great Wall, the city also offers an endless mixture of theatres, museums, discos, all kinds of restaurants and shopping malls, which will amaze you and delight you.

4 But beyond all of that, this is a city of millions of friendly people who love to meet people from around the world. They believe that if the 2008 Olympics is held in Beijing, it will help to enhance the harmony between our culture and the diverse cultures of the world. And I guarantee, their gratitude will pour out in open expressions of affection for you and the great movement that you guide.

5 Within our cultural programs, education and communication will receive the highest priority. We seek to create an intellectual and sporting legacy by broadening the understanding of the Olympic ideals throughout the country.

6 Cultural events will unfold each year from 2005 to 2008. We will stage multi-disciplined cultural programs, including concerts, exhibitions, art competitions, and camps, which will involve young people from around the world. During the Olympics, these activities will also be held in the Olympic Village, and in the city, for the benefit of the athletes.

7 Our ceremonies will give China's greatest—and the world's greatest—artists a chance to celebrate the common aspiration of humanity and the unique heritage of Chinese culture and that of the Olympic movement.

8 With a concept inspired by the famed Silk Road, our torch relay will break new ground, traveling from Olympia through some of the oldest civilizations known to man—Greek, Roman, Egyptian, Byzantine, Mesopotamian, Persian, Arabian, Indian, and Chinese. Carrying the message "Share the Peace, Share the Olympics," the eternal flame will reach new heights as it crosses the Himalayas over the world's highest summit, Mount Qomolangma, which is known to many of you as Mount Everest. In China, the torch will pass through Tibet, cross Yangtze and Yellow Rivers, travel the Great Wall, and visit Hong Kong, Macau, Taiwan, and the 56 ethnic communities who make up our society. On its journey, the flame will be seen by and inspire more human beings than any previous relay.

9 I am afraid I cannot give you the full picture of our cultural programs within such a short period of time. Before I end, let me share with you one story. Seven hundred years ago, amazed by his incredible description of a faraway land of great beauty, people asked Marco Polo whether his stories about China were true. And Marco answered: What I have told you was not even half of what I saw. Actually, what we have shown you here today is only a fraction of the Beijing that awaits you.

10 Ladies and gentlemen, I believe Beijing will prove to be a land of wonders to all of you—to athletes, spectators, and the worldwide television audience alike. Come and join us.

11 Thank you, Mr. President. Thank you all. Now, I would like to give the floor back to Mr. He.

Choices and Change

Barbara Bush

Barbara Bush's commencement address at Wellesley College on June 1, 1990, was ranked among the top 50 American speeches of the 20th century. Bush was invited to speak by the senior class when their first choice, Alice Walker, author of *The Color Purple*, could not attend. In protest, about 150 students, one-fourth of the graduating class, signed a petition charging that Bush was not a good role model for career-oriented women and had "gained recognition through the achievements of her husband," President George H. W. Bush.

The petition touched off a storm of controversy. Throughout the month before Bush's speech, educators, newspaper columnists, politicians, and others debated the petition and the larger issue of women's role in American society. The media spotlight became so bright that Bush's speech was broadcast live by all the major television networks. Adding to the occasion was the presence of Raisa Gorbachev, wife of Russian President Mikhail Gorbachev, who was in America for a state visit.

Video A.2
View "Choices and Change."

In her speech, Bush dealt with one of the most important issues facing modern women—how to balance their careers with their commitments to friends and family. With a blend of grace and humor, she explained the choices she had made in her life, talked about the importance of friends and family, and stressed the values of tolerance, diversity, and compassion. She capped off her remarks by suggesting that someone in the audience might follow in her footsteps and one day preside over the White House as the president's spouse. "I wish him well," she added, to thunderous cheering and applause.

Bush's performance won rave reviews. NBC News anchor Tom Brokaw called it "one of the best commencement speeches I've ever heard," while the *New York Times* judged it "a triumph." Many Wellesley students who had been critical of Bush beforehand were also impressed. "She was wonderful and funny," one of them stated. "She could have addressed more women's issues, but she was sincere and she won our hearts."

The text of this speech is taken from a recording and includes a number of impromptu comments and other changes from the version published in the press.

1 Thank you very, very much, President Keohane; Mrs. Gorbachev; trustees; faculty; parents; and, I should say, Julia Porter, class president; and certainly my new best friend, Christine Bicknell. And, of course, the Class of 1990.

2 I'm really thrilled to be here today and very excited, as I know all of you must be, that Mrs. Gorbachev could join us. These are exciting times. They're exciting in Washington, and I had really looked forward to coming to Wellesley. I thought it was going to be fun; I never dreamt it would be this much fun. So thank you for that.

3 More than 10 years ago, when I was invited here to talk about our experiences in the People's Republic of China, I was struck by both the natural beauty of your campus and the spirit of this place. Wellesley, you see, is not just a place, but an idea—an experiment in excellence in which diversity is not just tolerated but is embraced.

4 The essence of this spirit was captured in a moving speech about tolerance given last year by a student body president of one of your sister colleges. She related the story by Robert Fulghum about a young pastor who, finding himself in charge of

some very energetic children, hits upon the game called Giants, Wizards, and Dwarfs. "You have to decide now," the pastor instructed the children, "which you are—a giant, a wizard or a dwarf."

5 At that, a small girl tugging at his pants leg asks, "But where do the mermaids stand?" And the pastor tells her there are no mermaids. And she says, "Oh yes there are; I am a mermaid."

6 Now, this little girl knew what she was, and she was not about to give up on either her identity or the game. She intended to take her place wherever mermaids fit into the scheme of things. Where do the mermaids stand—all of those who are different, those who do not fit the boxes and the pigeonholes? "Answer that question," wrote Fulghum, "and you can build a school, a nation, or a whole world."

7 As that very wise young woman said, "Diversity, like anything worth having, requires effort." Effort to learn about and respect difference, to be compassionate with one another, to cherish our own identity, and to accept unconditionally the same in others. You should all be very proud that this is the Wellesley spirit.

8 Now, I know your first choice today was Alice Walker—guess how I know!—known for *The Color Purple*. Instead you got me—known for the color of my hair. Alice Walker's book has a special resonance here. At Wellesley, each class is known by a special color. For four years, the class of '90 has worn the color purple. Today, you meet on Severance Green to say goodbye to all of that, to begin a new and a very personal journey to search for your own true colors.

9 In the world that awaits you beyond the shores of Lake Waban, no one can say what your true colors will be. But this I do know: You have a first-class education from a first-class school. And so you need not, probably cannot, live a paint-by-numbers life. Decisions are not irrevocable. Choices do come back. And as you set off from Wellesley, I hope that many of you will consider making three very special choices.

10 The first is to believe in something larger than yourself, to get involved in some of the big ideas of our time. I chose literacy because I honestly believe that if more people could read, write, and comprehend, we would be that much closer to solving so many of the problems that plague our nation and our society.

11 And early on I made another choice, which I hope you'll make as well. Whether you're talking about education, career, or service, you're talking about life, and life really must have joy. It's supposed to be fun.

12 One of the reasons I made the most important decision of my life—to marry George Bush—is because he made me laugh. It's true, sometimes we've laughed through our tears, but that shared laughter has been one of our strongest bonds. Find the joy in life because, as Ferris Bueller said on his day off, "Life moves pretty fast, and if you don't stop and look around once in a while, you're gonna miss it." (I'm not going to tell George you clapped more for Ferris than you clapped for George!)

13 The third choice that must not be missed is to cherish your human connections, your relationships with family and friends. For several years, you've had impressed upon you the importance to your career of dedication and hard work—and, of course, that's true. But as important as your obligations as a doctor, a lawyer, a business leader will be, you are a human being first, and those human connections—with spouses, with children, with friends—are the most important investment you will ever make.

14 At the end of your life, you will never regret not having passed one more test, winning one more verdict, or not closing one more deal. You will regret time not spent with a husband, a child, a friend, or a parent.

15 We are in a transitional period right now, fascinating and exhilarating times, learning to adjust to changes and the choices we—men and women—are facing. As an example, I remember what a friend said on hearing her husband complain to his buddies that he had to babysit. Quickly setting him straight, my friend told her husband that when it's your own kids, it's not called babysitting!

16 Now, maybe we should adjust faster; maybe we should adjust slower. But whatever the era, whatever the times, one thing will never change: Fathers and mothers, if you have children, they must come first. You must read to your children and you must hug your children and you must love your children. Your success as a family, our success as a society, depends not on what happens in the White House, but on what happens inside your house.

17 For over 50 years, it was said that the winner of Wellesley's annual hoop race would be the first to get married. Now they say the winner will be the first to become a CEO. Both of those stereotypes show too little tolerance for those who want to know where the mermaids stand.

18 So I want to offer a new legend: The winner of the hoop race will be the first to realize her dream. Not society's dreams—her own personal dream. And who knows? Somewhere out in this audience may even be someone who will one day follow in my footsteps and preside over the White House as the president's spouse. And I wish him well!

19 Well, the controversy ends here, but our conversation is only beginning. And a worthwhile conversation it has been. So as you leave Wellesley today, take with you deep thanks for the courtesy and the honor you have shared with Mrs. Gorbachev and with me. Thank you. God bless you. And may your future be worthy of your dreams.

Yes, We Can

Barack Obama

Many factors contributed to Barack Obama's election as President of the United States, but none was more important than his remarkable gifts as an orator. At every step of the way from his emergence on the national stage in July 2004 to his election in November 2008, he was propelled forward by speeches that appealed to the country's desire for change and hope for a better future. Millions of Americans thrilled to his message and saw him as a refreshing new leader who could restore the nation's vitality and sense of purpose.

There is no better example of Obama's ability to energize listeners than his "Yes, We Can" speech of January 8, 2008, the night he lost the New Hampshire Democratic Party primary to Hillary Clinton. Given Clinton's experience and name recognition, most experts predicted that she would overpower Obama as the campaign proceeded into other states. Knowing that he could not allow his supporters to become discouraged, Obama responded with the most inspiring speech of his campaign.

Rather than dwelling on the loss in New Hampshire, he focused on everything the campaign had achieved so far in the face of steep odds. The desire for change, he said, was creating a "new American majority" whose creed was "Yes, We Can." Using his voice in perfect harmony with his words, he repeated the phrase "Yes, We Can" in multiple sentences as the audience chanted it in response. "Together," he concluded, "we will begin the next great chapter in the American story with three words that will ring from coast to coast, from sea to shining sea: Yes, we can."

The impact of the speech was electric, both on the immediate audience in Nashua, New Hampshire, and on the millions of people who watched it on national television. From that point on, "Yes, We Can" became the mantra of Obama's campaign, and today it is part of the global lexicon.

1 Thank you. Thank you. Well, first of all I want to congratulate Senator Clinton on a hard-fought victory here in New Hampshire. She did an outstanding job. Give her a big round of applause.

2 You know, a few weeks ago, no one imagined that we'd have accomplished what we did here tonight in New Hampshire. No one could have imagined it. For most of this campaign, we were far behind, and we always knew our climb would be steep. But in record numbers, you came out and you spoke up for change. And with your voices and your votes, you made it clear that at this moment, in this election, there is something happening in America.

3 There is something happening when men and women in Des Moines and Davenport, in Lebanon and Concord, come out in the snows of January to wait in lines that stretch block after block because they believe in what this country can be.

4 There is something happening when Americans who are young in age and in spirit, who have never participated in politics before, turn out in numbers we have never seen because they know in their hearts that this time must be different.

5 There is something happening when people vote not just for the party that they belong to, but for the hopes that they hold in common—that whether we are rich or poor, black or white, Latino or Asian, whether we hail from Iowa or New Hampshire, Nevada or South Carolina, we are ready to take this country in a fundamentally new direction. That's what's happening in America right now. Change is what's happening in America.

6 You, all of you who are here tonight, all who put so much heart and soul and work into this campaign, you can be the new majority who can lead this nation out of a long political darkness—Democrats, Independents, and Republicans who are tired of the division and distraction that has clouded Washington, who know that we can disagree without being disagreeable, who understand that if we mobilize our voices to challenge the money and influence that's stood in our way and challenge ourselves to reach for something better, there is no problem we cannot solve, there is no destiny that we cannot fulfill.

7 Our new American majority can end the outrage of unaffordable, unavailable health care in our time. We can bring doctors and patients, workers and businesses, Democrats and Republicans together, and we can tell the drug and insurance industry that while they get a seat at the table, they don't get to buy every chair. Not this time. Not now.

8 Our new majority can end the tax breaks for corporations that ship our jobs overseas, and put a middle-class tax cut in the pockets of working Americans who deserve it.

9 We can stop sending our children to schools with corridors of shame and start putting them on a pathway to success. We can stop talking about how great teachers are and start rewarding them for their greatness by giving them more pay and more support. We can do this with our new majority.

10 We can harness the ingenuity of farmers and scientists, citizens and entrepreneurs, to free this nation from the tyranny of oil and save our planet from a point of no return.

11 And when I am President of the United States, we will end this war in Iraq and bring our troops home. We will end this war in Iraq. We will bring our troops home. We will finish the job against al Qaeda in Afghanistan. We will care for our veterans. We will restore our moral standing in the world. And we will never use 9/11 as a way to scare up votes, because it is not a tactic to win an election, it is a challenge that should unite America and the world against the common threats of the 21st century—terrorism and nuclear weapons, climate change and poverty, genocide and disease.

12 All of the candidates in this race share these goals. All of the candidates in this race have good ideas. And all are patriots who serve this country honorably. But the reason our campaign has always been different, the reason we began this improbable journey almost a year ago, is because it's not just about what I will do as president, it is also about what you, the people who love this country, the citizens of the United States of America, can do to change it. That's what this election is all about.

13 That's why tonight belongs to you. It belongs to the organizers and the volunteers and the staff who believed in this journey and rallied so many others to join the cause. We know the battle ahead will be long, but always remember that no matter what obstacles stand in our way, nothing can stand in the way of the power of millions of voices calling for change.

14 We have been told we cannot do this by a chorus of cynics, and they will only grow louder and more dissonant in the weeks and months to come. We've been asked to pause for a reality check. We've been warned against offering the people of this nation false hope.

15 But in the unlikely story that is America, there has never been anything false about hope. For when we have faced down impossible odds, when we've been told we're not ready, or that we shouldn't try, or that we can't, generations of Americans have responded with a simple creed that sums up the spirit of a people: Yes, we can. Yes, we can. Yes, we can.

16 It was a creed written into the founding documents that declared the destiny of a nation. Yes, we can.

17 It was whispered by slaves and abolitionists as they blazed a trail towards freedom through the darkest of nights. Yes, we can.

18 It was sung by immigrants as they struck out from distant shores, and pioneers who pushed westward against an unforgiving wilderness. Yes, we can.

19 It was the call of workers who organized, women who reached for the ballot, a president who chose the moon as our new frontier, and a King who took us to the mountaintop and pointed the way to the Promised Land. Yes, we can to justice and equality. Yes, we can to opportunity and prosperity. Yes, we can heal this nation. Yes, we can repair this world. Yes, we can.

20 And so tomorrow, as we take the campaign south and west, as we learn that the struggles of the textile workers in Spartanburg are not so different than the plight of the dishwasher in Las Vegas, that the hopes of the little girl who goes to the crumbling school in Dillon are the same as the dreams of the boy who learns on the streets of L.A., we will remember that there is something happening in America—that we are not as divided as our politics suggest, that we are one people, we are one nation, and together we will begin the next great chapter in the American story with three words that will ring from coast to coast, from sea to shining sea: Yes, we can.

21 Thank you New Hampshire. Thank you.

Questions of Culture

Sajjid Zahir Chinoy

Seldom does a student commencement address upstage the featured speaker—especially when that speaker is a Pulitzer Prize winner from Harvard University. Yet that is exactly what happened when Sajjid Zahir Chinoy spoke to his fellow graduates at the University of Richmond on May 12, 1996.

Video A.3
View "Questions of Culture."

Born and raised near Bombay, India, Chinoy was selected to speak as the result of a campuswide competition. After describing the jumble of emotions that filled his mind as he came to the United States to attend school, he spoke movingly of the warm reception he received in Richmond and of how cultural differences can be overcome by attempting to understand other people.

Addressing his audience of 3,000 people extemporaneously and without notes, Chinoy received enthusiastic applause, and his remarks were widely reported in the press. His speech was so inspiring that the main speaker, Harvard psychiatrist Robert Coles, began his address by paying tribute to Chinoy. "I've been to a number of commencements," said Coles, "but I've never heard a speech quite like that."

After graduation, Chinoy attended graduate school at Stanford University, where he earned his PhD in economics. The text of his speech has been transcribed from a recording and is reprinted with permission from Chinoy and the University of Richmond.

1 Distinguished guests, faculty, staff, students, ladies and gentlemen, and, most of all, the Class of 1996:

2 I can visualize the scene again and again: 11:30 P.M., Saturday night, the fifteenth of August, 1992, Bombay International Airport, India. I was leaving home for the University of Richmond. And as I said that final goodbye to my parents, my family, and my friends; and as I saw hope, expectation, even a tinge of sadness, in their eyes; and as I stepped aboard the Boeing 747 in front, I knew my life had changed forever.

3 The next 36 hours on board the aircraft were a time of questions, of concerns, of tremendous uncertainty.

4 Had I made the right choice in leaving home? Had I made the right choice in leaving my parents, my family, my home? Had I made the right choice in leaving my country, my culture, my background? Had I made the right choice in choosing the University of Richmond?

5 And then, of course, there was that one nagging question, that one overriding concern: As one of only three Indian students on a Richmond campus of 3,000, would I ever fit in?

6 My country was different. My culture was different. My experiences were different. My background was different. My language was different. My accent was different. Would I ever fit in?

7 And so here I was, high above the clouds, grappling with questions of culture, of interaction, of ethnicity. What I didn't know was that 30,000 feet below, on the ground, the world was faced with these very same questions—the question of culture, the question of interaction, the question of ethnicity.

8 And so whether my aircraft took off from Bombay, where the Hindus and the Muslims lived together in a most fragile peace; or whether my aircraft was over Africa, where the Hutus and Tutsis of Rwanda and Burundi had long-standing animosity; or whether my aircraft was over Bosnia, where the Serbs, the Croats, the Muslims, and the Bosnians had broken yet another truce, the question was the same—could different cultures ever come together to reinforce one another?

9 Ladies and gentlemen, after that bumpy aircraft ride, this young Indian student had found his answer. He had been witness to the four most spectacular years of his life at the University of Richmond. The academics were great; the extracurriculars were great; his graduate plans were great.

10 But what left an indelible impact on his mind was none of this. No, instead it was those special moments, those moments of human interaction, those human relationships that can never quite be translated into words:

11 The time this young Indian student spent his first Thanksgiving dinner with his debate team coach. That Thanksgiving evening when I ate my first American turkey and saw my first American football game, not knowing the difference between a tackle and a touchdown. And yet, all of a sudden, just like that, this very different Indian student had become an inherent part of the great American tradition of giving thanks.

12 The time I spent my first Christmas Eve with my journalism professor. That Christmas evening when the relationship wasn't of a faculty member and a student anymore, but of two buddies who fought fiercely over every point in Ping-Pong.

13 The time I had a long and honest talk with an American friend on the eve of a calculus exam. I didn't learn much calculus that night, but what I did learn was that as different as we are—different countries, different cultures, different continents—inherently we are still the same.

14 The time in December 1992 when India was hit by communal riots, when violence and bloodshed were but a few hundred yards from my family and my home, and when my fantastic roommate from my freshman year sat up the entire night, giving me hope, strength, and courage at every step.

15 Yes, four years after that bumpy aircraft ride, I have found the answer to the question of culture.

16 I have found that it has taken just a little understanding, just a little sensitivity, just a little open-mindedness, just a little empathy on the part of this community—this University of Richmond community—to change my life like never before.

17 I have found that it makes no difference what culture you follow, what your background is, what your experiences are, what language you speak, what accent you have. The commonality of the human bond far transcends these superficial differences.

18 And yet look around at the world today. Look around at the very regions that were faced with the same question of culture that I was faced with four years ago.

19 Look at Bosnia, where, between 1992 and 1996, 300,000 people had been slaughtered—Bosnians, Serbs, Croats, Muslims—all because they came from a slightly different heritage or culture or history.

20 Look at Bombay, India. In one maddening week in 1992, 2,000 Indians—Hindus and Muslims—lost their lives fighting with one another. Two thousand human beings lost their lives.

21 Look at Africa, where, between 1992 and 1996, 1 million Hutus and Tutsis lost their lives. Just comprehend that for a moment. Between the time you were a freshman and a senior, 1 million lost their lives fighting over culture, over history, over background.

22 Yes, just look at the madness. The world has fought hard to highlight its differences. We have forgotten our inherent similarities. All because what was missing was a little understanding. Just a little sensitivity. Just a little open-mindedness. Just a little empathy.

23 Two similar questions of culture in 1992. Two diametrically opposite results in 1996.

24 And so, to the Class of 1996, I say go and distinguish yourselves like never before. Go get the best of jobs, the most rewarding of careers. Go to the best of graduate programs. And make a real difference in your communities.

25 But not for one moment, not for one moment, ever forget the memory of these four years—the memory that just a little understanding, just a little sensitivity, just a little open-mindedness, just a little empathy on your part can mean the difference between complete despair for one young boy in Bosnia and remarkable hope for another young boy at Richmond.

26 Thank you.

Notes

Chapter 1

[1]Pericles, quoted in Richard Whately, *Elements of Rhetoric*, 7th ed. (London: John W. Parker, 1846), p. 10.

[2]Stephen E. Lucas, "Public Speaking," in Thomas O. Sloane (ed.), *Encyclopedia of Rhetoric* (New York: Oxford University Press, 2001), pp. 640–647.

[3]Lü Xing, "An Historical Overview of Public Speaking Traditions and Practices in China and the West," in Wang Lifei and Li Ping (eds.), *English Public Speaking in Global Context: Challenges and Innovations—Proceedings of the First National Symposium of Public Speaking* (Beijing: Foreign Language Teaching and Research Press, 2009), pp. 36–41.

[4]Jonathan Adams and Max Hirsch, "English for Everyone," *Newsweek* (International Edition). August 20/August 27, 2007.

[5]Pang Jixian, Xing Zhou, and Zheng Fu, "English for International Trade: China Enters the WTO," *World Englishes* (2002), pp. 201–216.

[6]George A. Kennedy, *Comparative Rhetoric: An Historical and Cross-Cultural Introduction* (New York: Oxford University Press, 1998), p. 3.

[7]George A. Kennedy (trans.), *Aristotle on Rhetoric: A Theory of Civic Discourse* (New York: Oxford University Press, 1991).

[8]Patricia Bizzell and Bruce Herzberg (eds.), *The Rhetorical Tradition: Readings from Classical Times to the Present*, 2nd ed. (New York: Bedford/St. Martin's, 2001).

[9]Lü, "Public Speaking and China's Modernization," p. 36.

[10]Mary M. Garrett, "Chinese Rhetoric," in Sloane, *Encyclopedia of Rhetoric*, pp. 89–92.

[11]Xing Lu, *Rhetoric in Ancient China, Fifth to Third Century B.C.E.* (Columbia, SC: University of South Carolina Press, 1998), p. 3.

[12]William B. Gudykunst and Young Yun Kim, *Communicating with Strangers: An Approach to Intercultural Communication*, 4th ed. (New York: McGraw-Hill, 2003), p. 4.

[13]Stephen E. Lucas, "The Role of Public Speaking in China's English Language Curriculum," in Wang and Li, *English Public Speaking in Global Context: Challenges and Innovations*, pp. 3–24.

[14]John, Corbett, *An Intercultural Approach to English Language Teaching* (Clevedon: Multilingual Matters, 2003); Sandra Lee McKay and Wendy D. Bokhorst-Heng, *International English in Its Sociolinguistic Contexts: Towards a Socially Sensitive EIL Pedagogy* (New York: Routledge, 2008).

[15]Yin Suya, "Culture and Cultural Identity in Cross-Cultural Communication: Promoting Intercultural Communicative Competence Through Public Speaking Education," in Wang and Li, *English Public Speaking in Global Context: Challenges and Innovations*, pp. 47–62.

[16]M. Neil Browne and Stuart M. Keeley, *Asking the Right Questions: A Guide to Critical Thinking*, 8th ed. (Upper Saddle River, NJ: Pearson/Prentice-Hall, 2007).

[17]Mike Allen, Sandra Berkowitz, Steve Hunt, and Allen Louden, "A Meta-Analysis of the Impact of Forensics and Communication Education on Critical Thinking," *Communication Education*, 48 (1999), pp. 18–30.

[18]For other models of the speech communication process, see Stephen W. Littlejohn and Karen A. Foss, *Theories of Human Communication*, 8th ed. (Belmont, CA: Thomson/Wadsworth, 2008); Em Griffin, *A First Look at Communication Theory*, 7th ed. (New York: McGraw-Hill, 2009).

Chapter 2

[1]Alex Blyth, "How to Get the Most Out of Public Speaking Training," *Training Magazine* (June 14, 2006), p. 7.

[2]Daniel Goleman, "Social Anxiety: New Focus Leads to Insights and Therapy," *New York Times*, December 18, 1984.

[3]Cicero, *De Oratore*, trans. E. W. Sutton (Cambridge, MA: Harvard University Press, 1942), p. xxvi.

[4]Digby Jones, "Public Speaking Tests the Nerves of Most Directors," *Birmingham Post*, August 25, 2003.

[5]Quoted in Bert E. Bradley, *Fundamentals of Speech Communication: The Credibility of Ideas*, 6th ed. (Dubuque, Iowa: W. C. Brown, 1991), p. 36.

[6]Elayne Synder, *Speak for Yourself—With Confidence* (New York: New American Library, 1983), p. 113.

[7]Sharon Aschaiek, "Conquer Your Fear of Public Speaking," *Toronto Sun*, March 16, 2005.

[8]Lilly Walters, *Secrets of Successful Speakers* (New York: McGraw-Hill, 1993), pp. 32–36.

[9]Dick Cavett, quoted in Steve Allen, *How to Make a Speech* (New York: McGraw-Hill, 1986), p. 10.

[10]Chris R. Sawyer and Ralph R. Behnke, "Reduction in Public Speaking State Anxiety During Performance as a Function of Sensitization Processes," *Communication Quarterly*, 50 (2002), pp. 110–121.

[11]Richard L. Johannesen, Kathleen S. Valde, and Karen E. Whedbee, *Ethics in Human Communication*, 6th ed. (Prospect Heights, IL: Waveland Press, 2008). p. 13.

[12]Kenneth Blanchard and Norman Vincent Peale, *The Power of Ethical Management* (New York: Ballantine Books, 1988), p. 64.

[13]Joseph Gibaldi, *MLA Handbook for Writers of Research Papers*, 6th ed. (New York: Modern Language Association of America, 2003), p. 66.

[14]Bruce Perry, *Malcolm: The Life of the Man Who Changed Black America* (Tarrytown, NY: Station Hill, 1991), p. 380.

Chapter 5

[1]Quoted in Halford R. Ryan, "Harry Emerson Fosdick," in Bernard K. Duffy and Halford R. Ryan (eds.), *American Orators of the Twentieth Century* (New York: Greenwood Press, 1987), p. 148.

[2]Saul Alinsky, *Rules for Radicals*, (New York: Random House, 1971), p. 81.

[3]Research shows that speakers are usually more persuasive when they attempt to refute opposing arguments rather than ignoring them. See Richard M. Perloff, *The Dynamics of Persuasion: Communication and Attitudes in the 21st Century*, 3th ed. (New York: Lawrence Erlbaum Associates, 2008), pp. 249–250.

Chapter 6

[1]Eliot Aronson, *The Social Animal*, 10th ed. (New York: Worth, 2008), pp. 92–93.

[2]This point was made by James A. Winans in his classic *Speech-Making* (New York: Appleton-Century-Crofts, 1922), p. 141.

[3]Joel Best, *More Damned Lies and Statistics: How Numbers Confuse Public Issues* (Berkeley: University of California Press, 2004), provides a fascinating look at the use and misuse of statistics in speeches and other public discourses.

[4]Mike Allen et al, "Testing the Persuasiveness of Evidence: Combining Narrative and Statistical Forms," *Communication Research Reports*, 17 (2000), pp. 331–336.

[5]For research confirming the importance of citing sources when presenting evidence, see Rodney A. Reynolds and J. Lynn Reynolds, "Evidence," in James Price Dillard and Michael Pfau (eds.), *The Persuasion Handbook: Developments in Theory and Practice*, (Thousand Oaks, CA: Sage, 2002), pp. 429–430.

[6]Richard M. Perloff, *The Dynamics of Persuasion: Communication and Attitudes in the 21st Century*, 3rd ed. (New York: Lawrence Erlbaum Associates, 2008), pp. 251–254.

Chapter 8

[1]Dorothy Sarnoff, *Speech Can Change Your Life* (Garden City, NY: Doubleday, 1970), p. 189.

[2]Sarnoff, *Speech Can Change Your Life*, p. 190.

Chapter 10

[1]Dorothy Sarnoff, *Speech Can Change Your Life* (New York: Doubleday, 1970), p. 71.

[2]Annmarie Mungo, "A Child Is Born," *Winning Orations, 1980* (Mankato, MN: Interstate Oratorical Association, 1980), pp. 49–50.

[3]Edward Bliss Jr. (ed)., *In Search of Light: The Broadcasts of Edward R. Murrow, 1938–1961* (New York: Knopf, 1967), p. 276.

Chapter 11

[1]Daniel J. O'Keefe, *Persuasion: Theory and Research*, 2nd ed. (Thousand Oaks, CA: Sage, 2002), p. 185.

[2]See Mark L. Knapp and Judith A. Hall, *Nonverbal Communication in Human Interaction*, 6th ed. (Belmont, CA: Wadsworth, 2006), pp. 12–15.

[3]Richard M. Perloff, *The Dynamics of Persuasion: Communication and Attitudes in the 21st Century*, 3rd ed. (New York: Lawrence Erlbaum, 2008), pp. 235–239.

Chapter 12

[1]For a compendium of research on this subject, see Richard E. Mayer (ed.), *Cambridge Handbook of Multimedia Learning* (New York: Cambridge University Press, 2005).

[2]Douglas R. Vogel, Gary W. Dickson, and John A Lehman, *Persuasion and the Role of Visual Presentation Support: The UM/3M Study* (Minneapolis: University of Minnesota School of Management, 1986).

[3]Joe Ayres, "Using Visual Aids to Reduce Speech Anxiety," *Communication Research Reports*, 8 (1991), pp. 73–79.

[4]See Stephen Few, *Show Me the Numbers: Designing Tables and Graphs to Enlighten* (Oakland, CA: Analytics Press, 2004), for an authoritative look at the art of statistical graphics.

[5]For research on this point, see Richard E. Mayer and Cheryl I. Johnson, "Revising the Redundancy Principle in Multimedia Learning," *Journal of Educational Psychology*, 100 (2008), pp. 380–386.

[6]For additional information on the effective use of visual aids, see Garr Reynolds, *Presentation Zen: Simple Ideas on Presentation and Delivery* (Berkeley, CA: New Riders Press, 2008).

Chapter 13

[1]John R. Johnson and Nancy Szczupakiewicz, "The Public Speaking Course: Is It Preparing Students with Work-Related Public Speaking Skills?" *Communication Education*, 36 (1987), pp. 131–137.

[2]Andrew D. Wolvin and Diana Corley, "The Technical Speech Communication Course: A View from the Field," *Association for Communication Administration Bulletin*, 49 (1984), pp. 83–91.

[3]Richard E. Mayer, Sherry Fennell, Lindsay Farmer, and Julie Campbell, "A Personalization Effect in Multimedia Learning: Students Learn Better When Words Are in Conversational Style Rather Than Formal Style," *Journal of Educational Psychology*, 96 (2004), pp. 389–395.

Chapter 14

[1]Gerald R. Miller, "On Being Persuaded: Some Basic Distinctions," in James Price Dillard and Michael Pfau (eds.), *The Persuasion Handbook: Developments in Theory and Practice* (Thousand Oaks, CA: Sage, 2002), pp. 3–16.

[2]This view of the interaction between speaker and listener reflects cognitive processing models of persuasion in general and the Elaboration Likelihood Model in particular. For a concise explanation of the latter, see Em Griffin, *A First Look at Communication Theory*, 7th ed. (New York: McGraw-Hill, 2009), pp. 193–204.

[3]There is a great deal of research confirming the need for persuasive speakers to answer potential objections to their arguments. See, for example, Chasu An and Michael Pfau, "The Efficacy of Inoculation in Televised Political Debates," *Journal of Communication*, 54 (2004), pp. 421–436.

[4]Richard M. Perloff, *The Dynamics of Persuasion: Communication and Attitudes in the 21st Century*, 3rd ed. (New York: Lawrence Erlbaum, 2008), pp. 355–357.

[5]Daniel J. O'Keefe, *Persuasion: Theory and Research*, 2nd ed. (Thousand Oaks, CA: Sage, 2002), pp. 218–219.

[6]Edward L. Fink, Deborah A. Cai, Stan A. Kaplowitz, Sungeun

Chung, Mark A. Van Dyke, and Jeong-Nam Kim, "The Semantics of Social Influence: Threats vs. Persuasion," *Communication Monographs*, 70 (2003), pp. 295–316.

[7]Perloff, *The Dynamics of Persuasion*, pp. 283–285.

[8]John C. Reinard, "The Empirical Study of the Persuasive Effects of Evidence: The Status after Fifty Years of Research," *Human Communication Research*, 15 (1988), pp. 37–38.

[9]Michael T. Stephenson, "Examining Adolescents' Responses to Antimarijuana PSAs," *Human Communication Research*, 29 (2003), pp. 343–369.

[10]Rodney A. Reynolds and J. Lynn Reynolds, "Evidence," in Dillard and Pfau, *Persuasion Handbook*, pp. 429–430.

[11]In classical systems of logic, reasoning from particular facts to a general conclusion was known as induction. Contemporary logicians, however, have redefined induction as any instance of reasoning in which the conclusion follows from its premises with probability, regardless of whether the reasoning moves from specific instances to a general conclusion or from a general premise to a specific conclusion. In this scheme, reasoning from specific instances is one kind of inductive argument—as are causal reasoning and analogical reasoning. See, for example, Howard Kahane and Nancy Cavender, *Logic and Contemporary Rhetoric: The Use of Reason in Everyday Life*, 10th ed. (Belmont, CA: Thomson Wadsworth, 2006).

[12]In classical systems of logic, reasoning from a general premise to a specific conclusion was known as deduction. But just as contemporary logicians have redefined induction (see Note 11), they have redefined deduction as any instance of reasoning in which the conclusion follows from its premises with certainty. Some deductive arguments move from general premises to a specific conclusion, but others move from specific premises to a general conclusion. Most speech textbooks confuse reasoning from principle, which is one form of deduction, with deductive reasoning in general.

[13]For more on fallacies and methods of reasoning, see Douglas Walton, *Informal Logic: A Pragmatic Approach,* 2nd ed. (Cambridge: Cambridge University Press, 2008).

[14]George Campbell, *The Philosophy of Rhetoric,* ed. Lloyd F. Bitzer (Carbondale, IL: Southern Illinois University Press, 1988), p. 77.

[15]Research on fear appeals, for example, has demonstrated that messages devoted exclusively to arousing fear in the audience are usually less effective than are messages that combine fear appeals with reasonable explanations of how to eliminate or cope with the source of fear. For an excellent review of that research, see Perloff, *Dynamics of Persuasion,* pp. 263–280.

Chapter 15

[1]For both speeches, see "Remarks by President Clinton and President Nelson Mandela at Presentation of the Congressional Gold Medal to President Nelson Mandela," September 23, 1998. Accessed at *http://clinton4.nara.gov/WH/New/html/19980923–977.html*

[2]James C. Humes, *Roles Speakers Play* (New York: Harper and Row, 1976), p.33–34.36.

Chapter 16

[1]In the interest of readability, I have edited the text to correct obvious misstatements, vocalized pauses, incomplete phrases, and the like.

Photo Credits

About the Author

iii: Lu Haitao/Oriental Morning Post

Chapter 1

2: Stefan Wermuth/Reuters/Landov; 5: © Jeff Mitchell/Reuters/Corbis; 7: © Photodisc/Getty Images; 9: © Tom Grill/IPN Stock

Chapter 2

16: Fred Prouser/Reuters/Landov; 19: © Abdelhak Senna/AFP/Getty Images; 23: © Peter Yates/-Corbis; 25: © Roger L. Wollenberg/UPI/Newscom; 29: The McGraw-Hill Companies, Inc./Erica S. Leeds, photographer

Chapter 3

32: © Cow Studio-Mad/Photo Library; 32: © Jacque Brund 2005/Design Conceptions; 37: AP Photo/Bebeto-Matthews

Chapter 4

44: © Chris Ware/The Image Works; 44: © Mark Lewis/TSI/Getty Images; 47: © Tom Smart/The New York Times/Redux; 51: © DLILLC/Corbis; 53: © Jose Luis Pelaez, Inc./Corbis

Chapter 5

58: AP Photo/The Greenwich Time, Bob Luckey; 58: Tim Shaffer/Reuters/Landov; 61: © Bob Daemmrich/The Image Works; 63: © Marwan Naamani/AFP/Getty Images; 67: © David Young-Wolff/PhotoEdit, Inc.

Chapter 6

72: © Ramin Talaie/Corbis; 77: AP Photo/Christopher Pfuhl; 81: Mannic Media/McGraw-Hill, Inc.

Chapter 7

88: © RubberBall/Age Fotostock; 91: David Karp/-Bloomberg News/Landov; 93: © Bill Aron/PhotoEdit, Inc.; 99: Kevin Lamarque/Reuters/Landov

Chapter 8

102: © Bob Daemmrich/The Image Works; 105: © Joel-Gordon Photography; 107: © Digital Vi-sion/Creatas; 109: © Henning Kaiser/AFP/Getty Images; 113: © Jim Young/Reuters/Corbis

Chapter 9

118: © Joel Gordon Photography; 118: © Joel Gordon Photography; 121: © Chris Stock-Photography/Alamy; 125: AP Photo/Doug Mills

Chapter 10

130: Kevin Lamarque/Reuters/Landov; 133: Fred Prouser/Reuters/Landov; 135: AP Photo/Paul Franz; 138: © Lynn Goldsmith/Corbis; 141: © James Rulison/NewSport/Corbis

Chapter 11

146: © Tim Wimborne/Reuters/Corbis; 149: Joel Page/AP Photo; 151: © Patitucci Photo/Aurora Photos; 153: Fred Prouser/Reuters/Landov; 155: © AFP/Getty Images

Chapter 12

160: © Andrea Mohin/The New York Times/Redux; 160: © Digital Vision/Alamy; 165: Mannic Media/McGraw-Hill, Inc.

Chapter 13

179: AP Photo/Harry Cabluck; 183: Claro Cortes IV/Reuters/Landov; 185: © Suzanne DeChillo/The New York Times/Redux; 187: Denkou Images/drr.net

Chapter 14

197: © Suzanne DeChillo/The New York Times/Redux; 201: © Mark Lewis/TSI/Getty Images; 204: © Ramin Talaie/Corbis; 207: © Rachel Epstein/PhotoEdit, Inc.; 209: AP Photo/Dennis Cook; 211: © Tim Pannell/Corbis; 213: Steve Pope/Bloomberg News/Landov; 216: © Mariela Lombard/Zuma Press

Chapter 15

225: AP Photo/Daian Dovarganes; 229: © Scott London

Chapter 16

234: 21st Century English Newspaper; 237: Foreign Language Teaching and Research Press; 241: 21st Century English Newspaper; 244: 21st Century English Newspaper; 247: Foreign Language Teaching and Research Press